HARRY S. ASHMORE

A member of the Board of Directors of the Center for the Study of Democratic Institutions since 1954 and Chairman of its Executive Committee since 1959, Mr. Ashmore was elected Executive Vice President in 1966.

While executive editor of the Arkansas *Gazette* in 1957, Mr. Ashmore and his newspaper won the first double Pulitzer Prizes in history, in the Little Rock integration controversy. He also has been editor of the Charlotte (N.C.) *News*.

He was editor-in-chief of the *Encyclopaedia Britannica* from 1960 to 1965; is currently editor of the 1968 *Britannica Perspectives;* and is the author of a number of books, including *The Negro and the Schools, An Epitaph for Dixie, The Other Side of Jordan* and *The Man in the Middle*. Mr. Ashmore also directed a survey of bi-racial education for the Fund for the Advancement of Education.

Born in Greenville, S.C., in 1916, he is a graduate of Clemson College and a Nieman Fellow of Harvard University. In World War II he rose in rank to lieutenant-colonel of infantry. He served as personal assistant to Adlai E. Stevenson in the 1955-56 presidential campaign.

WILLIAM C. BAGGS

William C. Baggs has been associated with *The Miami News* since 1946 and has been its editor since 1957. During his residence as editor, the *News* has three times won the Pulitzer Prize, the most distinguished award in American journalism.

Prior to service overseas, in World War II with the Air Force, Mr. Baggs was associated with the *Star and Herald* in the Republic of Panama. In addition to newspaper writing, he has contributed articles to such national publications as the *American Scholar* and *The New York Times Magazine,* has been a contributor to the *Encyclopaedia Britannica,* and has appeared on national and local television forums.

He is a member of the Board of Directors of the Center for the Study of Democratic Institutions and a member of the executive committee of the National Citizens Advisory Council to the Community Relations Service. In 1961 he was the Chief of the United States Mission and the personal representative of the late President John F. Kennedy in the conferences that established the Caribbean Organization.

ELAINE H. BURNELL

Mrs. Burnell is an editorial associate on the staff of the Center for the Study of Democratic Institutions. Born in Shanghai, where her American parents were in residence, she lived in China and Japan for seventeen years. She was graduated from Smith College with high honors in history and was subsequently selected for the Naval Japanese Language Postgraduate School at the University of Colorado. During World War II, she was a WAVE officer assigned to Naval Intelligence. She has been an editorial researcher for the *Encyclopaedia Britannica* and was for several years an editor and positions analyst at the Library of Congress.

MISSION TO HANOI

MISSION TO HANOI

A Chronicle of Double-Dealing in High Places

A Special Report from the Center for the Study of Democratic Institutions

by

Harry S. Ashmore
and
William C. Baggs

With a Chronology of
American Involvement in Vietnam
Compiled and Narrated by
Elaine H. Burnell

A BERKLEY MEDALLION BOOK
PUBLISHED BY G. P. PUTNAM'S SONS
DISTRIBUTED BY BERKLEY PUBLISHING CORPORATION

G. P. PUTNAM'S-BERKLEY MEDALLION EDITION,
SEPTEMBER, 1968

G. P. Putnam's Sons
200 Madison Avenue,
New York, N. Y. 10016

Berkley Publishing Corporation
200 Madison Avenue,
New York, N. Y. 10016

BERKLEY MEDALLION BOOKS ® TM 757,375

Printed in the United States of America

For Luis Quintanilla,
whose enterprise made the first journey
possible and whose company
made it bearable

CONTENTS

Prologue: *The Uses of Demi-Diplomacy*   1

1. *The Hard Way to Hanoi*   13

2. *Of Culture and Politics*   27

3. *Uncle Ho*   41

4. *Return to Foggy Bottom*   52

5. *Fulbright's Law*   62

6. *The Double Deal*   73

7. *Assault by Innuendo*   88

8. *Decline and Fall*   100

9. *The Second Round*   112

10. *Waiting for the Word*   128

11. *The Piece of Paper*   143

12. *The Long Voyage Home*   159

Post-Mortem: *The End of Precedent*   174

A Chronology of American Involvement in Vietnam
                  by Elaine H. Burnell   197

Bibliography   360

MISSION TO HANOI

Prologue

THE USES OF DEMI-DIPLOMACY

The dominant problem of our age, Robert Maynard Hutchins has said, is to lay to rest two myths that have divided the world throughout the twentieth century. One is the proclaimed belief of the Communist International that survival of the Marxist revolution requires the demise of liberal democracy. The other is the conviction of the prevailing American leadership that the politicians who run contemporary Communist regimes still mean what Marx said.

This thesis and antithesis canceled World War II's brief promise of a new order, and produced instead a diplomatic ice age called the Cold War. The harsh polarization of world opinion has been accompanied by a spate of small hot wars which the so-called superpowers are able to feed but usually find difficult to douse. The mythology Hutchins referred to originally posed two monoliths facing each other across a line in Central Europe roughly dividing the world East and West, and it has proved its durability by surviving the advent of a third, China, which has turned on both. Meanwhile, much of the southern hemisphere has spun into chaos.

In broad, general terms these matters have been a necessary concern of the Center for the Study of Democratic Institutions, which Hutchins founded at Santa Barbara, California, after his departure from more traditional educational pursuits at the University of Chicago. The Center, privately financed by some thousands of members, undertakes no conventional research, accepts no public or industrial subsidy, and considers its interests confined only by the broad limits implied by its title. Hutchins has defined its function as a continuing effort to clarify the basic issues of our time and widen the circles of discussion about them.

In 1964 the Center saw in the late Pope John's encyclical, *Pacem in Terris,* an opportunity—indeed, an obligation—to participate in a vital effort to thaw the Cold War. With much encouragement from the leaders of the United Nations, and the initial approbation of the new administration of Lyndon Johnson, the Center employed the papal message as the thesis for an international convocation in New York in February 1965.

The gathering, called to consider what *Pacem in Terris* had termed the requirements of peace, was described in *Life* as "an extraordinary assemblage of the world's shakers and movers." John K. Jessup wrote:

The guest list would have done credit to a U.N. Charter meeting or a state funeral: the Secretary-General of the U.N.; the President of the Assembly and two former presidents; the Vice-President and Chief Justice of the U.S.; an associate justice and four U.S. senators; Belgium's Foreign Minister Paul-Henri Spaak; the Italian Vice-Premier Pietro Nenni; leading officials from Russia, Poland and Yugoslavia; two justices of the World Court; Historian Arnold Toynbee and Theologian Paul Tillich; all told more than two thousand delegates from twenty nations of the Communist, neutralist and free worlds.

If Jessup lapsed into the vocabulary of the Cold War to describe the composition of the convocation, it must be conceded that events were underscoring his usage. As the delegates were assembling in New York the first major escalation of the United States aerial offensive against North Vietnam was getting under way. In the months to come the broad issues on the *Pacem in Terris* agenda would be reduced to sharp and urgent focus by the explosion of what for a decade had been (ideology provides the choice of title) a minor-league civil war/revolution/insurrection/war of national liberation far across the China Sea.

In June 1965, three Under Secretaries of the UN—Ralph Bunche, C. V. Narasimhan, and José Rolz-Bennett —along with veteran diplomats from a half-dozen foreign countries, came to the Center in Santa Barbara to help evaluate results of the New York convocation. The mood of the gathering was dark. Escalation of the war in Vietnam, they reported, was already imperiling the fragile East-West *détente* which had made possible *Pacem in Terris.* Unanimously they urged that the Center try again, with the main effort this time on bringing in the mainland Chinese.

A year later, at the Palais des Nations in Geneva, the Center assembled advisers from the ten nations and the United Nations—all persons who had participated in the first convocation or were familiar with the undertaking.*

* Alastair Buchan, director, Institute for Strategic Studies, England; Jean Chauvel, ambassador and diplomatic counselor to the government of France; Mrs. Kiyoko Cho, professor, International Christian University, Tokyo; Xavier Deniau, ranking Gaullist member of the Foreign Affairs Committee of the French National Assembly; William O. Douglas, associate justice, United States Supreme Court; Mohamed El-Zayyat, under secretary for foreign affairs, United Arab Republic; Albert A. Gore, United States Senator from Tennessee; Nokolai N. Inozemtsev, director, Institute of World Economics and International Relations, Academy of Sciences, USSR; Manfred Lachs, professor of international relations, Warsaw University; George S. McGovern, United States Senator from South Dakota; Pierre Mendès-France, former premier of France; Dmitri D. Muravyev, secretary-general, Institute of Soviet-American Relations, USSR; C. V. Narasimhan, chef de cabinet, United Nations; Luis Quintanilla, former ambassador and professor of international relations, University of Mexico; Edgar Snow, author and journalist; Sonn Voeunsai, ambassador of Cambodia to France.

Hutchins put two questions to them: How could we persuade Peking to participate in *Pacem in Terris II?* If we could not, was there any point in going ahead?

The first question drew a variety of suggestions, all admittedly doubtful. The answer to the second was yes. And the participants on their own motion added an item to the agenda that was to determine the character of the second convocation—and set in motion the train of events that twice would take the authors of this chronicle behind the lines in Vietnam.

The senior Russian at Geneva, N. N. Inozemtsev, observed that while those present might agree among themselves that Vietnam was only one among urgent issues of coexistence, the world no longer thought so; the fighting in Southeast Asia was bound to dominate any program we might devise for *Pacem in Terris II.* This suggested a concentrated effort to bring Hanoi into the convocation, and thereby to initiate a direct American contact that conceivably could open the way for diplomats to make a formal move toward peace negotiations.

The three Frenchmen responded with enthusiasm, and they bore impressive credentials. Pierre Mendès-France headed the French government at the time of the defeat at Dien Bien Phu and the subsequent Geneva Accords; Ambassador Chauvel is an old China hand who had recently returned from Peking via Hanoi; and Xavier Deniau had served in then-French Indochina as a foreign service officer. They agreed to arrange with the North Vietnamese legation in Paris to transmit to Hanoi a letter suggesting a meeting with representatives of the Center.

In late August 1965, under a Prague postmark, there arrived in the ordinary mail a polite letter to Hutchins in Santa Barbara saying that such a meeting was not possible at that time, but pointedly leaving the door open. It was signed Ho Chi Minh.

It is still impossible for a U.S. national to obtain an

entry visa to China, and so the Center's overture to the People's Republic to consider participation in *Pacem in Terris II* was borne westward by a remarkable Mexican intellectual, Luis Quintanilla, now teaching at the University of Mexico after a distinguished diplomatic career. As a former ambassador in both Moscow and Washington, an old-line Mexican *revolucionário* who maintains a yacht in Acapulco, and a recognized authority on Buddhism, Don Luis seemed to bridge the ideological gap about as well as anyone.

In Peking, in the October 1966 season of revolutionary celebration and massive Red Guard demonstrations, Quintanilla got as far as an audience with Foreign Minister Chen Yi, from whom he received a lengthy lecture on the inevitability of World War III, and the certainty of the ultimate Chinese triumph. He read this correctly as an indication that the Center's invitation to *Pacem in Terris II* would not be accepted, but he did wangle permission to leave China by way of Hanoi. There he was granted a private audience with Ho Chi Minh, in the course of which the President indicated that he would consider receiving U.S. representatives of the Center for further discussions. Quintanilla subsequently informed Ho that the Center would send its executive vice-president, Harry S. Ashmore, and a member of its Board of Directors, William C. Baggs, editor of *The Miami News*.

Hanoi's acceptance of this proposal automatically produced a new relationship between the State Department and the Center. The Department could grant us clearance to join our Mexican colleague in a mission to North Vietnam only by acknowledging the legitimacy of the undertaking. When we were asked to keep the trip secret as long as possible, and to clear our passports at the U.S. consulate in Hong Kong to avoid any possibility of a news leak in Washington, the Department was recognizing that we might open up a useful channel of communication with the North Vietnamese. Finally, we were asked to make a number of inquiries in Hanoi on the Department's behalf.

We agreed to the conditions, although secrecy could be only temporary, since it was understood that Baggs ultimately would write a series of articles for his newspaper, and that at some point Hanoi's reaction to the Center's invitation to *Pacem in Terris II* would require a public announcement. This, however, was all to the good in the Department's view, since it would provide an excellent cover in case of premature publicity.

As it turned out, the story of our visit broke while we were still in North Vietnam. Harrison Salisbury of *The New York Times,* who had been cleared just ahead of us, departed from Hanoi the day we arrived, January 6, 1967. He picked our names off the manifest of the weekly International Control Commission plane which provides the only means of entry for U.S. citizens.

By the time we got back to Los Angeles on January 15, Salisbury's articles had already created a national furore. By documenting the extent of civilian casualties produced by saturation bombing of some North Vietnamese cities and towns the veteran *Times* editor had refuted official U.S. claims that the air attack was confined to pinpoint bombing of "concrete and steel" targets of immediate military value. The initial Washington reaction was a concerted effort to discredit Salisbury by attacking his veracity and, in the case of some administration fuglemen in the press, his loyalty.

As professional observers who had covered most of the ground Salisbury described, and some he did not, we found ourselves in considerable demand. However, at the State Department's request we managed to hide out for some days after our return, and to meet privately in Washington with the Department's top echelon. These briefings went on intermittently for a day and a half, and covered in detail the two-hour conversation we had had with Ho Chi Minh.

Ashmore then returned to Los Angeles to meet the press and deliver a considerably expurgated report on the Hanoi tour at a public meeting of the Center's Founding Members. In Miami, Baggs began a series of twelve articles for the *News,* which were distributed nationally by the Associated Press. Our reports were a vindication of Salisbury, and as a result we encountered the first private signs of what would later become a public monument of official displeasure. But, as we had agreed to do, we continued to avoid any suggestion that we had had any but routine contacts with the State Department or had opened up any significant new channel of communication with Hanoi.

As the spring lengthened, our relationship with the State Department took on a pronounced schizoid quality. There were those in high places there and elsewhere in the administration who seemed to regard our open channel to Ho Chi Minh as valuable and who sought to use it, not as an instrument of negotiation, but as a means of exchanging exploratory views without compromising the official position of either side. But there were also those of equal or higher rank who seemed to be opposed to any kind of exchange with Hanoi, and in the first round they prevailed. This led to a calculated campaign to sabotage the impending *Pacem in Terris II* convocation, scheduled for late May in Geneva, which the North Vietnamese had indicated they would attend.

In October 1967, we decided to make public some of this extraordinary background maneuvering. This was done in an article by Ashmore, "The Public Relations of Peace," in *The Center Magazine,* which revealed for the first time that two contradictory letters had been sent to Ho Chi Minh by official Washington the previous February—one written in collaboration with the State Department and transmitted by us as representing the views of "high officials," and the other signed by President Johnson and sent through diplomatic channels in Moscow. The hard-line Johnson letter, which actually stiffened the previous conditions for negotiation, obviously canceled the deliberately conciliatory letter we had been given to believe represented the prevailing view of the administration, and the Johnson letter was summarily rejected by Ho. This seemed to us a clear case of double-dealing, and we said so.

In the ensuing public controversy with the State Department we were accused of exaggerating the importance of our own role and of revealing confidential matters in a spirit of personal pique. The general line taken by the Department was that it had available many channels to Hanoi, official and unofficial, and in good faith tried to use them all for what they were worth. Even if this were true, it begged what we insisted was the central question: Why, if the Presidential letter was going forward, did the State Department use us to send any letter at all? The minimum result would be to confuse an obviously delicate situation, and the maximum result was what did obtain—the disruption of all effective contact with Hanoi for many months, during which the war increased in intensity.

The explanation for this contradictory performance, we came to believe, was that the leading critic of the administration's foreign policy, Senator J. William Fulbright, had become involved in our negotiations with the State Department at President Johnson's own request. To have refused to make any response at all to the feeler Ho Chi Minh had transmitted through us would have confirmed the Senator's frequently voiced suspicion that the administration's talk of willingness to negotiate was window-dressing to conceal from the American public its actual commitment to a military resolution of the conflict. Since Fulbright knew of the letter the State Department sent through us, and did not know of the contradictory hard-line letter drafted for the President two days before, he might have assumed that the failure of Ho Chi Minh to respond to our letter was evidence of recalcitrance on the part of Hanoi—an almost certain misunderstanding had not Hanoi taken the unusual step of releasing the Johnson correspondence along with Ho's sharp reply.

As a result of these experiences, we began to operate under what we have come to call Fulbright's Law: Don't trust the State Department. This, of course, produced a reciprocal reaction: the State Department clearly no longer trusted us, if indeed it ever had. Yet, remarkably enough, even in these strained circumstances our relationship with the Department continued on a minimal working basis. The practical reason was that we did have a direct channel to Hanoi, and it continued to remain open, and to elicit indications that the North Vietnamese were willing to come to the conference table when the United States was prepared to treat them as co-equals. For those who were sincerely working for a negotiated settlement —and certainly there were such among those with whom we dealt—we provided a possible opening that could not be prudently ignored. Moreover, the very fact of our public controversy with the Department had made us so conspicuous that the hard-liners were inhibited from taking overt action to remove us from the picture entirely. The administration was hoist on the President's remembered pledge that, despite the military evidence to the contrary, he was committed to negotiation.

Across the months of accelerating conflict Hanoi remained responsive to every contact the Center initiated, and we continued to keep the State Department fully informed. At the end of March 1968 we were readmitted to Hanoi, and arrived there, bearing messages from the State Department, three days before Lyndon Johnson made his surprise announcement that he was altering the bombing pattern and withdrawing from the Presidential race. We also came out of Hanoi bearing messages, those which prescribed the procedure for the first formal contact between the warring parties. This sent us once again into the inner reaches of the State Department as the sparring began over the site for the proposed talks.

We found the change in political temperature occasioned by the journey from Hanoi to Washington no more marked than it is in the passage from Foggy Bottom to Capitol Hill—where we went to deposit in an executive session of the Senate Foreign Relations Committee the same information we had delivered to senior members of the State Department.

We have come to believe that this overt hostility among men in high places in Washington involves a great deal more than their immediate division over U.S. policy in Vietnam, grave though that is and has been. The tension is both product and symptom of an alarming corrosion of the nation's foreign policy-making process. This condition was evident at every stage of the peculiar case history in which we have been involved during the past two years.

Ours has been an uncommon vantage point. If our unofficial, and usually suspect, status denied us access to a good deal of pertinent information in both Hanoi and Washington, it also has left us free of the inhibitions that attend official envoys. We were messengers and observers, not negotiators, and we never confused our role by our actions, or in our own minds. We were paying our own way, or the Center was, and we asked nothing of the State Department except clearance. As private persons we had no personal stake in the larger official policies that hedged about the essentially procedural questions of contact between the two parties which we considered ourselves authorized by the State Department to discuss.

The North Vietnamese with whom we dealt understood that while we have been sharp critics of the administration's conduct of the Vietnamese war, and were obviously anxious to see the conflict ended, we could not be counted among those radical American peace activists who, on moral grounds, had transferred their sympathies, and for all practical purposes their political allegiance, to Hanoi. To the Vietnamese we provided an opportunity for frank discussion with Americans who could be presumed to present to them a fair estimate of prevailing public opinion and political reality in the United States. Similarly, some, at least, of the American officials with whom we dealt accepted our ability to report and appraise the views expressed to us by Ho Chi Minh and his associates without any undue coloration of personal bias.

Finally, in the matter of maintaining secrecy we were bound only by our consciences, not by the sometimes stifling formal restrictions that beset the public servant. We made it clear from the outset that, while we would treat as confidential any restricted matter we might receive from official persons on either side, we would exercise our own judgment as to when we would publish information we had gathered and transmitted on our own. On this basis we withheld a good many of the facts of both visits so long as we thought their publication might jeopardize the possibility of negotiations.

By the fall of 1967 we were convinced that this was no longer the case so far as Hanoi was concerned; the exchanges in which we had been involved after the first trip had been canceled by internal maneuvering within the Johnson administration. This, it seemed to us, not only freed us from our voluntary restraint, but imposed an obligation to make the facts known—for they constituted one of the first fully-documented challenges to the administration's professed willingness to go anywhere at any time to talk peace with the North Vietnamese.

So it is in the case of the second journey. By the time this book appears, the negotiations we helped get under way during the first week of April 1968 will have bogged down in the aftermath of the unseemly quibbling that marked the opening rounds, or they will have moved on to deal with the substantive questions that must be faced by both sides if there is to be a negotiated settlement. In either case we believe this record to be pertinent.

The narrative deals with events of the last two years in which we were involved, or of which we have personal knowledge. These took place, however, as part of a continuum that goes back to the end of World War II. That record, taken from official documents and other primary sources, is covered in the Vietnam Chronology prepared by Elaine H. Burnell. We have presented the chronicle and the chronology in this volume in the hope that they can be considered as pointing up the lessons of the past misconduct of our foreign affairs in the light of renewed prospects for peace in Southeast Asia.

1

THE HARD WAY TO HANOI

It is a long way from the neon and concrete pyramids of Los Angeles International Airport to the little-used airfield that serves the embattled capital of the Democratic Republic of Vietnam. Now, in the first week of the year 1967, we had traveled those 10,000 miles. Behind us lay the vacant reaches of the Pacific, the journey south through the cloud cover that usually huddles along the China coast, and all but a few minutes of the ten hours of waiting and flying time required to travel on from Phnom Penh, Cambodia, where commercial air travel reaches the end of the line. Just ahead was Hanoi, surprisingly freckled with lights; abruptly our World War II-vintage transport slanted down toward the dimmed-out landing strip as though the French crew were anxious to duck beneath any possible line of fire.

For these two Americans such an arrival in a combat zone induced a kind of somber, middle-aged nostalgia. The pocked runway announced itself through the thumping wheels as an Oriental cousin to the African and Italian fields Baggs had flown from during a tour with the bombers in World War II. Inside the old plane the mixed cargo of uniformed Sikh soldiers of the International Control Commission, diplomatic couriers guarding their pouches, and studiedly anonymous civilians was not different from the company Ashmore had kept in the days when he flew back from the German front on liaison for a long-disbanded infantry division.

Only the smiling Vietnamese girls who glided into the scant light around the ramp bearing delicate bouquets provided a new touch for two veterans of the European Theater. But this gentle gesture of welcome was soon submerged in memories, even though we still clutched their long-stemmed blossoms after we had been hunched into the narrow back seat of an old Russian Volga sedan and aimed toward the city.

In early January 1967, the U.S. Air Force had struck Hanoi proper only a few glancing blows, and our subsequent examination of the results would reveal that our countrymen either were guilty of inordinately sloppy bombing or were carrying on a macabre heckling campaign. However, on the narrow road in from the airport, which lies beyond the broad Red River and requires passage across the temptingly exposed Long Bien Bridge, there was ample evidence of what the bombardiers could do when they put their talents to it. In the industrial suburbs our dimmed headlights began picking up the shadowy forms of men and women, and beyond them the heaped rubble of blasted buildings they were using to patch up bomb craters in the road. It was a frieze out of the valley of the Moselle.

This sense of *déjà vu* would stay with us when we traveled through the scarred countryside to the south of the capital, making our way into areas where the American bombers had been operating entirely without restraint. It rained steadily while we were in North Vietnam on this first visit, and it would rain again when we came back after fourteen months. All wars are cold and wet—or at least all our wars have been.

Before we could get within range of the aerial assault

that has screamed and crumped across the Democratic Republic of North Vietnam since February 1965, we had to surmount a series of obstacles that ranged from maddening to whimsical.

There are American correspondents of our acquaintance who have put in more time in the anterooms of DRV legations in Paris, Algiers, Prague, Moscow and Phnom Penh than they would have spent in Hanoi had they received the visas they unsuccessfully pleaded for. Such official blessing is absolutely essential; without a DRV visa you can't get aboard the decrepit International Control Commission airplane that provides one of the two means of entry to the embattled country. The only other way is by air or rail from the People's Republic of China—through which *no* American is granted passage these days.

The odds are only slightly better for those who try the southern route. Except for a dozen or so peace activists who have established their own channels and usually proceed without regard to State Department travel restrictions, we know of only three other Americans who have been cleared by Hanoi for entry since the United States declared open season on DRV territory in alleged retaliation for an attack on American destroyers in the Gulf of Tonkin.

Four of this select company were practicing correspondents and the other, Ashmore, still bears the journalistic cachet. On the American end of the long trek this simplified matters, since newsmen are placed in one of the few categories entitled to consideration for passport clearance to countries on the State Department's banned list: North Vietnam, the People's Republic of China, Cuba, and Albania. But at the jumping-off point usually designated by the DRV—Phnom Penh, Cambodia—an established reputation for having a way with words can be fatal.

The monarch of that delightful country, Prince Sihanouk, has a distaste for American journalists so pro-

nounced it led him several years ago to break off
diplomatic relations with the United States. In the Cambodian legations a U.S. citizen's application for a tourist visa
is set aside while a clerk thumbs through a massive black-
list that looks as though it might well combine the contents
of the professional directories published by *Editor and
Publisher* and *Broadcasting*.

In Hong Kong, where we twice ran the gauntlet, Baggs
attempted to interrupt the rise in tension by commenting
to the young lady engaged in this perusal: "You certainly
don't have to worry about us. We can assure you that we
haven't robbed any banks in Cambodia."

"Oh, we don't mind bank robbers in Cambodia," she
replied, "only those clever, clever journalists."

On the ground in Phnom Penh, our Mexican colleague,
Luis Quintanilla, who travels on a diplomatic passport
and leaves no doubt that he is entitled to it, ran interference for us as we nervously made our way through immigration, carefully listing our profession as education, and
our purpose as tourism. We made it, but in the process
we learned that an old friend who had preceded us by a
week had had no such luck.

Louis Lomax, the Los Angeles author and television
commentator, had counted on picking up a tourist visa at
the Phnom Penh airport upon arrival, as Americans are
usually allowed to do. But his professional reputation had
somehow preceded him, and the adamant Cambodians
sent him ricocheting off to Bangkok, Thailand, the next
stop for west-bound airliners.

Noel Deschamps, the Australian ambassador who
looks after American interests in the current absence of
U.S. diplomatic representation, tried to intervene on Lomax's behalf, but could get him no more than permission
to leave the airport between planes. The North Vietnamese simply returned Lomax's unissued visa to their
files, and he has never since been able to get any response
to his efforts to retrieve it.

With this precedent at hand Ambassador Deschamps advised us to stay out of sight, which is not easy for two tall, round-eyed Americans and a voluble Mexican in a small city populated by small brown people. We found that our visas were in order at the DRV representation, but we also found that the Tuesday ICC plane we had counted on boarding had been canceled, as it frequently is. The next flight was on Friday, which gave us almost a week in which to blend, as best we could, into the light January flow of European and American tourists passing through Phnom Penh on their way to the magnificent ruins at Angkor Wat.

In these musical-comedy circumstances we found it hard to take the ebullient, gregarious Cambodians seriously, the same failing that doubtless got the United States into trouble with the Prince in the first instance. The Khmers, the native stock which traces its blood lines south and west to India and Indonesia, have been embattled for centuries. They count as their natural enemies the yellow races who surround them, the Chinese, the Vietnamese and most particularly the Thais. To make matters worse, the Chinese and Vietnamese generations ago infiltrated the Cambodian cities and towns and since the departure of the French have come to dominate the country's limited manufacturing and commerce.

Prince Sihanouk, who declared an end to the Khmer royal line by abdicating the throne and having himself elected chief of state, functions as a sort of back-country Machiavelli, as perhaps he has to. One broad boulevard in Phnom Penh is named for Mao Tse-tung, another for Lenin, and still another for John F. Kennedy. But along with the elephants, the pagodas and the ubiquitous Buddhas, the pedicabbing tourist also encounters a sharp reminder of the extent to which the escalating war next door has intruded upon the Prince's political juggling act. In the park along the bank of the Mekong River the most conspicuous monument is the crumpled remains of an American bomber shot down over Cambodian territory.

In even more marked fashion American military power has spilled over into the poor, landlocked territory of Laos, where the ICC plane puts down en route to Hanoi. The Ho Chi Minh Trail snaking south through the Laotian jungles is a prime target for U.S. bombers, and there is no secret about our logistic support for the Royal Laotian troops of Prince Souvanna Phouma, who have been fighting for years against the Communist-backed Pathet Lao.

Vientiane, the dusty, bedraggled Laotian capital, is a scene straight out of a Graham Greene novel. The main industries are diplomacy, made possible by the remarkable fact that all the great powers maintain major embassies here, thus furnishing local social events with a rare combination of senior representatives of the United States, Communist China, Russia, North Vietnam, and even the Pathet Lao; smuggling and dope running, which make use of the proximity of the Chinese poppy fields and the upper reaches of the Mekong; and espionage, which employs this pathetic little city as an international spy drop of the magnitude of Lisbon in World War II.

The shadow of the American presence is long in Vientiane, and grotesquely distorted. The two great monuments of American aid are a Holiday Inn-style hotel on the river-front populated mostly by conspicuously anonymous Westerners, and a vast, bustling airport whose ultramodern terminal building is already falling into decay. Out on the flight line, however, there is the epitome of Yankee efficiency. Any day the drowsy Laotians can look out and watch the lumbering take-off of scores of huge cargo planes bearing the insignia of Air America, the CIA's well-known front. These are loaded with munitions and supplies to be airdropped to those who are defending the Laotian and American Ways out in the steaming hills.

In the past the rear areas of a shooting war have had a feeling of transience about them, the smell of canvas shelters that can be struck when the war moves on, or ends. But in Vientiane the natives fade into a sort of dim backdrop, and the Westerners in the foreground give the impression that they have come to stay.

We once mentioned this to Senator J. William Fulbright, who for some time has been using his Foreign Relations Committee as a pulpit from which to warn that the United States is drifting into a kind of unintentional imperialism, spreading our bounty and arms around the globe in an effort to impose *Pax Americana*.

"Naturally the Americans in a place like Laos dig themselves in," the Senator said. "Their control of American military force and American aid allows them to run a little country like that to suit themselves. Under what other circumstances could they exercise power on such a scale? We give them other titles but we have created a new breed of pro-consuls, and I'm not sure Washington any longer has any real control over them. I imagine Rome had the same trouble with Pontius Pilate."

The objective of this encircling American might, for which Laos and Cambodia are no more than casual overshots, is a narrow strip of territory which extends more than a thousand miles south from the China border, lying between a rugged mountain spine and the shore of the South China Sea. In the lower half American ground forces try to search out and destroy dissident Vietnamese in person; in the North the assault is more detached, launched from above and beyond, by planes bearing bombs and rockets from bases in Thailand and carriers at sea, and by bombarding naval vessels lying offshore.

Americans have now dumped more high explosive on Vietnam than was detonated over all of Germany in World War II, and have employed the most extensive use of napalm and defoliation chemicals in history. The most

telling measurement of the effect of this mighty effort
would be an accurate tally of the corpses it has produced,
but this is not to be had.

In the South, where the toll is surely greater, no one
believes the casualty figures put out by either side—in
part because it is in the tradition of all defense ministries
to exaggerate enemy losses and minimize their own, but
primarily because in this kind of war there is often no
way to distinguish soldier from civilian, to determine
from which direction the lethal blow came, or to be sure
that all the bodies will ever be found.

In the tightly organized, completely mobilized North,
where you have the feeling that every last grain of rice is
accounted for, there undoubtedly are statisticians who
know exactly what the casualty yield per pound of American explosive has been. But there are no total figures
available to visiting correspondents, or to the Vietnamese
population. In a Communist country you are told only
what is believed to be good for the cause—and it appears
that the custodians of the morbidity reports quite reasonably figure that a high casualty figure would depress
local morale and cheer the enemy, while a low figure
would only spur the enemy to redouble his efforts.

At the site of a given bombing, however, you can obtain a pretty fair estimate of what happened. Some discount must be made for propaganda; your escorts are in a
position to determine what you will inspect, and we found
they had an understandable tendency to pick out the remains of schools, hospitals, orphanages, pagodas, and in
one notable instance, a leprosarium. Still, there was the
inescapable fact that, no matter how selective the process,
our guides had no trouble turning up scores of such exhib-
its as we made our way a hundred kilometers down
Route One, the main highway from Hanoi to Saigon.

Nor were we amateurs at this kind of grisly sightseeing.
Baggs, after all, had dropped enough bombs during
World War II to know a military target when he saw one,

and the difference between a hit and a near-miss; and Ashmore in the same war had been on the receiving end of enough strikes (including a good many launched by the U.S. Army Air Corps) to have some basis for estimating type and effect.

We kept a joint log, since we knew we would be interrogated by Defense Department experts upon our return from the first trip, when Hanoi was still presumably off-limits and the fiction was being maintained that our airmen were restricted to "strictly military targets." The following quotation from this laconic compilation is taken from the entry of January 7, 1967, when we looked over three bomb sites in Hanoi proper, and another in the suburbs:

The third strike was on Nguyen Thiep Street, one-half mile northeast from downtown Hanoi, said to be in the most densely populated section of the city. We counted 52 homes totally destroyed. These were old buildings made of brick and plaster, built close together on both sides of the street. The entire roof of a pagoda was missing, as was the Buddha from the altar. We talked to a boy, Nguyen Thi Quynh, 13, who said he was present on the evening of the bombing. He said the air alert had given him time to get out of his house, but not to the shelter. He had not been hurt. He didn't know, or wouldn't say, how many people had been killed. "Many" was the best we could get. Some 30 yards away, down the street, was the rail line to Haiphong, elevated at this point, and still apparently undamaged. It was only a rail line, with an open passenger shed, and if it was a legitimate target it had been missed.

Another entry from the same day:

Late in the afternoon we visited the Viet Ba School, said to have been bombed on December 2 and again on December 14. It is a general school, from the first through the tenth grades, and is five kilometers south of Hanoi, a couple of hundred yards off Highway One. We counted eight bomb craters around the school, 1000-pound size by World War II standards. One of the two large classroom buildings was

sliced half in two, and the remains of the ruined section left
no wall more than two feet high. The other building had no
roof, doors or windows. Smaller buildings on the grounds had
suffered less damage but were uninhabitable. The school compound is situated all by itself, and it appears it must have
been deliberately selected as a target. A mile away, across the
highway—too far to have accounted for a near-miss by the
worst-trained pilot—was a truck park; a mile away in another direction was a storeyard for sewer pipe; and a half
mile away was the main rail line south. There was no evidence that these had been touched.

This pattern was repeated over and over when we
passed beyond the restricted zone. The highway, and the
parallel narrow-gauge rail line, had been pounded repeatedly, and the permanent bridges were long since gone, to
be replaced overnight by the light, hand-crafted pontoon
and bamboo structures which are a serviceable Vietnamese specialty. Whatever military targets had been in
Phu Ly, a rail and road junction town 59 kilometers
south of Hanoi, had been destroyed along with everything
else—including the dwellings of a now-vanished population of 7,700. This was a clear case of saturation bombing, undertaken over a ten-day period in October 1966,
according to the Vietnamese, who believe it was intended
as an object lesson for Hanoi, just up the road. Elsewhere, however, we found what seemed to be an almost
random pattern of strikes.

In Nam Dinh, a textile center with a prewar population
of 90,000 and the country's third city, the most conspicuous military target was a large, old-fashioned steam-gen-
erating plant clearly marked by its high stacks. It stood
untouched, its old generators humming loudly, while a
few blocks away ten residential blocks had been systematically leveled. Another log entry, from the record of our
tour of Nam Dinh:

On either side of Dhan Dinh Pheng Street the greater part
of nine square blocks was demolished. This again was a com-

munity of private homes. For a long while ours was the only car on the streets. Now and then a man or woman hauling carts would appear, or a bicycle, or a wagon drawn by water buffalo. We saw a few old lorries, and a few pedestrians. In these early daylight hours Nam Dinh is all but deserted, in preparation for the almost daily raids that usually begin around 9:30 a.m. and continue until 3:30 p.m. Still, our escorts claim, every one of the textile mills is still operating, and certainly they show no signs of heavy damage from the outside. The answer is that the people go to the countryside during the day, when the planes come, mostly low-level attack craft off the carriers. In the late afternoon they come back and go to work.

There are no casualty estimates in our log. In the worst of the areas we inspected the answer obviously would have been that the number of dead depended upon the number present, for a few would have been left moving after the planes passed on. The Vietnamese understood this early, and evacuation has been the order of the day. In Hanoi, still only lightly damaged when we went back in 1968, the school children, the university students, the old and the infirm, have been gone since 1966.

We could believe that it is probably true, as the North Vietnamese claim, that even if our bombers totally destroyed their shabby but still lovely old capital, it would do no more than inconvenience the war effort in the South. Hanoi already is a city stripped to the essentials. Only those who are necessary to pump daily life into the capital remain, and many of these sleep elsewhere. In the early morning, when the moon still floats over the sou trees which form a kind of pleasant green roof for the city, you can see workers streaming in from outlying precincts. They glide by noiselessly on bicycles, which are more common in Hanoi than taxicabs are in New York City, and they come on foot or in carts drawn by oxen or in trucks which grumble along the dimly lighted streets. The city closes down during the middle hours of the day, which is the usual time for the American bombers to appear. When we returned in April 1968, this was still the pattern, although the bombardment by then had taken out all the industrial suburbs and bedroom communities right up to the edge of the city proper, which must have added considerably to the daily commute.

When the on-again, off-again bombing in the vicinity of Hanoi is explained in Washington it is usually justified as a canny employment of something called "measured pressure." Looking at the result on the ground, we wondered if the ultimate American restraint didn't result from the fact that all the Socialist nations and more than a dozen of our Western allies in effect protect the city with hostages—members of the legations that occupy walled villas along the tree-shaded avenues that here, as in all the old Indochinese towns, carry the look of provincial France. Among its other defensive assets, Hanoi quite evidently counts on the fact that it could provide the trigger for World War III.

Here, of course, is the source of the frustration of the American generals and admirals who promised to bomb the North Vietnamese to the conference table if their commander-in-chief would only take off the wraps. They had precedent with them. Their enemies in the first great air war had concentrated their heavy, essential industries in areas like the Ruhr and the Saar and the Japanese home islands, and the Axis powers couldn't keep their mechanized armies in the field once these vital plants were bombed out of action.

But the Vietnamese have precious little such heavy industry, and an army that travels as light as any Americans have faced since Sitting Bull's. When the bombers began to appear over their cities and towns they simply went into the countryside, taking along with them such essentials as small generators and light fabricating equipment, and even putting together portable breweries to produce the beer that is about the only luxury item Communist puritanism and wartime rationing have left in the staple diet.

Back in Washington, in the deserted Pentagon on a tranquil Saturday afternoon, we passed these observations and conclusions along to the man who then had his hand on the military controls. Robert McNamara presumably already had gone over the record of a lengthy interview we had had with a Defense Department team, and now he put a series of probing questions of his own.

The point, we told the Defense Secretary, was that North Vietnam was not a primary production center but a supply line; the stuff the guerrillas required for their operations in the South had to pass through the country, but it was made somewhere else—in Russia and Czechoslovakia mostly, with some light matériel originating in China. Obviously the bombing was doing a good deal of damage, but it was not effectively halting the flow of men and goods to the South. Moreover, it had served to unify the people of the North rather than to intimidate them. What we had to offer was only supplemental evidence; the real test of the failure of the bombing policy lay in the evident fact that our adversaries in the South had been growing progressively stronger ever since it began.

The Secretary said bluntly that he knew this was so, that he had never thought the bombing of North Vietnam could be justified in purely military terms. He had led the argument within the administration for the two long bombing pauses in 1966 and 1967, he told us.

"The decision to bomb the North was political," he said, "and those of us who tried to halt it took a beating when the Vietnamese didn't make any political response to the bombing pauses. The generals and admirals covered us up with aerial photographs of supplies moving South while they had to hold their fire. Then they put the issue to the President as one of protecting our own troops."

A year later McNamara made public his view of the essential military futility of the bombing assault on North Vietnam, stating it in the place most likely to raise White House hackles, the Senate Foreign Relations Committee. Not long after, the man who was once rated the strongest and most favored member of the Johnson administration left the Defense Department for the relatively restful obscurity of the World Bank.

2

OF CULTURE AND POLITICS

In downtown Hanoi, near the dignified government houses of the vanished colonial regime, an old hotel lifts four high-ceilinged floors above a wide brick sidewalk penetrated at intervals by spreading sou trees. In the rear there are still remnants of a garden with summer houses, its promenades interrupted by concrete entrances to the bomb shelters which provide the latest modern conveniences for guests and staff.

The hostelry the French called the Métropole has been pointedly rechristened Reunification House, and the Vietnamese, who use it primarily to quarter the few visiting foreigners they allow into their war-torn country, have made other predictable changes. The capitalist elegance has been stripped away. Heavy, square, utilitarian chairs line the section of the lobby which once must have been a sort of semitropical Peacock Alley, and the usual drink served over the high zinc bar is tea or coffee or the mild Vietnamese beer.

Still, it does not unduly strain the imagination to turn the calendar back forty years and visualize a conversation over aperitifs between an intense young French intellectual named André Malraux, who spent much time here, and a visiting British literary fellow called Somerset Maugham, who frequently traveled these parts and in his short stories caught the essence of seedy colonial hauteur. Malraux would have been certain that revolution was coming, and Maugham would have doubted it. And in a way both would have been right.

It would not be the Marxist revolution plotted in Paris, Moscow and Peking by a worldly poet named Ho Chi Minh that finally broke the grip of the colonial French, but a blundering, belated imperial venture by the distant Japanese. It would not be agents of the Comintern who joined Ho in the jungle to help him pick up the pieces after the Japanese defeat, but bright young American officers of General Wild Bill Donovan's Office of Strategic Services. And it would be the least revolutionary of recent American Presidents, Dwight D. Eisenhower, who guaranteed Ho's final triumph by turning down the urgent demand of John Foster Dulles and the Joint Chiefs of Staff that he send an American invasion force to bail out the returned French armies at Dien Bien Phu.

The Vietnamese intellectuals who come to dine with their foreign guests in the private rooms at Reunification House treat this aspect of their national history with a combination of amusement and outrage. The official American pronouncements, intended to sound as though the defense of the Thieu-Ky regime in Saigon is a key campaign in a holy war, appear to leave them undecided whether to laugh or cry. Ho Chi Minh himself, now the venerable father of his country, wryly reminded us in his impeccable English that he had once spent a good deal of time in New York, and inquired, "Tell me, gentlemen, is the Statue of Liberty standing on her head?"

It takes a good deal of doing to reassure the Vietnamese leaders that, while the lady who dominates New York Harbor may be tilted slightly, she continues to hold up her torch. Still we felt obligated to try as we worked our way through the series of briefings, cultural entertainments, and chopstick-wielding dinners laid on for us by the Committee for Cultural Relations with Foreign Countries.

Our official hosts, we discovered, run their guests around an entirely different track from that laid out for the American peace activists, who are handled by the DRV Committee for World Peace. On our first visit the World Peace people were squiring a group of passportless American lady pacifists and a couple of investigators for Lord Russell's war crimes trial, and when we returned they had under their auspices the distinguished novelist, Mary McCarthy, and Professor Franz Schurmann of the University of California.

Similarly, we learned that our fellow journalists who came in on straight press credentials, Harrison Salisbury of *The New York Times,* David Schoenbrun, and Charles Collingwood of CBS, were put on still another circuit. Their escorts were provided by the press section of the foreign ministry, and they were generally assisted by the amiable Australian free-lance writer, Wilfred Burchett, who seems to be the only English-speaking Westerner allowed regular entry to Hanoi. It was somehow touching to see Burchett get off the plane at Phnom Penh, where he maintains his residence these days, buss the cheek of his attractive Bulgarian wife, and inquire after their pet bear with the insouciance of a Westchester commuter.

We would occasionally share breakfast or lunch in the boardinghouse-style dining room of Reunification House with our fellow countrymen, or compare notes over a drink of the hard stuff, mostly Russian and Polish vodka, kept behind the bar for the outlanders. Otherwise we were politely but firmly taken on our separate ways by the English-speaking escorts who were always on hand when we came off the surprisingly modern self-service elevator.

This, however, was an act of consideration, not of surveillance. The Vietnamese start the day early, before sunrise, and work late, but they usually build several hours of siesta into the middle of the day's schedule. In these intervals we were free to wander about the city on foot unattended, and frequently did so, being greeted with unfailing courtesy everywhere we went despite our conspicuous foreign look. It was, of course, evident that if anybody cared to keep track of us we were as easy to locate as two redwoods in a grove of dwarf pines, and that we could hardly gather any forbidden information since no one outside the middle and upper reaches of the official bureaucracy speaks anything but Vietnamese.

During these untended intervals the special etiquette of the Reunification House lobby approved an exchange of greetings with our fellow guests, and, when the language barrier permitted, casual conversation with the assorted Poles, Russians, Rumanians, Czechs, French, Cubans and Japanese. The one exception was the visiting Chinese comrades, who wore drab, unadorned uniforms, traveled in coveys like quail, and stared stonily past any face equipped with round eyes. We would watch them pass through, and then exchange shrugs and waves of the vodka glass with the equally snubbed Russians across the way.

The correlation of age and status works out so that most Vietnamese of ministerial and subministerial rank are French-educated, graduates of colonial academies in Vietnam for the most part since only an exceptional few went on to Paris in the old days. There is, however, a sharp division by generation. After Dien Bien Phu, French continued to be taught in the secondary schools, but it is no longer a required second language. Now Russian, Chinese, and even English are also offered; and while nobody we talked with knew, or was willing to say, which foreign language is the most popular, there is a marked drop-off of bilingualism of any kind among the younger people—perhaps a natural consequence of the fact that anybody under 40 has been at war since puberty.

Among the French-speaking senior Vietnamese officials to whom we were exposed, only Ho Chi Minh had a command of English sufficient to warrant his using it in serious conversation. Since our French is inadequate, this meant the use of interpreters to translate from Vietnamese into English and back at any time the talk turned to matters of moment.

The Vietnamese seemed to be fairly well supplied with translators with an adequate command of written English, but many of these had trouble with the spoken version. Apologetically, they pointed out that after all they had very little chance to practice. These interpreters seemed to occupy a special status as semischolars, probably not unlike that of the traditional Mandarin class in other years.

With one exception of indeterminate age, who said he had spent a year or so at Yale but seemed reluctant to supply any details of his sojourn, all had learned their English in Vietnamese schools and in special classes at the university, and kept their ears in trim by listening to short-wave broadcasts from the BBC's overseas service, Voice of America, and the U.S. Armed Services Network in Saigon. The absence of any tutelage by those who speak English as a native tongue, and of any experience outside their own isolated society, usually produced an accentless, almost mechanical speech pattern. This disembodied quality carried over into the small talk in which they eagerly indulged between interpreting chores.

This is an overt mark of the insularity imposed upon the North Vietnamese a generation ago by the Japanese occupation and maintained since by the requirements of their revolution. Cultural isolation, of course, has been compounded by the U.S. intervention in the South, and perhaps as significantly by the widening political and ideological division between the embattled DRV's indispensable allies, Russia and China.

The government boasts that despite total wartime mobilization it has been able to maintain the educational drive that has wiped out illiteracy and has opened up an educational system that reaches its apex with a tenfold increase over the limited opportunities for university and technical education provided by the French. The claim was borne out by our limited observation; the attractive, well-printed newspapers seemed to be widely circulated and read in even the backwoods villages, and everywhere along the muddy roads there were gaggles of local and evacuated children of all ages heading to and from makeshift schools.

But, as some of the intellectuals conceded in informal conversation, the educational system of necessity is closed and inward-looking. The fact that this was a matter of concern to some highly placed members of the new regime seemed to us worth noting. To a classic Marxist theoretician a closed educational system would not pose a problem but would afford a glorious opportunity to guarantee that only the pure doctrine reached the malleable minds of the young.

On our second visit, in 1968, we renewed our acquaintance with one of the most outspoken of these intellectuals, a literary man who seemed to enjoy some sort of special scholarly status and, so far as we could divine, was burdened by no official duties. With heavy irony and obvious relish he pointed out that the American bombing of the North had provided the Marxist bureaucrats with a key device they had so far been denied. In the face of the strong Oriental family tradition, no one had previously dared undertake the separation of children from their peasant and bourgeois parents in order to provide a school system on the Russian model, and thereby guarantee that their revolutionary education would be uncorrupted by any carryover from the decadent past. Now

American bombing of the cities and towns has made such segregation of school children not only possible but mandatory, and even the youngest see their parents only on week-end visits. "Your President Johnson has done what Ho Chi Minh would never have dared to do," our sardonic friend said. "Your bombers may have given us our first generation of Vietnamese Red Guards."

Our social life was assisted greatly by our traveling companion, Don Luis Quintanilla. His mother was French, he was educated at the Sorbonne, and he is by temperament one of the true gallants of our time—a fast man with a toast, a serious student of Oriental culture, and a sympathizer with all revolutions everywhere. With it all, he still has reflexes conditioned by a thousand embassy dinners, and he gracefully extricated us from dead-end conversations when we were brought under siege by our hosts' polemics.

"My sons here," he would explain, "are pure *Americanos*. I am a different breed, a *Norte Americano,* but also a Mexican. So if you feel it necessary to call President Johnson and Secretary Rusk reactionary butchers please address me. I may not agree with you, but I do not have a personal duty to be offended."

Actually, there were remarkably few such contretemps. The Vietnamese naturally display a grave courtesy, relieved by flashes of humor, and the flying of the red flag does not seem to have produced here, as it apparently has in China, any effort to suspend the ancient traditions of Oriental hospitality. In no case was there a display of personal animosity against us as loyal citizens of the country that was spreading death and destruction across their homeland.

It is, of course, an old Communist ploy to make a forensic distinction between the peace-loving American people and the imperialist warmongers who control the American government. But we came away with the con-

viction that more than this was involved in the attitude of
the Vietnamese officials with whom we talked seriously
—and this was particularly marked in the case of Ho Chi
Minh. There was no mark of insularity apparent at the
upper levels of the hierarchy, and no lack of sophistication.

As we progressed through the schedule laid out for us
we began to note that the propaganda content was dropping day by day. For the first three days we were taken
regularly to the villa occupied by our host Committee, or
to the headquarters of an appropriate agency, and exposed to a series of specialists called in for what were evidently set briefings. Thus we were subjected to the DRV
version of the military victory over the French, which has
become their great national saga; the legal and political
background, and the consequences of the Geneva Accords; the case against the United States for "unprovoked
aggression against a sovereign power"; and the alleged record of atrocities committed by the Americans, which included not only statistics and photographs but the living
exhibit of a napalm-seared boy of 16.

It appeared to us that the cast of characters at these
affairs was steadily becoming more political, and so was
the tone of the conversation. On Wednesday afternoon,
when we arrived at the Committee's headquarters for
what we had been told would be another discussion of
Vietnamese culture, the company was composed of highly
placed officials who clearly wanted to explore the ramifi-
cations of a negotiated settlement of the war with the
United States.

Technically, the senior man present was Pham Ngoc
Thuan, chairman of the Committee of Cultural Relations,
who carries the rank of minister in the government. But it
had been evident from the time we met him at the airport
that the man who was automatically in charge of any
meeting he attended was Hoang Tung, editor of the principal Party paper, *Nhan Dan,* official spokesman for the

government, president of the journalists' association, and member of the Party's central committee. This time he had with him Tran Cong Tuong, who is the equivalent of the American Attorney General and was one of the original Vietnamese delegates to Geneva; Luu Quy Ky, who edits the official National Liberation Front publication; and other lesser lights. Hoang Tung opened by saying that the time had come to be frank and specific about the matters that stood in the way of a settlement between his country and ours.

It was a wide-ranging conversation, brutally frank on both sides at times, but without heat. Our log entry for that day, January 11, shows that we got around to deescalation, which was then considered more likely than a cease-fire; the possibility of preliminary talks while the fighting went on; and the matter of ultimate troop withdrawal by both sides. We noted also the lack of response to our probing on such matters as the role of the NLF, which we regarded as perhaps more significant than anything that was said.

That evening we were back on the cultural circuit as guests of honor at a musicale at the Committee's villa, featuring a troupe of girl singers who had just returned from a guerrilla-style USO tour in the South after covering more than a thousand kilometers on foot to cheer the troops at the front. They wore the colorful, very feminine kimonos of the Montagnard tribes in place of the usual neat white blouses and black trousers of the workaday dress, and they were a fetching sight as they sang sweetly, accompanying themselves on long-necked stringed instruments that resembled undernourished mandolins. In the course of one lilting number, which we had concluded was a gay love song, the girls suddenly lifted their instruments to shoulder-height, pointed them skyward, and broke into an unmistakable rat-a-tat-tat—the climax of their ballad being, as we were gleefully informed by our hosts, the shooting down of an American plane.

During an interval in the festivities we told Hoang Tung we had thought the afternoon's conversation most useful, but that since our visit was drawing to a close and the formalities were now behind us, it might be that something a little more private was in order. He agreed, and said he would send his car next morning to fetch us to his newspaper office. "It will be a little chilly there," he warned us, a wide grin breaking his normally expressionless face into a mass of deep wrinkles, "but maybe our talk will heat it up."

We discovered what Hoang Tung meant when we arrived at the editorial headquarters of *Nhan Dan*. His office is located in what once had been the residence of the colonial French commandant, and overlooks one of Hanoi's downtown lakes. It was raining, as always, and a cold, wet wind blew through the large upstairs room where we sat huddled in our overcoats.

The temperature outside was 42 degrees and the temperature inside the office also was 42. Tung apologized for the chill. We asked if he would please close the windows, explaining that we were, respectively, from California and Florida, and possibly had suffered from some thinning of the blood. This, Tung explained, unfortunately was impossible: "Your Mr. McNamara bombed out several of my windows."

Tung went on to dryly express his conviction that it would do no good to replace the glass. He was confident that "your Mr. McNamara" would simply bomb his windows out again.

We were to discover that our host kept the needle handy, easing the sting with his marvelous grin and his meticulous courtesy, but never letting us forget that we were adversaries first and guests second.

Quintanilla had stayed behind at Reunification House, feeling that the conversation might be franker with only the two Americans involved, so we were alone except for

Tung's highly competent interpreter, and a silent male secretary who took extensive notes in Vietnamese. The conversation ran for more than three hours, interrupted only by the occasional intrusion of black-pajamaed girls bearing tea, coffee, peanuts, candy, and tiny glasses of sweet Vietnamese cherry liquor. Tung always halted the talk and personally supervised the service, and once he barked at a particularly awkward girl. Then he gave her the healing grin and explained, "We Socialists are too democratic to have very good servants. Actually, all these girls are members of the staff of *Nham Dan*. This one writes articles on education."

There are few such light moments, however. Tung began by suggesting that we give him a frank appraisal of what we thought our country's basic aims were in Vietnam. He would simply listen, he said, and ask questions only for clarification—and for the most part he did restrain himself, only occasionally breaking in with a substantive objection. In the final hour of the morning he recited in one-two-three order his understanding and interpretation of what we had said, rejecting some points outright, offering rebuttal to others, and adding some additional views he said were necessary to a full understanding of the position of the DRV. It was not a process intended to establish areas of agreement, but it did dispose of a lot of irrelevancies and pare the discussion down to basic differences, which, of course, were formidable.

Shortly before noon the street-side loudspeakers which carry the air raid warnings broke into the musical interlude which provides a daily preface to the reading of the news. As a rousing patriotic air poured in through the broken windows Hoang Tung brought the conversation to a close.

"You tell me you believe your government is prepared to accept a negotiated settlement of the war which would not require the NLF to simply surrender or disappear," he said. "If this is so, President Johnson obviously has changed his mind. Why did this happen?"

We explained our view that there had always been a faction in the Johnson administration opposed to direct military intervention in Vietnam on pragmatic grounds. These dissidents argued that escalation of the attack against the North within the necessary bounds of a limited war could not produce a victory, or force a settlement on American terms. Now they could point to the increased effectiveness of the NLF campaign in the South since the bombing began, as incontrovertible evidence that the United States had been caught in a military stalemate. Events, we believed, were pushing Mr. Johnson to recognition that the impasse could be broken only by a negotiated settlement, or an application of force on a scale that carried with it the risk of launching World War III.

We cited the lengthy conversation we had had earlier in the week with Colonel Ha Van Lau, the urbane general staff officer who serves as the DRV representative to the International Control Commission and who would turn up in Paris a year and a half later as deputy chief of the Vietnamese mission when a meeting with the United States finally did materialize. Our session with the colonel had quickly passed into a stage of military shop talk, in which he pointed out that the great advantages of terrain, mobility, and popular support that accrued to native guerrilla forces had canceled out the absolute air superiority enjoyed by the United States in the South, and had largely offset the superior firepower of the heavy armament available to the American ground forces.

Under our questioning Colonel Van Lau had estimated that the NLF and the DRV regulars could stand off an American expeditionary force of up to two million men. "At some point," he conceded, "our ability to resist would break. But then the matter becomes academic so far as we are concerned, for the Socialist countries would intervene and it would no longer be our war, but the beginning of World War III." It was clear that China was the Socialist country primarily on the colonel's mind.

We agreed with Colonel Van Lau's estimate, we told Hoang Tung—and, more important, so did some of the senior American generals, most notably those of the Army, whose predecessors had split with their colleagues on the Joint Chiefs of Staff fourteen years ago, recommended against the proposed invasion in support of the French at Dien Bien Phu, and persuaded President Eisenhower not to run the risk of bogging down an American expeditionary force in a land war on the mainland of China.

Hoang Tung nodded and reached for his needle. Throughout the conversation he had been jotting notes on the back of a folded sheet of coarse paper, and now he turned it over to display a piece of wire service copy fresh from a teleprinter. "Perhaps," he said, "you would like to hear what your President said yesterday in his State of the Union message. This is what they will be reading over the loudspeakers in a few minutes."

Lyndon Johnson had unequivocally restated his previous pledge to support the government of South Vietnam in its effort to resist what he called aggression, had proclaimed that American forces were gaining significant victories against the NLF and the DRV, and had asked for a 6 percent increase in the income surtax in order to finish the job. "We will stand firm in Vietnam," he had said. "I think you all know that our fighting men there tonight bear the heaviest burden of all. With their lives they serve this nation, and we must give them nothing less than our full support—and we have given them that—nothing less than the determination that Americans have always given their fighting men."

We could only reply that LBJ was a politician who already had occupied at least two positions on Vietnam, and was quite capable of assuming a third. Hoang Tung laughed, walked us to the front door, and told us that principals in his government would want to talk with us after he had reported our conversation to them. He would make arrangements, he said, and send for us at the hotel.

In mid-afternoon word came that Ho Chi Minh was expecting us at 5 p.m. at the old governor's Palace.

3

UNCLE HO

He is called the father of his country, the
George Washington of Vietnam, and there
isn't any point in protesting the cliché; if the independent
nation that has emerged from the debris of the old
French colony survives, Ho Chi Minh must be recorded
as its sire. For more than thirty years he industriously im-
pregnated his countrymen with the seeds of rebellion, and
his first rewards were prison and exile. He used his time
in the French jails to write and reflect, and established
himself as a poet of more than passing talent. He devoted
the years abroad to perfecting his organizational skills
and seeking the support he would have to have when he
launched what his sometime compatriot, Mao Tse-tung,
would term a war of national liberation.

The record shows that Ho sought help wherever he
thought he might find it. In 1919 he was in Paris publishing an angry weekly, *The Underdog,* when Woodrow Wilson arrived with his heady talk of the sacred principle of
self-determination of peoples. Ho was moved to address a
petititon to the peace conference at Versailles, and in the
light of later history it was a remarkably restrained document. He did not ask for autonomy for his country, only
for freedom of press and assembly. Even so, the Jefferso-
nians at Versailles were not impressed. Ho never received

an appointment with any member of the American delegation, or of any other.

In the course of his long exile he put in at many of the
world's great cities, including New York, and found that
there simply was no sale among any of the majority political parties of the West for the idea of liberating colonial
peoples. So Ho Chi Minh, like most of the rebels of his
age, found sympathy and tutelage among the more radical
minority parties of the European Left. A year after he
was spurned at Versailles he allied himself with Marcel
Cachin in the dispute that split the French Socialists and
led to the founding of the French Communist Party. He
was launched on the course that would lead him to the
discovery that practical assistance was available for his
cause only in the Union of Soviet Socialist Republics, the
new colossus committed to the proposition that revolution anywhere outside its own immediate orbit was in the
Russian interest.

An extended and wide-ranging conversation with Ho
Chi Minh left us with no reason to doubt his fealty to the
Communist crusade, or his conviction that his country's sal-
vation requires collective organization along Marxist lines.
Yet, even to questions that cut close to the ideological
bone, he offered us no response that could be described as
doctrinaire. The summary impression was one of a stubbornly independent, highly skeptical cast of mind. In this
vein he readily assumes the role of a man who often has
been sold down the river, who now accepts the record of
the past without undue rancor, but who is bound and determined not to be taken again.

He recited Franklin Roosevelt's frequent profession
that he had no intention of permitting the reinstatement
of colonialism in Southeast Asia after World War II, and
pointed to the subsequent American support of the Allies'
decision to turn over the reoccupation of Vietnam to
Chiang Kai-shek's armies and the local British command,
thus paving the way for the return of the French. He re-

called that Dwight Eisenhower's historic decision not to intervene at Dien Bien Phu had been followed a few weeks later by John Foster Dulles' move to launch the train of events that led to American support for the Diem government in the South and the abrogation of the agreement to hold nation-wide elections. But he could remember items on the other side of the ledger too—most notably the decision of his old comrades in the French Communist Party to stand by the tricolor when the Free French armies were sent back to take over the colonial reins from the Vichyites who had collaborated with the Japanese.

"We have learned the lesson," Ho said. "We have been taught to be nationalists by two thousand years of our history. We are reasonable people, and we want an end to this war. But the freedom and independence of Vietnam will never again be negotiable."

It is as a revolutionary liberator that Ho has earned his place in the contemporary Pantheon, but, despite the violence that has marked his career, his easy manner and benign presence place him in the wing with Gandhi rather than alongside the tough, abrasive Mao. He is universally called Uncle Ho by his countrymen, not as an Oriental mark of respect for his 78 years, but as evidence of genuine affection. Unlike traditional Marxist leaders, and the residual monarchs in the surrounding countries shaken out of French Indochina, he employs none of the trappings of the personality cult. There are no monuments to Ho in Hanoi, no squares bearing his name, and there are far fewer Presidential photographs and portraits on display in public buildings than one would find in Washington, D.C.

Nor does he carry his lack of ostentation to the other extreme and make it an aggressive mark of identity, as in the case of Fidel Castro's combat fatigues. He is an urbane gentleman, perfectly at home in the elegant parlor of the Governor's Palace where he received us. If he chooses to live elsewhere, in a simple, one-bedroom residence on the spacious grounds, this seemed only a matter of comfort and common sense for an elderly bachelor. He obviously had no objection to using the Palace for ceremonial occasions and as a place to entertain visitors, and no effort has been made to temper the high style inherited from the French.

His appearance has been accurately caught in the photographs usually published in this country—the thinning white hair, the high narrow forehead and prominent cheekbones, the Mandarin-style moustache and beard, and the trademark beige pajama-style native garb and sandals. What does not come through is any suggestion of the extraordinary mobility of expression which thoroughly gives the lie to the legend of the inscrutable Oriental. As he talked, his amusement, disdain, anger, curiosity, and doubt passed across his features like wind-ripples on a pond. His voice is soft but distinct, and rather lower in pitch than is usual among the Vietnamese.

He used his fluent French for his reunion with Luis Quintanilla, and then turned to greet us in English, and to express his regret that because of the others present he would now have to resort to Vietnamese and thus deliver our conversation to the mercy of the interpreters. The others were Hoang Tung, and Ho Chi Minh's personal aide who serves as a living reminder of his own lost youth, the charming, animated To-Huu, who must be regarded as poet laureate of the DRV.

We inquired after the President's health, and he gave us a quizzical look that indicated his awareness that this question was of great and pointed interest to the State Department and to other chanceries around the globe.

"I am holding up very well. I have only this one bad habit," he replied, waving one of the American cigarettes he chainsmokes, "but I guess I am now too old for it to hurt me much. I have never had time to get married and raise a family—I tell the Vietnamese people they are all my children—and so I can live quietly and simply. I sleep well, even with your bombing."

Certainly he was in full vigor at the end of this dismal January day, and he cut short the pleasantries and moved straight on to business. "Please forget protocol," he said in English. "Please feel at home. Can we talk among ourselves—in confidence?"

We assured him that we could, subject to the understanding that we would report the conversation in full to the high officials of the State Department with whom we had talked before beginning our journey. We had no official status, we emphasized, no authority to negotiate or act as agent for our government, but we thought we could adequately report the prevailing views in Washington and accurately convey his in return. Ho indicated understanding and approval, and addressed himself directly to the two of us—or perhaps, in his mind, to Lyndon B. Johnson.

Once the pleasantries were over, there was no intervention from Quintanilla, Hoang Tung, or To-Huu. At the end of an hour we made a tentative move to leave, but Ho waved us back to our chairs. He had greeted us on the stroke of five, and it was three minutes to seven when he walked us to the front door to bid us farewell on the high front steps of the Palace.

There was no feeling of the well-rehearsed set piece about any part of Ho's relaxed discourse. It ranged freely and naturally in response to our questions, bringing in personal anecdotes and allusions to American history, taking on a sharp edge at times but never lapsing into polemics. Frequently he broke in to correct the interpreter's English rendering of his replies, and he often addressed us directly in asides.

At one point, in response to Ho's quotation of Abraham Lincoln, Baggs observed that our host's simple, unaffected life style reminded him of the Carl Sandburg story about a pompous visitor who came into the Presidential office to find Lincoln standing with his foot on the edge of the desk, busily polishing his boot. "Good heavens, Mr. President," he said. "Do you shine your own shoes?" "Certainly, sir," Lincoln replied. "Whose do you shine?" Ho laughed, held up his white-socked foot in his cross-strapped sandal, and said, "It's a good story, but I couldn't very well follow suit."

These excursions, however, never took Ho far from the two main points he obviously wanted to make—that there could be no productive talk about a settlement in Vietnam until the United States halted the bombing, and that if this condition were met there was no other barrier to negotiations that might lead to peace.

"Your government must understand this," he said. "We are not at war with the United States, we have committed no hostile act against your territory. We are supporting our fellow Vietnamese in the South in their war of liberation, but this is a matter among Vietnamese, not an attack against the United States. Yet your bombers are attacking our territory every day, your naval vessels are committing hostile acts within our territorial waters, your artillery is firing across the demilitarized zone. No self-respecting independent nation can tolerate this. While these acts of war go on you cannot expect us to come to the negotiating table. To do so would be not to negotiate a settlement, but to sue for peace—to surrender. This we shall never do.

"When you ask what would we do in return if you stop the bombing it is like being asked by a Chicago gangster who has held you up at gun-point what you are willing to pay him not to shoot you. The answer is that when the bombing stops the talks can begin. If the United States wants to begin talks with the DRV your government knows what to do—stop the bombing."

This basic proposition was not new. To our knowledge

it had been formally conveyed to Washington by Secretary General U Thant of the United Nations, and by the Canadian diplomat, Ambassador Chester Ronning, who had twice visited Hanoi as an informal emissary from the United States, and it had doubtless also percolated through foreign diplomatic channels. As the proposal seeped into the press later in the spring it brought on one of the most unseemly quibbles in the tortuous history of these backstage contacts—the public quadrille danced for many months by Secretary Rusk and his associates over the question of whether the North Vietnamese leaders had ever said talks "would" begin after a bombing halt, or only that they "could" begin. If it was only "could," the rationale went, the United States couldn't possibly take the chance of moving first because our wily Communist foes might take advantage of our good faith by tossing in new conditions.

With this likely prospect in mind, we suggested to Ho that a near-paranoid suspicion of the DRV was endemic in some quarters in Washington, and that it would be useful if we could be as specific as possible in reporting any conditions he might be setting on negotiations. Could we say that he was willing to guarantee talks without further condition if the bombing were halted? He replied with some asperity:

"I am not willing to guarantee anything under these conditions. I am also a suspicious man, and I have reason to be. You are Americans, and so I assume you are businessmen. Well, I am a businessman, too, and I want to see the goods before the price is established. When the bombing stops we can talk. Then we will have seen the goods."

If he was unyielding on the bombing, however, Ho was quite evidently using his conversation with us to convey to Washington his willingness to make other major concessions. At that time Hanoi still stood officially on the four points regularly proclaimed in Hoang Tung's

Nham Dan as conditions for negotiation: (1) withdrawal of American troops, (2) respect for the military provisions of the Geneva Accords forbidding foreign intervention, (3) settlement of internal affairs in South Vietnam "in accordance with the program of the National Liberation Front," and (4) peaceful reunification of North and South without foreign interference. As the talk went on, Ho made it clear by indirection that all of these four points had been dropped as conditions for opening talks, or considerably modified—which meant that while they would certainly turn up as items on the agenda, Ho was conceding in advance that they were negotiable.

Although he refused to consider any prior guarantee of reciprocal military action, he made a point that could be taken as opening the way for the kind of mutual deescalation Washington was then demanding as the price of a bombing pause. The United States, Ho said, made a great deal of the fact that North Vietnam continued to supply the NLF during previous suspensions of the aerial attack —charging that this enabled its enemies to strengthen their position in the South and imperiled the American forces there. Well, he said, so did the United States continue to send in men, weapons, and supplies during these bombing pauses, and he went on to charge that the original purpose of the bombing was to provide a shield behind which American troops could be moved in to take over the fighting from the collapsing South Vietnamese armies. "If the United States wants to talk about a halt to the build-up of the fighting forces in the South let it first stop building up its own side," he said. "If that were done and the bombing stopped there would be much to talk about."

On the matter of troop withdrawal he said, "I realize that President Johnson has pledged that the United States has no ambition to maintain a permanent military force in Vietnam. Frankly we find this hard to believe when we see the huge permanent military installations you are building in the South, and we also understand from experience that the conditions about free elections are the kind that have been used before to justify continued intervention. However, on our side, we realize that it is not possible to simply stop fighting and remove such a huge military force overnight. We would expect that it would take some time for the Americans to depart after an armistice is arranged."

Did that mean he would consider a phased withdrawal, along the lines Mr. Johnson had suggested? You could call it that, he replied—the terminology was not important, only the fact that as an *ultimate* objective the Vietnamese people had to be guaranteed the right to run their own affairs without outside interference.

The National Liberation Front was made conspicuous by the absence of specific mention in Ho's discourse. The only direct reference came in passing praise of the gallant fighting men at the front, where Ho still did not concede that DRV regulars were engaged. We circled warily around the matter of whether the DRV continued to insist, as it once had, that the NLF must be represented at any talks with the United States, and suggested that we had reason to believe our government might be willing to yield on this point.

Ho replied, "There are no other conditions for initiating talks once the bombing is stopped." Here he brought up the matter of "face," conceding that he understood that the Johnson administration had some troublesome commitments to the South Vietnamese regime and to its other Asian allies—and strongly implying that he had similar "face" problems of his own. The implication here was that Ho recognized that if he insisted on NLF representation he would have to accept Saigon—a point that would later take on much significance as the maneuvering began on the Paris talks. Vietnam's other active allies, China and the Soviet Union, came into the conversation only in passing, as "our Socialist brothers."

On the matter of reunification Ho was more precise.

Vietnam, he insisted, was one country, and ultimately it must be united under one government—that one, we gathered, clearly being his own. But there was no reason the South could not be governed separately for a while, provided the government were truly representative, as the present "puppet regime" in Saigon certainly was not. Such a government, he continued, would have no difficulty collaborating with the DRV, and he had no doubt that in time the two regimes would work out a true and lasting union. This, of course, constituted tacit acceptance of a coalition government in the South.

We asked if he could give us an idea what "in time" meant in this context. He replied, "It could be ten years, or longer. That is not important, so long as the Vietnamese people are free to work out their own destiny. They will see to it that Vietnam is again one country. I may not live to see it, but I have no doubt that this will come. All our history demands it."

As the conversation moved toward the final exchange of felicitations Ho assumed his avuncular role for a moving peroration. We had thanked him for his courtesies, and noted that we had been touched by the cordial reception we Americans had received from all his countrymen, even those who were immediate victims of our own country's bombing attack.

"We respect the American people," he replied. "The American people are an intelligent people, and they are a peace- and democracy-loving people.

"The American soldiers are sent here to kill and get killed; but if they came to help, as technicians, then we would welcome them as friends, as brothers.

"But now they come to kill and get killed. This is a shameful thing.

"This may be difficult for you to believe. I am grieved not only when the Vietnamese people are killed. I am also grieved when American soldiers are killed. I sympathize with their parents.

"So I tell our people they must always be prepared to welcome the Americans—not when they come, as now, as soldiers bearing arms, but when they come, as they may again one day, to offer us help in rebuilding our country. If this sounds strange to you, look at our record with the French. When the fighting ended at Dien Bien Phu a close and cordial relationship grew up between Hanoi and Paris. The French are now our warm friends, and we are proud to acknowledge the Gallic flavor in our modern culture.

"So, please believe me when I say I would be more than happy to welcome President Johnson to this Palace if he came in peace. We are prepared to hold out the hand of friendship to any country that accepts Vietnam as a free and independent nation."

We would, we told him, communicate any reaction to these sentiments after we had conveyed them to official Washington, and asked if we should transmit our reply through Hoang Tung. "Mr. Hoang Tung will always be glad to hear from you on any matter," he said. "But if you have a message for me why not send it direct? And if your State Department desires to make any official contact, any of our legations abroad will be available to arrange it."

It seemed to us that the metaphorical telephone of Dean Rusk's standard Vietnam speech, which he claimed always went dead when he tried to make a connection with Hanoi, was ringing loud and clear.

4

RETURN TO FOGGY BOTTOM

Back at Reunification House, we sat down with Luis Quintanilla to pool our impressions of the conversation with Ho Chi Minh while they were still fresh, and to reduce our common impressions to writing. Next day, when Hoang Tung came to the hotel for a final private session he suggested that it would be useful if we reviewed with him our notes on the session with the President. This, he said, had been suggested by Ho Chi Minh himself, and we were, of course, happy to oblige.

The final version of these notes, as certified by Tung, thus constituted an informal but accurate statement of the current position of the North Vietnamese government on the procedural matters involved in starting negotiations —and provided a fair indication of how the DRV might be expected to proceed once the discussion reached the substantive issues involved in a settlement of the war in the South.

There was also evidence of some tempering of the DRV attitude in Hoang Tung's report that Ho Chi Minh had taken under consideration the Center's invitation to participate in the *Pacem in Terris II* convocation in Geneva the following June. The significance here was that the invitation had not been rejected out of hand, as had seemed likely since the proposed session would require a representative of the DRV to join publicly in a panel discussion with a spokesman for the Saigon regime.

As we compared the key passages in Ho's conversation with the main points made in the extensive briefings we had undergone in the State Department, it seemed to us there were definite prospects for movement. In the weeks before our departure we had talked with Under Secretary Nicholas deB. Katzenbach and William P. Bundy, the Assistant Secretary for East Asian and Pacific Affairs, who had brought in some of the Vietnamese experts in his section. All of these generally held to the hard administration line, which treated North Vietnam as a Communist puppet state engaged in unprovoked aggression against a free and independent neighbor, South Vietnam. But behind this façade there seemed to be recognition that, short of the total defeat of the guerrilla forces fighting so effectively in the South, there would have to be some compromise political solution which would give the NLF a role in the government of South Vietnam.

Bundy had declined to make any but the most heavily qualified response to our queries about the U.S. attitude toward a possible coalition in Saigon, but he had come back pointedly to the proposition that the Geneva Accords could provide a basis of settlement. And although there were sharply conflicting interpretations of those loose agreements, they did envision the ultimate unification of Vietnam, thus establishing a common goal and confining the disagreement to the means of reaching it.

The first of these conversations in Foggy Bottom took place in the second week of November 1966, when we reported Quintanilla's message that Ho Chi Minh would receive representatives of the Center, and requested passport clearance for the two of us. Quintanilla had already made a full report on his own findings in Hanoi to the United States ambassador to Mexico, Fulton Freeman, and this had been relayed to the Department and read with apparent interest by Katzenbach and Bundy.

We were encouraged to go ahead and contact Hanoi, although Katzenbach asked us to delay the trip until he could be sure that we would not interfere with unspecified "other things" that might be shaping up. As it turned out, it took almost a month to receive final clearance from the DRV for Ashmore and Baggs, and at this point Katzenbach asked us to wait until after the first of the year— presumably because of backstage diplomatic maneuvering accompanying the Christmas bombing pause.

As a result we had two lengthy background briefing sessions in Foggy Bottom more than a month apart. In addition to their obvious interest in impressions they could use to augment or attack their own intelligence reports, the State Department people wanted us to make certain soundings on specific matters—notably on prisoner exchange. After the first briefing session we prepared a confidential memorandum for our principals at the Center setting forth our understanding of the U.S. position as it had been presented to us. Copies of this went to Katzenbach and Bundy, noting that we wanted to make certain that we had not inadvertently done violence to their views. This written summary was before them when we met again in late December for our final session before departure, and no demurrer was indicated.

The memorandum made clear our understanding of the nature and limitations of our mission, in which we would "function as private citizens, with no obligation to our government except to keep the State Department informed." We added that "we could foresee no eventuality in which we would be in position to do more than transmit information and impressions, that if anything in the nature of a specific proposal emerged in our conversations it would of necessity require some official action on both sides, at which point we would fade from the scene."

After summarizing the five main areas covered in the

briefing under headings ranging from "military strategy" to "general settlement," we set down for the record the conclusions we had drawn from what we had heard:

Bundy laid particular stress on the fact that the United States had not yet indicated willingness to recognize the NLF as a full participant in any cease-fire negotiation; the maximum inference that can be drawn from any of the several statements on "unconditional" negotiations by the President, Secretary Rusk and Ambassador Goldberg is that NLF representatives could take part as members of the North Vietnamese delegation but would not, as Bundy put it, have a place on the front row with a name card. This, obviously, is directly related to the stress also laid on the fact that no coalition with the NLF would be considered at this time.

In one sense this might be seen as a trading point; we probably can't know unless it were actually made how the U.S. would react to a flat offer by Hanoi to come to the table with the NLF as a full-scale participant. As indicated above, the State Department recognizes that any *ultimate* settlement will require some sort of negotiation with leaders of the force that is doing most of the fighting in the South; by the same token that considerable number of South Vietnamese who have participated in or supported the NLF effort must *ultimately* participate in the new government unless they are exterminated or exiled—which U.S. policy certainly does *not* contemplate. There is, however, a real problem of how to get from here to there, and it would be a mistake to write off the issue of NLF representation as a relatively minor matter of face for either side.

To negotiate a cease-fire directly with the NLF would by implication recognize its political legitimacy; once this line is bent the stake is raised to acceptance of the NLF in a coalition government. The issue has been avoided so far by insisting that we would deal as a principal only with North Vietnam, which we treat as a separate power intervening in the independent nation of South Vietnam; conversely, Hanoi can keep the coalition issue alive by treating the conflict as one in which it plays only a supporting role to the NLF. The importance of all this toe-dancing is that all concerned think it is quite probable at this stage that the NLF, with support from

the North, would soon dominate any conceivable coalition—
by undemocratic means, the State Department contends . . .

The moral and ideological arguments about containing militant Communism in Asia (and those on the other side about
crushing capitalist imperialism) may still carry some weight
at some levels in our government, and in Hanoi's, but we
would not judge that they are much on the minds of the
pragmatic men who deal directly with the Vietnamese problem. In our own view these surface protestations have become propaganda symbols that identify the several positions
in an old-fashioned game of power politics that has degener-
ated into a stalemated war through a series of miscalculations
and outright blunders . . .

This still leaves a considerable basket of snakes to be un-
tangled. But there is one compelling fact that lends hope: We
are confident that American policy is based on the premise of
ultimate withdrawal from Vietnam; removal of the U.S. military presence is, of course, also the ultimate goal of North
Vietnam and the NLF; it is, indeed, with only some qualification as to what ought to be achieved first on the part of
some of those in the immediate neighborhood, a goal shared
by all the great and small powers—except China. If the belligerents are already united by circumstances on this common
objective it should not be impossible to find a political formula to achieve it without entailing evidently unacceptable
sacrifices of position or principle on either side. We believe
the United States is in fact willing to explore a wide range of
possibilities, looking, we would judge, primarily to some formula involving elections, and is fairly flexible as to details, including the possible involvement of some existing or newly
created international agency. . . .

It is now evident that the basic elements of the position
outlined in this memorandum represented the policy toward which the United States would haltingly move
across the next bloody year and a half—the essential formulation American negotiators would take with them to
the Paris meetings with the Vietnamese in May 1968.
Under the circumstances in which it had been presented
to us we had no reason to doubt that this was the prevail-

ing view of the State Department, and that the obvious discrepancies with the public "hard line" were accounted for by the bargaining room any professional negotiator tries to leave for himself.

The farewell dinner at Reunification House was a cheerful, optimistic affair all around. Hoang Tung obviously felt that our digest of the long conversation with Ho Chi Minh constituted a reasonable bid for further talks, and so did we. We assured our hosts that they would be hearing from us soon, one way or another, and began the long air journey home.

At Tokyo, as arranged before our departure, we sent an abbreviated message through the U.S. Embassy indicating that we had seen Ho Chi Minh and had some pertinent information to convey. We were asked to come on to Washington as soon as possible, and to try to remain under cover if we could. This we managed for a full week after we landed at Los Angeles, but it required a good deal of outrageous dissembling to the old journalistic comrades who were pursuing us in the wake of Harrison Salisbury's reverberating reports from North Vietnam in *The New York Times*.

At the State Department the "debriefing" went on intermittently for two days, and this time Katzenbach and Bundy were joined by Averell Harriman, the roving ambassador who had been designated by President Johnson to devote full time to seeking a peaceful settlement in Vietnam. We had known Harriman for some years, in his previous incarnations as New Deal cabinet officer, governor of New York, and Democratic Presidential aspirant, and it was a pleasant reunion.

We had brought back nothing that could be described as a hard proposition from Hanoi, but in context it appeared that Ho had met all the stated American conditions for opening negotiations except a guarantee to close the border between North and South Vietnam in return for a cessation of the bombing. Privately, most Washington insiders conceded that the so-called "infiltration" guarantee was an unrealistic demand under the circumstances. The North Vietnamese could hardly agree to halt the maintenance and supply of fighting forces dependent upon them unless they were prepared to leave them wholly at the mercy of the massive American expeditionary force roaring through the countryside on its "search and destroy" mission. The most that could reasonably be expected was a much more modest reciprocal gesture as a manifest of good faith, and we could report that Ho Chi Minh appeared to us to be inviting such a proposal. In any case, the way was wide open for a further probe—either through us, or directly through diplomatic channels —without any risk of compromising the official U.S. position.

It seemed evident to us, too, that time was a considerable factor. We could report our strong impression that Ho Chi Minh was in excellent mental and physical condition the day we saw him, but this was at best a fleeting glimpse of a man in his late seventies. On any actuarial basis the Vietnamese President was an increasingly poor risk as he neared the end of a hard life, and if he was in fact willing to move toward a compromise settlement prudence demanded that he be taken up on it. With his great personal standing and universal popular support he probably could sell any reasonable compromise to his associates, including the supporting Chinese, but there was no guarantee that his successor would enjoy similar freedom of action. We summarized these main points in a memorandum to Bundy dictated in the Department:

There appears no question but that Ho makes the decisions in Hanoi. The NLF is independent to a degree, although it confers with the DRV on all important matters. There is some Chinese influence in the NLF. We are told on what we think is as reliable authority as you can get in Hanoi that about 20 percent of the NLF is Communist, and that the majority sentiment in the NLF is nationalist, and very much in favor of a neutralization of Southeast Asia. It seems inevitable that some measures of conflict are going to grow between the NLF and the DRV. At the moment General Giap [Commander of the DRV Army] plans strategy for both the DRV and NLF. It is our opinion that Ho Chi Minh, because of his immense prestige in the country, could probably, at this time, persuade the NLF to abide by any decision he makes.

Based on our many conversations with government persons, it is our opinion that the leadership in the DRV is going to become collective and of an uncertain mood after Ho passes from the scene. It is quite possible that all kinds of influence, including Chinese, could insinuate themselves into power after Ho. . . .

In the circumstances, the remarks of Ho impress us as an offer to come to the table and the elements in the offer are simple enough: we stop the bombing and he will talk.

We had an attentive audience, and in the beginning no reason to doubt that what we said was being taken seriously. The Department's Vietnamese experts manfully swallowed their irritation at having persons they regarded as diplomatic amateurs instruct them in their own specialties, and if any of the professional hard-liners entertained the notion that we were innocent dupes who had been taken in by a wily old Red he did not voice it in our presence.

However, there were passing indications that our report was being received with something less than acclaim in precincts beyond those where we were immediately engaged. We did not expect to be greeted as returning heroes, but we thought we would arouse some simple curiosity as the only Americans who had talked politics privately with Ho Chi Minh since the attack on his country was launched more than two years before. We were, it is true, functioning at the highest level in the State Department, but it also began to be evident that we were limited to a narrowly proscribed circuit. Secretary Rusk, although we passed him in the corridor outside the Under Secretary's office, never stopped in to ask a single question of his own—and hasn't until this day.

We began to suspect that Katzenbach might be telling us something by indirection with his constant reminders that we must not be impatient, that it took time to get a reading on such delicate matters, that we didn't really appreciate the kind of problems the government would have with its Asian allies if it began to move toward negotiations, and that, after all, the Department had other channels available to it and was constantly checking other sources. He even resorted to the hoary cliché with which foreign service officers traditionally brush off unwelcome views—a man can't possibly have a valid opinion on a diplomatic matter unless he enjoys the privilege of reading the secret cables. This was doubtless true, we replied, unless he had been out talking to the people the men who send the secret cables ought to be talking to, but can't reach.

Governor Harriman in his turn improved a social interlude by telling us how so few people appreciated the pressures brought to bear on an American President in a situation like that posed in Vietnam. Every time Lyndon Johnson made a conciliatory move, as he had done repeatedly with his bombing pauses, the generals and admirals moved in with evidence of men and supplies moving south, he said, and obviously no commander-in-chief could thus leave his own boys at the mercy of the enemy. If the North Vietnamese would just give a little bit in return, it would give the peacemakers a leg to stand on.

All of this, Harriman continued, was bad enough, but the pressure on the President was compounded by the fact that his unhappy plight aroused no sympathy among those intellectual critics he referred to, more or less accurately, as "your friends." Instead of praising Mr. Johnson for not escalating the war any more than he had to, these ingrates (most were Democrats, of course) blamed him for making it as big and costly as it was. They ought to stop talking about getting out of the war, the governor said, and support those who were trying to keep the war from getting any bigger.

We agreed that things were tough all over, and left Washington a good deal less sanguine than we had been when we arrived.

5

FULBRIGHT'S LAW

Although the State Department is a notorious sieve, through which presumably confidential information constantly leaks, most often with im-
petus from within, the fetish of secrecy is still enshrined
in the executive suites on the seventh floor. Beyond the
legitimate requirements of diplomacy, and the human
conceit that derives pleasure from knowing something no
one else knows, the eccentricities of President Johnson
have endowed the buttoned lip with high survival value
during the brief epoch of the Great Society. The monu-
mental Presidential tantrums occasioned by his encountering even the most innocuous information in the press
before he has had a chance to divulge it himself are a
matter of historical record, and undoubtedly the fear of
provoking such outbursts has had much to do with shaping, and misshaping, public policy.

We suspected that this, rather than any real concern
that Hanoi might be upset by premature disclosure of our
findings there, occasioned the obsessive departmental
concern that we not follow our journalistic instincts and
publish all we knew. We agreed to limit our public statements to our general impressions and to avoid any
suggestion that we were in any way involved in matters
that might lead to a break in the military impasse. Our

own primary interest, of course, was in trying to promote a settlement of the war, and since it takes two to negotiate we had no disposition to send Lyndon Johnson up the wall.

This was a simple if uncomfortable matter to arrange so far as the public prints were concerned. However, when Senator J. William Fulbright, Chairman of the Senate Foreign Relations Committee, requested that we testify at a closed session, and a similar bid came from a select group of the House of Representatives, the danger of premature publicity became a secondary consideration; now the obvious political implications were paramount. Hanoi could hardly be displeased if influential legislative leaders who supported a negotiated settlement in Vietnam were apprised of Ho Chi Minh's conciliatory attitude as expressed to us; but the same could hardly be said for the hard-liners in the Johnson administration. Even so, on the assumption that to do otherwise might undermine the position of the pro-negotiation faction in the administration, we acceded to a telephone request from Katzenbach that we not testify before any Congressional committee.

As days went by without any further word from the Department, however, we began to feel concern that we might have been pushed into a dead end and muzzled in the process. On January 25 Baggs sent a personal and confidential letter to Governor Harriman, stating:

It is our thinking, from the experience and conversations we had in Hanoi, that a response of some nature should be sent in order to keep this channel open. Perhaps it should be so informal that we could simply pass along our impressions and maintain for both parties this rather flexible and uncommitting position which is possible with unofficial persons.

In any event, we are confident that the appropriate persons in Hanoi do expect some kind of word, private or otherwise, to what we regarded as the next possible thing to a hard and formal proposal. We do not believe we can overemphasize our conviction that a response, in some form, would be most useful in many ways at this time.

At about the same time, acting entirely on his own, Luis Quintanilla had presented a kindred argument to his personal friend, Ambassador Freeman, in Mexico City. He suggested that if the State Department were not disposed to act directly, he would send a message to Ho Chi Minh over his own signature stating that he was doing so with the U.S. ambassador's knowledge and consent. He dictated a draft at the embassy which proposed that (1) a secret preliminary meeting be held at once, (2) the aim would be to arrange a cessation of hostilities and the discussion would be without agenda, and (3) the bombing of the North would be halted when conversations were agreed to, but this would be done without initial public announcement.

Perhaps the most significant aspect of this proposal was the reaction to it. Quintanilla was told there were five specific objections to the message as he had drafted it: It suggested that the North Vietnamese speak for all Vietnamese; it suggested that the NLF is a legitimate political body; it did not refer to the Geneva Agreements, which might provide a basis of eventual settlement; it did not stipulate simultaneous withdrawal of North Vietnamese troops; and it did not refer to the Saigon government. It was clear that Ambassador Freeman and his staff were well versed in the current State Department line and were not disposed to encourage any departure from it. Quintanilla informed us of his meeting with Freeman on February 1, and at the same time Freeman reported the conversation to the State Department and asked for instructions.

Meanwhile, by inadvertence, President Johnson became personally involved in the matter. We had no extended contact upon our return with Senator Fulbright, but we had talked with him by telephone to explain that we had agreed not to appear before his committee, even in executive session. A few days later the Senator came to Miami to make an address, and after his talk he dropped by Baggs' residence. Baggs reiterated to the Senator our reasons for declining to testify before his committee. While Baggs did not go into the details of the conversation with Ho Chi Minh, he did indicate that we had returned from Hanoi much encouraged over the prospects of a negotiated settlement. Fulbright inquired as to the reaction of President Johnson, and Baggs said that he and Ashmore had no way to measure it since neither had talked to him. The Senator was astonished; and a few days later, at a White House social function, he had an opportunity to raise the question with Mr. Johnson.

Fulbright pointed out that Mr. Johnson had known us for many years and urged that, even if he chose to make some discount because of our known opposition to his Vietnam policy, he ought to have the benefit of a first-hand account on such a vital matter from a couple of supposedly competent reporters. The President's reply was perhaps the most splendid *non sequitur* of the entire episode. "I'd like to see them, Bill," he said, "but you know I can't talk with everybody who's been over there talking with Ho Chi Minh." When this exchange became public knowledge some months later, David Brinkley of NBC observed that Mr. Johnson was speaking of "a multitude of two."

The White House conversation, as it turned out, did pink the nerve that controls Mr. Johnson's hyperactive consensus reflex. We were summoned back to Washington forthwith by the State Department, and Fulbright received two lengthy telephone calls from the President. He was concerned, he said, that the Senator not get the idea that Ashmore and Baggs weren't being taken seriously, and that his administration wasn't prepared to follow up any opening that might lead to negotiations. He had issued instructions, he said, that anybody in the government we thought useful to see would be available to us. That could include Secretary Rusk if we insisted, but he added that it was his own feeling that we would be better off dealing with Under Secretary Katzenbach—who, he noted, was likely to be disposed toward peace since he once had been a prisoner of war himself.

The upshot of this remarkable exchange was that the President asked Fulbright to be present at our next session at the State Department. Fulbright felt he had no option but to agree—although, as he told us when we joined him at dinner upon our return to Washington on February 3, he was convinced that nothing useful could come of it.

This mordant view was not confined to the privacy of the dinner table. The meeting was set for 10 a.m. next morning and the company gathered in Katzenbach's office in the Saturday morning quiet of a nearly deserted building. We sat on a sofa in what amounted to no-man's-land as Fulbright faced Katzenbach, Harriman and Bundy, and a second row of lesser functionaries, across the spacious office.

He was present, Fulbright began, only because the President had asked him to come, and he had to say in all candor that he thought he was wasting his time and theirs. "The trouble is that I believe we ought to negotiate a settlement of this war in Vietnam, and you don't," he said. "You're all committed to a military victory, and all this talk about being willing to go to the table doesn't mean a damned thing and you know it."

He wasn't being personally critical, he said, since he understood that they had to be loyal to their departmental policy. "Of course we haven't seen much of Secretary Rusk lately, since he no longer honors our invitations to appear before the Committee, but over the years I have spent many, many hours questioning him about what we're doing in Vietnam. I know what Dean Rusk thinks, and that's what you've got to act on—and so we go ahead treating this little piss-ant country as though we were up against Russia and China put together.

"You don't have to tell me what kind of pressure

you're under from the military. The air force chief, General McConnell, is from Arkansas and still considers himself a constituent of mine. He comes by to see me and tells me what wonderful weapons he's got and begs me to help him get a chance to use them so we can get the war over with. I don't blame the general—that's the business he's in, and of course he wants to use his new hardware and prove how well it works.

"But the way it works is to kill off a bunch of backward people, and for no purpose that serves any conceivable legitimate national interest of this country. How can you keep on talking about defending a friendly nation from aggression when the only people the United States military hits with its bullets and bombs are Vietnamese —not Chinese, or Russians, or any other monolithic Communists, just little, sawed-off Vietnamese fighting us on their own soil? It ought to say something to us, too, that these little fellows fight so well when they're against us, and so poorly when they're on our side.

"Well, you all know how I feel. You've heard me say it over and over for years, and obviously you are not paying any attention, since the State Department goes right on with the same old bankrupt foreign policy, making the same mistakes over and over. All you people over here think of is power, and so you have this country throwing its weight around all over the world, and if anybody points out that this is not only immoral but it isn't even working you say they're isolationist, or unpatriotic, or maybe both. I say you're caught in a trap and you can't get out because you won't do the one thing you've got to do—admit you're wrong and start off in a new direction.

"That's what I mean by the arrogance of power, and I'm prepared to bet that you're going to prove me right by hanging so many conditions on whatever reply you send to Ho Chi Minh you'll make sure he'll turn you down, and then you'll use that as an excuse to step up the bombing even more."

This, we concluded in retrospect, was about as stringent a political charge as we had ever heard detonated in the course of something less than sheltered lives. If the aplomb of the Senator's adversaries survived it, it was with visible effort; the impassive expressions stayed in place but the telltale crimson crept up toward the hairlines, and the response, when it came, tended to arrive in blurts. And it consisted, in fact, of not much more than the assurance that those present, at least, were just as desirous of peace in Vietnam as was the Senator, and were trying hard to get some kind of negotiations going. The trouble with Fulbright's position, Katzenbach complained, was that he talked as though there was only one side to the question, and Harriman added that there were a great many stubborn realities involved that couldn't simply be swept under the rug.

Bundy brought the exchange back down to conversational pitch by producing a draft letter he said had been worked up in his section as a possible reply to Ho Chi Minh. The channel we had established, he said, seemed to be highly useful, and he thought we ought to employ it once again to transmit the Department's views informally rather than running the risk of direct official contact.

We found the proposed letter unduly turgid, and Bundy agreed that it might well be simplified and improved. It was arranged that we would return after lunch and the three of us would rework the draft. Harriman, who had told us earlier that the White House had instructed him that we were to have a "blank check" on appointments, had set up a date for us with Defense Secretary McNamara, and we headed for the Pentagon as the gathering began to disintegrate with the approach of noon.

Foggy Bottom was bare of taxis, so we hitched a ride to a cab stand with Fulbright, who, with admirable consistency, continued to berate the State Department in private with the same asperity he had displayed in the presence of the country's leading architects and practitioners of foreign policy. It was in this conversation that he enunciated what we have come to refer to as Fulbright's Law.

"I've been up against these fellows, one way or another, for the past 26 years," he said, "and the one lesson I have learned is that you can't trust them. It's mutual, of course—they don't trust you, either, and they'll tell you that's the first rule of diplomacy.

"We talk about the Russians acting on the principle that the end justifies the means, but let me tell you that you have just been in the ultimate citadel of that policy. These State Department people figure they're entitled to use you, in any way they see fit, to further what they call the national interest, but the national interest is whatever they decide it is and can sell the President.

"Their big weapon is secrecy; they let you have just as much of the pertinent information as serves their purpose and hold back the rest. And you'll find the classification system gets some rapid revision when you cross them and they begin leaking out whatever they've got that can serve to discredit you.

"If you want a laboratory example you can look at the Tonkin Gulf Resolution. As chairman of the Foreign Relations Committee I took the lead in putting that Resolution through the Senate, and they've been using it ever since to justify escalating the war. I never would have endorsed it if I had been given the facts, nor would a majority of the Senators have supported it. You can call that dissembling, or you can call it lying—but it comes out the same way. It's a hell of a way to run a foreign policy."

We joined Bundy in his office that afternoon for the preparation of what would turn out to be the key document in another laboratory example of Fulbright's Law at work. The letter to Ho Chi Minh was reworked completely by the two of us, and then reviewed line by line with Bundy. By the time we had agreed on text and tone the day was drawing to a close. We took a draft copy to Governor Harriman when we joined him at his Georgetown house for cocktails, and arranged to meet Bundy back at the Department in mid-morning, which would give him time to clear the letter where necessary—which we took to mean with Secretary Rusk and the White House.

When the draft was returned to us on Sunday morning only a few minor changes had been suggested, and we dictated the final version to a secretary. Bundy volunteered to deliver the mailing copy and two carbons to us at Senator Fulbright's residence, where we were going for a farewell luncheon—a gesture which acknowledged the fact that the Senator was entitled to see what had been wrought in our joint effort. Here is the full text of the letter to Ho Chi Minh, as signed by Ashmore and mailed by him on Sunday afternoon, February 5, at Dulles International Airport:

Mr. William Baggs and I have made a full report to appropriate officials of the United States Government on our recent conversation with you in Hanoi. Ambassador Luis Quintanilla has communicated his views to the U.S. Ambassador in Mexico City.

The State Department has expressed itself as most grateful for your thoughtful approach to the possibility of an ultimate settlement of the hostilities between the United States and the Democratic Republic of Viet-Nam.

In our several discussions with senior officials of the State Department they took occasion to reiterate points we believe are already known to you. They emphasized that the U.S. remains prepared for secret discussions at any time, without conditions, and that such discussions might cover the whole range of topics relevant to a peaceful settlement. They reiterated that the Geneva Accords might be the framework for a peaceful solution.

They expressed particular interest in your suggestion to us that private talks could begin provided the U.S. stopped bombing your country, and ceased introducing additional

U.S. troops into Viet-Nam. They expressed the opinion that some reciprocal restraint to indicate that neither side intended to use the occasion of the talks for military advantage would provide tangible evidence of the good faith of all parties in the prospects for a negotiated settlement.

In the light of these concerns, they expressed great interest in any clarification of this point that you might wish to provide through a communication to us.

Speaking now wholly for ourselves, we believe the essential condition for productive talks is an arrangement under which neither side stands to gain military advantage during the period of negotiation. To achieve this end it may be that preliminary secret discussions would be helpful to determine the outline of a possible peaceful settlement.

As we see it, these are practical considerations that have nothing to do with questions of "face." There is no doubt in our minds that the American Government genuinely seeks peace. As private citizens our sole concern is in facilitating a discussion that will bring all matters at issue to official consideration. It is in this sense that we convey these comments, and invite any reply you may wish to make, which of course we would report to our government in complete discretion.

May I take this occasion to renew our thanks for the courteous and considerate treatment we received in Hanoi throughout our visit, and for the honor of our most useful conversation with you.

If you feel that further personal conversation with Mr. Baggs and me is in order we would of course return to Hanoi at your convenience.

If this final version bore some of the weaseling touches of the usual committee effort, it still seemed to us virtually certain to elicit some response from Hanoi, and the expectation got a sort of backhanded official endorsement in a secret telegram sent by the Department to Ambassador Freeman in Mexico City instructing him to spike the proposed Quintanilla message. The message said in part:

Question of sending Hanoi some appropriate response has been thoroughly explored in meeting this morning with Baggs and Ashmore and they have agreed on general lines of message they would send as their personal impressions based on conversations in Washington. We think this kind of message is far better designed to explore possibilities of keeping this channel open than Quintanilla's proposed draft. At same time it would avoid danger, definitely posed by Quintanilla's draft, of over-burdening this particular channel and of confusing messages reaching Hanoi through other reliable means.

In our view best solution would be for Quintanilla to associate himself with message being sent by Baggs and Ashmore, text of which will follow in immediately succeeding telegram.

In conveying this to Quintanilla you should once again assure him that we recognize the devotion to peace which has inspired his efforts and express our belief that given his experience with diplomatic practice over the course of many years he will be first to understand reasons for discretion and prudence in such delicate matters if there is serious interest in achieving successful outcome.

Quintanilla of course acceded, and on February 7 sent a brief cable to Hanoi, via Hoang Tung, associating himself with the views expressed in our letter. On February 15 we received, as requested, cabled confirmation from the DRV representation in Phnom Penh that the letter had been received there and transmitted to Hanoi. It was, as we were to discover, at least five days too late.

6

THE DOUBLE DEAL

We had calculated on the basis of past performance that it ordinarily takes about two
weeks to receive a response to a message to Hanoi, what
with shaky communications by mail or cable coupled with
the natural caution of the recipients. The cabled acknowledgment of our letter on February 15 indicated that nine
days had been used up outward bound (the international
date line knocks 24 hours off the calendar computation).
As the month drew to a close with no response, Quintanilla proposed sending a message that would require some
sort of answer. On February 27 from Mexico City he cabled Hoang Tung:

REPLY TO LETTER HARRY ASHMORE FEBRUARY 5 REFERRED TO
IN MY TELEGRAM OF FEBRUARY 7 IS SO VERY IMPORTANT ASH-

MORE AND BAGGS ARE RETURNING HANOI VIA ICC PLANE
MARCH 10. FURTHER DELAY WILL HAVE ADVERSE EFFECT.
PLEASE ACKNOWLEDGE RECEIPT OF THIS CABLE TO ME.

Quintanilla's effort produced a response, but its effect
was to head off our return trip to Hanoi before it began.
On March 2 Hoang Tung cabled:

USA UNDERTAKING NEW SERIOUS STEPS OF WAR ESCALATION
AGAINST DRV. VISIT TO HANOI AS REQUESTED BY ASHMORE AND
BAGGS NOT OPPORTUNE. SINCERELY

73

Quintanilla relayed this message to us, and also discussed the matter with Ambassador Freeman at the U.S. Embassy. He had drafted a response which he showed the ambassador, who said he would prefer that no message of any kind be sent, but that if Quintanilla insisted he would not quarrel with the proposed text. So, with what might be called State Department nondisapproval, the following went to Hoang Tung on March 7:

WE SINCERELY BELIEVE IT WOULD BE SERIOUS MISTAKE TO INTERPRET "NEW UNDERTAKINGS" REFERRED TO IN YOUR TELEGRAM OF MARCH 2 AS AN INDICATION OF ANY CHANGE IN ATTITUDE REFLECTED IN ASHMORE LETTER FEBRUARY 5 STATING THAT THE UNITED STATES REMAINS PREPARED FOR SECRET DISCUSSIONS AT ANY TIME WITHOUT CONDITIONS. WE CAN ASSURE YOU THIS CONTINUES TO BE ENTIRELY HONEST AND VALID. THEREFORE WE URGE YOUR IMMEDIATE REPLY TO ASHMORE LETTER.

Two weeks later we would understand that Freeman's effort to head off this message was probably intended to spare his Mexican friend the embarrassment of continuing to innocently endorse a conciliatory U.S. policy that no longer existed—if, indeed, it ever had.

We, like Quintanilla, had assumed that the "new undertakings" cited by Hanoi referred only to the resumption of bombing on February 14, after a six-day cessation for the Tet lunar new year holiday. However, on March 21 Ho Chi Minh made it clear that our exchange had been terminated not by aerial bombardment, but by a hard-line letter he had received from President Johnson on February 10.

Ho's release of the Johnson letter, along with his caustic reply, noted that it had been transmitted through Moscow and had arrived in Hanoi five days before ours did. A Presidential message, of course, would have taken precedence in any event, and this one effectively canceled the conciliatory tone and tentative openings we had offered on behalf of "high officials of the State Department." The

President restated conditions we had indicated Ho Chi Minh would not accept, and added a couple of new ones. There was even a preambular paragraph referring to previous futile efforts to establish contact that could be read as an advance disclaimer of the message we had forwarded on behalf of the State Department: "It may be that our thoughts and yours, our attitudes and yours, have been distorted and misinterpreted as they passed through these various channels. Certainly there is always a danger in indirect communication."

The President then laid down his own requirements for the beginning of talks:

There is one good way to overcome this problem and to move forward in search for a peaceful settlement. That is for us to arrange for direct talks between trusted representatives in a secure setting away from the glare of publicity. Such talks should not be used as a propaganda exercise but should be a serious effort to find a workable and mutually acceptable solution.

In the past two weeks I have noted public statements by representatives of your Government suggesting that you would be prepared to enter into direct bilateral talks with representatives of the United States Government provided that we ceased "unconditionally" and permanently our bombing operations against your country and all military action against it. In the last day, serious and responsible parties have assured us indirectly that this is in fact your position.

Let me frankly state that I see two great difficulties with this proposal. In view of your public position, such action on our part would inevitably produce worldwide speculation that discussions were under way and would impair the privacy and secrecy of those discussions. Secondly, there would inevitably be grave concern on our part whether your Government would make use of such action to improve its military position.

With these problems in mind, I am prepared to move further toward an end of hostilities than your Government has proposed in either public statements or through private diplomatic channels. I am prepared to order a cessation of bombing against your country and the stopping of further augmentation of the United States forces in South Vietnam as soon as I am assured that infiltration into South Vietnam by land and by sea has stopped. These acts of restraint on both sides would, I believe, make it possible for us to conduct serious private discussions leading toward an early peace.

I make this proposal to you now with a specific sense of urgency arising from the imminent new year holidays in Vietnam. If you are able to accept this proposal, I see no reason why it could not take effect at the end of the new year, or Tet, holidays. The proposal I have made would be greatly strengthened if your military authorities and those of South Vietnam could promptly negotiate an extension of the Tet truce.

As to the site of the bilateral discussions I propose, there are several possibilities. We could, for example, have our representatives meet in Moscow where contacts have already occurred. They could meet in some other country such as Burma. You may have other arrangements or sites in mind, and I would try to meet your suggestions.

The important thing is to end a conflict that has brought burdens to both our peoples, and above all to the people of South Vietnam. If you have any thoughts about the actions I propose, it would be most important that I receive them as soon as possible.

When the Johnson letter was made public the American and world press generally assumed that it was, as *The New York Times* described it, "designed to convey a hardening of the U.S position." This was denied by the State Department, whose spokesmen tried to argue that the President in fact was offering a substantial new concession. As William Bundy subsequently put it: "It added a very major action on our side, the cessation of reinforcements immediately. It proposed a very major action on the other side in response. There is a long series of proposals of a general sort in this area that have been made publicly and privately. I do not consider this to have been a hardening. On the contrary."

However, as we read the rough-textured Johnson letter

we could well imagine the reaction of the addressee. In his wry way, we thought, Ho Chi Minh doubtless would be amused by the President's fatuous argument that he couldn't stop the bombing because this would arouse suspicion that negotiations were under way and thereby impair their secrecy and subject the participants to the temptation to indulge in propaganda—this from a man who the year before had celebrated Christmas by dispatching coveys of senior diplomats to the capitals of the world as "salesmen of peace," and would follow up this Madison Avenue gesture a year later by making a personal Yuletide foray to the Vatican to pray with the Pope.

There was another secondary matter which would not amuse Ho at all—the effort to tie negotiations to the Tet holiday. Although Mr. Johnson referred to the "imminent new year holidays," Ho indicated in his reply that he had actually received the letter on the 10th, midway through the four-day Tet observance. And it was William Bundy who had warned, while we were drafting our own letter, that it would be a mistake to tie any proposal to Tet, since the announced bombing pause was of such short duration it would not allow reasonable time to consider a response and this would be considered intolerable pressure, if not implied blackmail. We had thought Bundy's appraisal correct when he made it, and we still do.

However, all of this was merely window-dressing. The Johnson proposal not only repeated his prior demand for a halt to infiltration to the south by land and sea, but also required that the border be closed before he took action to suspend the bombing. In contrast, we had worked for some time with Bundy on a softening expression for reciprocity in our letter, which finally resulted in the heavily qualified "some reciprocal response."

The Presidential prose guaranteed a prompt rejection. Ho Chi Minh indicated his contempt for the proposal by unilaterally making it public and firing back a few hun-

dred words of standard Communist polemics, in the
course of which he restated the four points he had so
conspicuously modified in his conversation with us. Then
he made the only reply the authors of the Johnson letter
reasonably could have expected:

In your message you suggest direct talks between the Democratic Republic of Vietnam and the United States. If the
United States Government really wants these talks, it must
first of all stop unconditionally its bombing raids and all
other acts of war against the Democratic Republic of Vietnam. It is only after the unconditional cessation of the U.S.
bombing raids and all other acts of war against the DRV that
the DRV and the U.S. would enter into talks and discuss
questions concerning the two sides.
The Vietnamese people will never submit to force, they
will never accept talks under the threat of bombs.

Publication of the Ho-Johnson letters left us with no
doubt that J. William Fulbright had been proved a proph-
et in good standing, and that Fulbright's Law was in
full force and effect. The result of this duplicity was to
give the administration another contrived excuse for further escalation of the war through the spring and summer, with a major build-up of American forces in the
South and intensification of the bombing attack on the
North. Moreover, we were aware that this was one of a
series of similar maneuvers that had canceled out previous tentative moves toward a negotiated settlement
when they seemed about to elicit a favorable response
from Hanoi.

David Kraslow and Stuart H. Loory of the Washington
Bureau of the Los Angeles *Times* documented five such
aborted efforts in their series on *The Secret Search for
Peace in Vietnam,* published after the preliminaries of the
Paris talks were announced. We had had considerable
first-hand knowledge of three of these as background for
appraising our own bizarre experience. The first, in January 1965, involved the late Adlai Stevenson, who had en-

couraged U Thant to complete arrangements for a secret meeting in Rangoon, Burma, only to have President Johnson undercut his UN ambassador and rule out U.S. participation. In November 1965, Giorgio LaPira, the former mayor of Florence, Italy, returned from Hanoi with word that Ho Chi Minh was ready to talk, and would do so without insisting on his previous demand that American troops be withdrawn; this time Dean Rusk scuttled the move with a set of complicating terms delivered to Italian Foreign Minister Fanfani, and this was followed by the first bombing of Haiphong. After the 37-day bombing pause which began in December 1965 as the background for the President's Christmas peace extravaganza of that year, Ambassador Chester Ronning, the Canadian expert on Asia, was called out of retirement to fly to Hanoi on behalf of the State Department, and was sufficiently encouraged by his preliminary findings to go back again in June 1966; a week after Ambassador Ronning's return from the second trip with a report that movement now seemed possible, American planes bombed the Hanoi area for the first time.

After reviewing our own experience with some of the principals involved in these episodes we concluded that the dim prospects for a negotiated settlement could not be harmed, and might possibly be improved, by exposure of the high-level double-dealing in which we had been involved. Ashmore included an abbreviated account of the dispatch of the two contradictory letters to Ho Chi Minh in an article on the background of the *Pacem in Terris* convocations he wrote for *The Center Magazine*. The article carefully avoided the details of our conversation with Ho, or any other information which might compromise a formula for settlement, but it did set forth the circumstances under which our letter had been drafted in the State Department. Ashmore charged:

This conciliatory feeler was effectively and brutally cancelled before there was any chance to determine what response Hanoi might have made. . . .

Any appraisal I can offer of what actually went on in the ultimate reaches of the Administration during this period is necessarily subjective. From beginning to end of our dealings with the State Department there was an almost total absence of candor on the official side. . . .

This may have reflected no more than an understandable discretion in dealing with outsiders who had often been critical of State Department policy. But I am convinced the cause runs much deeper in the case of the overriding question to which we never got a satisfactory answer—whether the Administration was really willing to negotiate a compromise settlement in Vietnam or was committed to a military victory. . . .

The theory that seems to me to fit about as well as any is that the President has taken a ping-pong approach to the problems he inherited in Vietnam. The extent of his personal ambition, so far as I can divine it, is to find a compromise that will permit him to get out of Southeast Asia without appearing to have suffered a major military and political defeat. The technique is to throw his weight behind the advocates of negotiation until do-it-now pressure from the generals and admirals becomes unbearable. Then he cuts the military loose for another turn of the screw, only to clamp down again when the opinion polls remind him how unpopular the Vietnam war really is. The double-dealing to which William Baggs and I were subjected seems to indicate that we passed through both phases.

When the text of the Ashmore article was released to the press on Monday, September 18, it produced a sharp reaction in Washington. The blunt charge of Presidential duplicity produced headlines in the morning papers across the country, and that afternoon the administration felt it necessary to send forth William Bundy to try to put out the fire. The State Department issued a lengthy official statement, and one of the first queries it elicited was why the rebuttal was so much more detailed and elaborate than any issued before under similar circumstances. This was only one of the uncomfortable questions the gentlemanly and obviously pained Bundy would have to field during the next fifty minutes.

First of all, there was a confusion about dates which became more embarrassing the more Bundy tried to explain it away. Ashmore had written that the President's letter to Ho was dated February 2, which meant that it must have been available to the State Department at least three days before the letter he sent to Ho was cleared by Bundy on behalf of his superiors. February 2 was the date given by the Department when it confirmed Ho's announcement of the Johnson letter on March 21, and provided the intelligence that the Presidential message had been forwarded from Moscow on February 8—a discrepancy in time, one of the reporters noted, that had been puzzling him ever since. Now Bundy was charging that Ashmore had been in error and that the Johnson letter in fact was dated February 8, the day of transmittal.

This issue threads through the transcript of the lengthy press conference, and was a recurring diversion to Bundy's effort to write off the Ashmore-Baggs channel to Hanoi as one of little consequence. The real action had been going on in Moscow, he said, where there was an actual face-to-face exchange between real live foreign service officers of the United States and the DRV. Here are the concluding passages of the official transcript:

Q: Bill, the implication of Ashmore's statement in his article, and I think he almost says it in so many words, is that he had a good thing going which would have very, very probably led to some kind of agreement to stop the war, and the President sent a very tough letter to Ho which knocked it all in the head.

Now, in very simple peasant language, this is what a lot of this whole controversy is about. Will you comment on this point?

A: Yes. I will comment to say that it's again obvious to any student of the relative weight to be attached to the chan-

nels as of that time that the direct channel in Moscow was by
far the most important. I think Mr. Ashmore yields to an understandable personal feeling that his own was the center of
the stage. I think the account I have given makes clear that it
was not, and in the nature of things could not be.

The question is what the sum total of the exchange is in
Moscow—which I have characterized as far as it's in the national interest to do—and of the President's letter, and what
Ho's reply is. And I think it's clear, if you take these all together, that the reading was that Hanoi had no desire to
move at that time.

Q: To what extent did the Baggs-Ashmore report have the
conversation with Ho—to what extent did that contribute to
the end product, namely the letter of February 8th by the
President?

A: I think I have already answered that question.

Q: I am not clear, Bill.

A: What I said was that it was obviously part of our total
information. I don't think it played a significant part, but it
was a part of our total stock of information.

Q: Could I ask Mr. Hightower's question another way: Are
you prepared to say that the President's letter was in no way
imaginable, conceivable, related to the Baggs-Ashmore—

A: No, I didn't say any such thing. I said it was based on
total analysis of all information over a long period of time
and in particular on the information, negative though it was,
of response to the various proposals made in Moscow to
other information that had reached us from other quarters
very recently and referred to in the President's letter and to
the totality of all we had.

Now, of course, in that total sense, what Baggs and Ashmore had given us was a part of it. So to say that it had no
impact was, I would say, my own summation—no significant
impact—but it was a part of the totality.

Q: But you will not say that the day that you drafted the
letter with Ashmore that you were in the process of drafting
the President's letter?

A: No, sir. I will not comment on the drafting of letters
written by the President of the United States.

Q: Well, this is the central point of his argument.

A: Not at all, Mr. Roberts, in the account I have given.

The exact day at which you come to a decision to handle a thing, it seems to me, is a matter that a government is entitled to let stand on the record.

Q: But you are trying to answer his accusation, and his accusation is that one-half of the Government didn't know what the other half was doing.

A: I have answered that question too. I have said that those who framed the response that was given to Mr. Ashmore were fully aware of all that was under way and contemplated in the other channel.

Q: Was the letter under way and contemplated at that time?

A: That's a question that I regard as a matter of Executive Privilege and not a matter on which any spokesman for the Administration should comment. The letter speaks for itself.

Q: But you stand by what you said before, that the letter was—

A: We will never comment on dates letters are written.

Q: You did say before—you originally told us it was written on the 2nd; you did.

A: No. I merely corrected the record on that, Chal.

Q: After it becomes—

A: If it was said at any time by any Administration spokesmen that it was February 2nd—and this is a matter that doubtless Bob McCloskey has got somebody looking up at this moment—that was in error. That letter was in its published form dated February 8th. I have told you the facts.

Q: I think when we were given the letter there was no date on it.

A: That quite often happens with correspondence. It's normally given a date corresponding to the date of transmission, which in this case was very early on the 8th.

Mr. McCloskey: I have the record of the transcript on that day. There's no reference to February 2 in the record on that.

A: I really don't know how the February 2 story got started, Chal, and I will have to leave it to one side.

Q: High officials in the Department of State told us that date.

A: Well, in that event we were wrong.

Q: Thank you, Bill.

Whatever other purpose it served, the press conference resulted in a further effort to pry up the lid of secrecy on the Moscow negotiations of which Bundy made so much in his effort to denigrate the Ashmore-Baggs channel. The enterprising Kraslow and Loory have since established that the Johnson letter did a good deal more than shoot down the effort of those the Department sought to dismiss as vagrant amateur peacemakers (just two more frustrated seekers after the Nobel Prize, Dean Rusk said off the record, and was promptly quoted). Two chiefs of state were treated in equally cavalier fashion—British Prime Minister Harold Wilson and Soviet Premier Alexei N. Kosygin, who were meeting in London during the critical period. *The Secret Search for Peace* series also cleared up the matter of dates which so plagued Bundy by establishing that there *was* a Presidential draft letter dated February 2, which was drastically hardened before it was actually dispatched to Ho Chi Minh on February 8:

To guard against any misunderstandings in the London meetings, which began Feb. 6, the Johnson Administration dispatched Chester L. Cooper, an expert in Vietnam diplomacy, to brief Wilson on the American position and to monitor the talks with Kosygin. . . .

Unnoticed, Cooper left Washington on February 2, the day the President told the world at a press conference that "just about any step" by North Vietnam could bring surcease from American bombing.

Cooper had seen the Feb. 2 draft of the President's letter and knew what had been happening in Moscow in the secret talks between John Guthrie, deputy chief of the American embassy, and Le Trang, his North Vietnamese counterpart.

Cooper took with him to London the latest version of an American negotiation scenario secretly designated Phase A–Phase B, which conformed to the draft he had seen of the President's letter. It was a flexible plan for de-escalating the war in such a manner that neither the United States nor North Vietnam would lose either face or military advantage.

Phase A–Phase B was no peace plan as such. It was more a plan to cool off the war in the hope that once that was accomplished serious negotiations involving the interests of all combatants—the Saigon regime and the National Liberation Front as well as the United States and North Vietnam—would result.

Phase A involved the cessation of American bombing of North Vietnam. It would only take effect, however, after Washington and Hanoi secretly agreed on Phase B—an act of de-escalation of the ground war on both sides. The United States would move first in Phase B as well.

The indication is that under the plan Cooper took to London, North Vietnam would be permitted to continue resupplying its forces in the South.

Wilson laid out the A–B proposal, and Kosygin responded by indicating that he could get a guarantee that the Vietnamese "would" come to the table if the bombing were halted as proposed in Phase A. This was a slightly more affirmative version of a recent statement by DRV Foreign Minister Nguyen Duy Trinh, and it attracted a good deal of attention when Kosygin reiterated it publicly in an internationally televised press conference. This was on February 9, and it brought forth the standard complaint from the White House: "Mr. Kosygin commented on the military action the United States should take but made no mention of the military action the other side should take." Dean Rusk went on to deplore what he called "a systematic campaign by the Communist side" to generate pressure for a bombing halt without even "elementary reciprocity."

This hardly sounded as though Phase A–Phase B was still on anyone's agenda—and indeed it shouldn't have been, since the February 8 version of the President's letter to Ho clearly reversed the essential points in the February 2 draft Cooper had seen before he set out for London. Remarkably enough, although the hard-line letter already had been dispatched to Moscow and had brought a halt to the Guthrie-Trang exchanges, no one bothered to inform the high-level negotiators in London. Here is the Kraslow-Loory description of the low-comedy scene that resulted:

Under the Phase A–Phase B Plan that Wilson had, on America's behalf, been presenting to Kosygin, the United States would make the first act of de-escalation. The Johnson letter turned this around and demanded that North Vietnam move first to end all infiltration before the bombing ended.

Wilson did not learn of the change in the President's letter to Ho making the turnaround. On Friday, February 10, Kosygin asked for the first time in the week that Wilson put into writing the American proposal he had been given orally. . . . He appeared eager to transmit the proposal to Moscow before departure.

After Kosygin had left 10 Downing St., where he had lunched, Wilson and Cooper, according to London sources, drafted a memorandum.

A copy was cabled to Washington, where it was received simultaneously in the White House Situation Room and the State Department Operations Center.

Wilson put the message in his inside coat pocket and went off to a 5:30 reception at the Soviet Embassy, where he spent 90 minutes. During the reception, Kosygin took Wilson into an anteroom and asked him if he had the message.

If there was anything wrong with the message, Wilson thought, he would have heard from Washington by then. He hadn't. He gave Kosygin the message and returned to 10 Downing St.

At about 10:15 p.m., London time (4:15 p.m. in Washington), when Kosygin left the embassy for the 10-to-20 minute ride to Euston Railroad Station, transatlantic chaos set in. The President and others, having read the cabled memo from Downing Street, became alarmed when they realized the inconsistency between it and the letter to Ho Chi Minh.

Rusk and presidential assistant Walt W. Rostow were summoned to the Situation Room. While Rostow contacted Wilson, the men in the room were drafting a new paragraph to substitute for the unsuitable section in the Wilson message to Kosygin. . . .

The substitute paragraph was dictated to 10 Downing St. It was now approaching 11 p.m. in London. Wilson dispatched one of his aides with orders to hand it personally to Kosygin at Euston Station.

The aide raced through London in his car. He dashed through the doorway of Euston Station, down the stairs, through the crowds and finally, out of breath, to Platform No. 1. He just made it.

Wilson, according to Kraslow and Loory, stiffened his British upper lip and "took it like a man." There is no record of how Kosygin reacted, which, under the circumstances, may be just as well.

7

ASSAULT BY INNUENDO

The public exchange between Ashmore and
Assistant Secretary Bundy, which reverber-
ated in the press for some weeks thereafter, only confirmed a condition that had existed for months—one we
would later describe in diplomatic parlance as a *détente*
based on mutual distrust.

The impending *Pacem in Terris* convocation made it
impossible for the State Department simply to write us
off. Even after the prospect that we might be instrumental
in opening negotiations with Hanoi apparently had been
disposed of, there was still Ho Chi Minh's indication that
he might be represented at Geneva. The North Vietnamese by now had accepted in principle our invitation to
join with the other Southeast Asian nations in a discussion of possible neutralization of the entire region. This
was a matter of considerable significance, since it meant
that Hanoi had agreed to permit its representatives to sit
down publicly with those of Saigon.

There is independent evidence that this tentative com-
mitment to *Pacem in Terris II* survived the post-Tet esca-
lation and the exchange of letters with President Johnson.
A senior Indonesian diplomat, Nugroho, then Deputy
Foreign Minister and soon to be assigned as his country's
Ambassador to Hanoi, told us in Geneva that the North

Vietnamese Ambassador in Djakarta had informed him right up to the beginning of May that Hanoi expected to be represented at the convocation. The decision to withdraw came in the wake of the new American aerial offensive launched in late April, which lifted the previous ban against direct attacks on major concentrations of civilian population.

Under date of May 19, just ten days before the convocation's scheduled opening, we received Hanoi's formal cancellation in a cable from Hoang Tung. "The USA talks 'peace and negotiations,' " the cable said, "only to camouflage new extremely serious escalation steps going even to the length of bombing Hanoi and Haiphong."

The invitation under consideration by the North Vietnamese had been accepted, and later was honored at Geneva, by Thailand, Cambodia, Laos, Indonesia, and Malaya. It stipulated that unless both sides in the Vietnam war were represented, neither side would be heard—a precaution against allowing the panel discussion to degenerate into a propaganda forum, and the only condition under which neutralist Southeast Asian countries could have considered participation.

By April the South Vietnamese were claiming foul. Marshal Ky announced in Saigon that he would demand a boycott of *Pacem in Terris II* on the ground that Ho Chi Minh had been invited and he had not. The State Department expressed its concern. All parties were again assured that Saigon would be represented if Hanoi or the NLF sent participants, but would not be invited to participate alone. Letters of invitation stipulating this condition were dispatched to two South Vietnamese whose names were supplied by the State Department. One was Ky's Foreign Minister, Tran Van Do.

Soon we began to encounter evidence that this contrived South Vietnamese issue was being used to undermine the convocation. In Bern the U.S. Ambassador, John S. Hayes, complained to Ashmore that in submitting the first invitation to Hanoi we had given Ho the option of blocking Saigon's participation by withholding his own. Ambassador Hayes did not seem to be interested in the explanation that this also worked in reverse, since Saigon could block Hanoi in the same fashion.

In Geneva we began to cross the trail of Roger Tubby, the U.S. Ambassador to UN organizations, who was busily denigrating *Pacem in Terris II* all around the diplomatic cocktail circuit. Many months later, when Senator Claiborne Pell of Rhode Island held up confirmation of Tubby's reappointment in protest against this activity, the State Department came to his rescue by confirming that he was acting under orders from Washington.

As it was perhaps intended to do, the issue publicized by Saigon had its repercussions in Eastern Europe. Although the conditions for the Southeast Asian panel had been covered with the Eastern bloc foreign ministries in the initial planning stage, sharp questions were now raised about the role of the South Vietnamese, particularly by the Soviets. Fred Warner Neal, the Claremont international affairs professor and Center consultant who handled these negotiations, reassured all concerned that unless both belligerents joined the panel neither side would be permitted to address the convocation. This condition, incidentally, had been rejected by National Liberation Front representatives in Prague and Moscow, who demanded that Saigon be barred as the price of NLF participation. Our refusal to consider this had terminated the negotiation.

Finagling over South Vietnamese representation continued into the convocation proper. As soon as Hanoi's cancellation was received we cabled the South Vietnamese Foreign Minister to inform him that, under our prior understanding, we were withdrawing our invitation. The response from Saigon was that Tran Van Do already had departed for Geneva, even though this was a good week ahead of time, and could not be headed off. He arrived in the company of the ranking public-relations expert from Saigon's Washington embassy, and politely forced us to reject his demand that he be allowed to address the convocation from the floor. Thus was created the kind of free-speech issue that is guaranteed to draw a glandular response from the American press.

Ironically, the presence of Tran Van Do in Geneva also provided the Russians with the stated reason for their last-minute withdrawal from the convocation. Negotiations with the Soviets are made thorny enough under any circumstances by their inordinate suspicion of the West and their honest difficulty in drawing a distinction between official policy and private action. Throughout the spring, Neal's dealings were beset by the steady worsening of Soviet-U.S. relations on all fronts. Then, in the week preceding the convocation, the situation suddenly deteriorated into the Arab-Israeli crisis, which amounted to a direct confrontation between the two great powers in the Mid-East.

It seems likely that a variety of factors contributed to the sudden Soviet decision to renege on long-standing commitments to *Pacem in Terris II*—one no doubt being Premier Kosygin's adventures in London at the time our own contact with Ho Chi Minh was being canceled by President Johnson. However that may be, the eleventh-hour telegram announcing withdrawal led off with the usual denunciation of the bombings in Vietnam and offered as its first point of substance: "We also bear in mind the fact that from the very beginning we were placed in difficult position as convocation sponsors had planned to invite representatives of Saigon regime, which having lost all support of its own people, is mere extension of external forces, etc., etc."

A dialogue requires at least two sides, as Mr. Johnson's former press secretary, Bill Moyers, was to observe in publicly writing off *Pacem in Terris II* because of the last-minute shortage of Russians. Actually, we came out pretty well on the East-West score.

Able Communist-bloc participants from Poland, Czechoslovakia, East Germany, Hungary and Rumania stayed on at Geneva despite the defection of their Soviet peers, and Peking's view was set forth by Professor Paul T. K. Lin of McGill University, a Chinese-Canadian citizen sympathetic to Mao's revolution. The insurmountable problem, it turned out, was arranging for comparable presentation of the foreign policy views of the Johnson administration.

We had not sought any formal blessing for the convocation from the State Department. At the outset we had pointed out that any open and reasonably balanced foreign policy dialogue was bound to include much criticism of the American position. Since we had no desire to stage an anti-U.S. lynching bee at Geneva, we asked the Department's cooperation in lining up competent spokesmen for the administration's views to be slotted in appropriate panels.

Our first choices were men of recognized intellectual capacity who had been intimately involved in the development and execution of contemporary U.S. policy but were now in positions where they could be presumed to be free of official inhibitions. Invitations went out in the fall to McGeorge Bundy, the recently retired White House foreign policy chief; former Under Secretary George Ball, with whom we had begun the discussions that led us finally to Hanoi; and Moyers. Bundy and Moyers declined early on grounds of prior commitment; Ball accepted tentatively.

We also suggested that the occasion might be appropriate for a major U.S. statement at the highest level. The convocation would bring together a predominantly intellectual international audience—precisely the kind of gathering where the American position most needed explanation and justification, and where any genuinely new effort toward thawing the Cold War could be launched under favorable auspices. Moreover, we had informal assurances from the Russians that they would match a leading American with a Soviet of equivalent weight. This would have made it certain that we also could bring in a major spokesman from the Third World. The obvious choices from the American side were President Johnson, Vice-President Humphrey, who had opened the first *Pacem in Terris* convocation in New York, and Secretary of State Rusk.

We also discussed with Defense Secretary McNamara the possibility that he might find in *Pacem in Terris II* an ideal forum for a major philosophical statement on the urgency of nuclear arms control. This, he had told us, had been much on his mind, since he recognized that powerful men on both sides were beginning to ignore the terrible truth about the deterrent and to think and speak of nuclear weapons as though it were possible to use them and survive. Humphrey was interested and sympathetic, but, like McNamara, he could not move until there was a signal from above. When the signal came in early spring it was first amber, and then bright red. By April, word was out in Washington that the White House wanted no administration participation in the *Pacem in Terris II* convocation.

As we pressed the State Department and Walt Rostow, McGeorge Bundy's successor at the White House, for promised assistance in lining up appropriate pro-administration participants outside official circles, it became obvious that we weren't going to get that either. At this stage Ball dropped out, and on our own motion we turned to UN Ambassador Arthur Goldberg, a one-time board member of the Center, whose special guarantee of independence permitted him to respond to our personal appeal—although, as it turned out, the UN's emergency session on the Israeli-Arab crisis kept him away from Geneva.

The legislative branch was theoretically beyond reach of the White House ban. However, Humphrey pointedly observed to Baggs that the five Senators on our guest list were all tagged by the administration as Vietnam doves. Baggs suggested that the Vice-President pick five of his own feather to insure balance. Humphrey did so, and these were promptly invited—or reinvited in the case of two who had already declined. Only one on Humphrey's list accepted, Senator Edward Brooke of Massachusetts, a Republican moderate who could hardly qualify as an administration spokesman.

Thus the list of those who might have presented the case for the Johnson policies with the authority of personal involvement and conviction was steadily whittled away until there could be only *pro forma* representation of the administration position in Geneva.

We had been neatly set up for a self-fulfilling prophecy, and the administration's many-sided public relations apparatus began pumping out the suggestion that *Pacem in Terris II* was being deliberately loaded against the United States and would probably turn out to be almost as biased as Bertrand Russell's Vietnam war crimes trial which was then circling for its ultimate landing in Stockholm.

Once administration strategists had decided to undermine the convocation they could count on a number of standard reflexes from the news media. The mere fact that we were committed to exploring the possibilities of coexistence with Communists was enough to unleash the journalistic True Believers. Among the certainties we could anticipate from the convocation's inception was that the Chicago *Tribune* would label it "Dumb and Disgraceful"; the New York *Daily News* would complain that pacifists had "snitched" the *Pacem in Terris* title from the late Pope John and applied it to a "hate-the-U.S.-on-account-of-the-Viet-War talkathon"; the Indianapolis *Star* would demand that the convocation's sponsors be jailed and fined under the Logan Act for illegally practicing diplomacy; William F. Buckley Jr. would characterize the Geneva meeting as the "Hutchins International Conference to Hate America"; and the right-wing Catholic press would rejoice in such lines as these from the Rev. Daniel Lyons, S.J., in *Our Sunday Visitor:* "Lenin called the free world apologists for Communism 'deaf mutes.' Stalin called them useful idiots. It might be said that both of these dominated the conference."

These standard vulgarities soon began to turn up outside their usually limited channels. It was apparently Alice Widener, whose column is syndicated to ultraconservative newspapers, who first dreamed up the Logan Act ploy. Her client editors gave it enough support to prompt the Associated Press to query the State Department as to whether our visit to Ho Chi Minh constituted a violation of the hitherto unenforced 1799 statute. The AP then compounded its gullibility by circulating a muddled account of the accusation after the Department had confirmed the obvious fact that the law manifestly could not apply to those who acted with its full knowledge and consent.

The most damaging attacks we sustained were the product of the Johnson administration's largely successful effort to implant in the American media the notion that the convocation was deliberately, and suspiciously, loaded against the United States. Until the very last this campaign was covert, which effectively prevented our countering it. The public, official position in Washington regarding *Pacem in Terris II* was initially benign, then neutral. It was not until May 23 that the State Department conceded to the Associated Press that the administration had in fact decreed a "hands-off" attitude.

After that, the wraps were off. The effort to discredit the convocation was carried openly into the hall at Geneva, where a State Department representative was on hand to "brief" the considerable concentration of reporters from the world communications media. This briefing consisted primarily of denigration, and had its effect with the general run of harried and ill-prepared correspondents.

. Upon arrival in Geneva, the Center's board chairman, Justice William O. Douglas of the United States Supreme Court, spotted a figure long familiar to him in Washington—a well-known CIA hand who had attached himself to the entourage of Foreign Minister Tran Van Do of South Vietnam. Van Do stayed around long enough to milk his alleged "barring" from the convocation of maximum publicity value and, whether by happenstance or the CIA man's inspiration, the Intercontinental Hotel, where the convocation headquartered, was suddenly overrun by a swarm of Vietnamese of all sizes and shades and, so far as we could tell, political persuasions.

Most of these were from the sizable colony of Vietnamese refugees in Paris, and some were doubtless attracted by understandable personal interest in a meeting where the fate of their country was under discussion. But some, certainly, were imported for the purpose of confusing the proceedings. These displayed the formidable talents of their guerrilla brethren, infiltrating the meeting hall despite the best efforts of the Swiss security guards, buttonholing delegates, spreading their printed propaganda material, and happily joining in the buffet meals served the delegates. Mrs. Crane Haussamen, the French-born wife of one of the Center's directors who assisted in screening those who sought credentials, swore she discovered a cheerful Vietnamese supplicant in her bathtub.

The result was predictable. Robert Lasch, editor of the *St. Louis Post-Dispatch,* wrote in a valedictory dispatch from Geneva:

Deprived of headline-making government participants who would have provided fodder for their typewriters, correspondents looked down very long noses at the whole affair. . . .

Less jaded observers, however, found it stimulating that a company of great intellectual diversity could short-circuit their governments and find large areas of agreement on key issues of war and peace. If governments and their spokesmen didn't like it, that was only to be expected.

Vietnam was an inescapable topic at *Pacem in Terris II,* and the general tension produced a remarkable side effect. Brig. Gen. Said Uddin Khan, an able Pakistani soldier-diplomat who had once served as chief of the United Nations peace-keeping mission in Indonesia, on his own motion called together the representatives of the Southeast Asian countries for a closed session. It was an impressive group: Sonn Voeunsai, Cambodian Ambassador to France; Nugroho, Indonesia's newly appointed Ambassador to North Vietnam; Princess Moune Souvanna Phouma, daughter of the Laotian chief of state, and Tianethone Chantharasy, general secretary of the Laotian Presidential Council; Tan Sri Ghazali Bin Shafie, permanent secretary for foreign affairs of Malaysia; Mamintal Tamano, Commissioner on National Integration, the Philippines; and Thanat Khoman, Foreign Minister of Thailand.

Represented in this gathering were the United States' most active supporter in Southeast Asia, Thailand, and North Vietnam's most consistent sympathizer, Cambodia, with the others ranging between these polar positions. All were countries upon which the United States could, and often did, exert formidable economic and political pressures. But in private their representatives made no bones about their growing concern over the destructive effects of the prolonged fighting—and their feeling that the war was rapidly nearing the point of no return.

This, they told General Khan, was the first time these highly placed functionaries had ever had a chance to discuss their common affairs on a private and unofficial basis. They came out of the closed session with a formal request that the Center organize on neutral ground some-where in Southeast Asia a similar but expanded gather-ing. The unanimous statement (signed by Sonn Voeunsai of Cambodia with a reservation about the utility of such a meeting while the Vietnamese war continued) pointedly sought to bring in the North Vietnamese:

It should be understood that invitations to participate on a full and equal basis would be extended to persons from North Vietnam, South Vietnam, and the rest of Southeast Asia. The objective of this conference would be to permit the people of Southeast Asia, without outside interference, to address themselves to the resolution of their own problems. . . . A continuation of this effort would provide a new, urgently needed opportunity for the resolution of cur-rent conflicts in Southeast Asia.

This proposal, particularly since it had drawn strong support from the pro-U.S. Thanat Khoman of Thailand, seemed likely to be of more than passing interest to the North Vietnamese. We had already replied to Hanoi's withdrawal from the public discussion at Geneva with a cable to Hoang Tung suggesting that we were prepared to arrange a wholly private session with the other Southeast Asian representatives. On June 1 Tung replied that time did not permit consideration of such a session before the Geneva participants dispersed, but that Hanoi would like to have more details. It was worked out that Baggs, who had already returned to Miami, would bring the State De-partment up to date and rejoin Ashmore in Paris on Monday, June 12, for a meeting with the North Viet-namese ambassador, Mai Van Bo.

It seemed to us significant that through the threatened shambles at Geneva this tenuous contact with Hanoi had held firm and was still functioning. Soon after President Johnson undercut us in the February exchange with Ho Chi Minh, the news broke in the world press that the CIA for years had been subsidizing what purported to be independent, respectable American foundations and educational institutes and using them for propaganda and presumably even for espionage purposes. Although the Center's precarious financial condition ought to have provided palpable evidence that we had no such blank-check resources, there was no doubt that the sensationalized reports of CIA activity had brought us under general suspicion in some foreign quarters.

We learned later that it was the blatant and heavy-handed finagling by the Johnson administration in regard to *Pacem in Terris II,* and the Center's refusal to yield to the pressure and permit the South Vietnamese to use the convocation for a propaganda festival, that recertified our independence. The harassed North Vietnamese were in a position to appreciate an organization that managed to bring upon itself a simultaneous boycott by Washington, Moscow and Peking.

8

DECLINE AND FALL

Although we had never been privy to the Phase A–Phase B negotiating scenario, we had arrived independently at the basic elements of the proposal Prime Minister Wilson inadvertently presented to Premier Kosygin in London as the United States' best offer for settlement in Vietnam. This was not a matter of profound diplomatic insight but of elementary logic. The bombing of the North, and the manner in which the administration proclaimed its purpose, made it impossible for the DRV to make any public concessions in advance of its termination without in effect offering to surrender and sue for peace. Some flexible, private, two-stage approach obviously would be required to break the impasse.

At one level, generally favored by President Johnson when he plays his peacemaker's role, the administration has employed a defensive stance to justify the bombing attack on the North, contending that this was a legitimate extension of the American military effort intended to deny sanctuary to the Northern aggressors. Such was the rationale of the Tonkin Gulf Resolution, which has since come under bitter attack by many of the Senators who supported it in the fall of 1964. But more candid officials in both State and Defense always have spoken bluntly of "bombing the enemy to the table."

The attack on the North actually did not begin until February 7, 1965—some months after the Tonkin Gulf incident, but very shortly after President Johnson had ruled out the Adlai Stevenson-U Thant negotiating proposal in late January on the ground that the United States would have to deal from a position of weakness. In the South both the civilian government and the army were near collapse, and the President's military advisers were warning him that he would have to provide American forces to take over the fighting or face the prospect of withdrawing the American presence.

According to the findings of Kraslow and Loory in *The Secret Search for Peace* series, a less painful alternative was presented to Mr. Johnson by his own White House staff. Here is their account, as published in the Los Angeles *Times:*

McGeorge Bundy, then the President's special assistant for national security affairs, among others, advised the President that a relatively short period of steady bombing would not only arrest the deteriorating situation but would also avoid the need for sending American combat troops to South Vietnam.

Of the two choices—American troops to fight in Asia or American bombing of North Vietnam—bombing was far more palatable to the American public.

Sources then on the White House staff now talk of Bundy's "three-month plan." Bundy, it is said, felt that after three months of sustained bombing Hanoi would be ready to make significant concessions.

The bombing, it was felt, would be something the United States could agree to stop doing in return for concessions by North Vietnam.

It didn't work.

In May, 1965, the United States did stop the bombing for five days in an effort to test the three-month thesis. Secretary of State Dean Rusk asked North Vietnam for significant reductions in the fighting if it wished the bombing pause to continue. Hanoi, receiving aid from Peking and Moscow, wasn't interested. It contemptuously returned American messages in Moscow and, through the British, in Hanoi.

Two years later, when we met with Mai Van Bo in Paris, the basic situation hadn't changed. Despite the death and destruction in the North, and the commitment of an American expeditionary force in the South heading toward the half-million-man level, the military stalemate continued.

Van Bo, a courtly, impassive career diplomat, represents his country not only in France but in all of non-Communist Europe. He has been the principal contact of most Americans seeking entry to Hanoi, and his availability has provided a sort of fever chart of the DRV's attitude toward negotiations.

At the time of our first *Pacem in Terris II* planning session in Geneva in June 1966 the freeze was on, and Van Bo declined to receive Fred Warner Neal for no reason other than his nationality; an aide at the legation explained that appointments were not available for Americans. The Center's initial letter to Ho Chi Minh was delivered to Van Bo on our behalf by our French colleague, Ambassador Jean Chauvel.

In June 1967, when we met him in the aftermath of the Geneva convocation, we found Van Bo correct and cordial. It was obvious, however, that his instructions were to listen and report, and that he had been given nothing to pass along to us. We were alone in a reception room at the unpretentious chancery on the Left Bank, except for Mrs. Crane Haussamen, who served as our interpreter, and an English-speaking member of the legation staff. There was the usual understanding that the conversation was off the record, but would be reported privately to the State Department. We delivered a copy of the resolution adopted by the Southeast Asians at the Geneva convocation and discussed the proposed meeting in some detail. Van Bo agreed to transmit the proposal for DRV participation to Hanoi, and asked if we had anything further to discuss.

Baggs had come away from his Washington briefing convinced that, while the Johnson hard line of February was still in effect, there were still those in State who would like to find an opening. He suggested to Van Bo that the absence of any tangible evidence of good faith on Hanoi's part tended to disarm those who were insisting that an honorable settlement on nonmilitary terms was still possible. The exchange that followed in the course of an hour-and-a-half conversation was summarized in our memorandum to Under Secretary Katzenbach, dictated in the State Department after our return to Washington on June 14:

Van Bo asked if we had any specific suggestions.

Ashmore replied that we could, on our own motion, offer to arrange a private meeting of influential persons from the United States on a wholly unofficial basis, if Hanoi desired the Center to make such arrangements. If, however, Hanoi desired to take the discussion to the official level—while still maintaining complete privacy—we could only offer to recommend such action to our government. Baggs added that he could say that he had every reason to believe that Washington would respond favorably to such a suggestion, because, he emphasized, he was personally convinced that Washington is willing to discuss all reasonable prospects to end the conflict.

Van Bo then asked what we thought might be the subject matter of such a meeting.

Ashmore replied that he understood that Hanoi now stands on the proposition that there can be no official discussion of the possibility of a settlement until the bombing of the DRV has been halted. Did this necessarily, he asked, preclude a preliminary discussion of a possible agenda for such a meeting—to be held privately and on the understanding that no further meeting would be held at all unless the bombing were in fact halted? This, he stressed, would not be a meeting as such, but an exploratory conversation, and would not be binding in any way upon either party to it. He noted that while both Washington and Hanoi had publicly indicated they would be willing to undertake discussions without any prior limitation on subject matter, it was certainly true in

Washington, and he assumed in Hanoi, that there were those who felt the ultimate negotiations would be greatly facilitated if some prior agreement on agenda could be reached, at least informally.

Van Bo evidenced considerable interest in this suggestion, and asked a series of questions to clarify the terms. At this point Van Bo said he would prepare very complete notes on our conversation and forward them to Hanoi.

Baggs said that Ashmore and he felt there was some measure of misunderstanding about whether Hanoi would begin talks with our government promptly after a cessation of the bombing. Van Bo said that his government would not refuse conversations between the two governments if the bombing were stopped unconditionally. Baggs and Ashmore asked twice more to make clear the position of Hanoi. Van Bo twice answered that Hanoi would talk if the bombing were stopped without conditions. . . .

Van Bo then summarized the main points we had made and asked if we had anything to add. We agreed that his summary was accurate and indicated that we had completed our conversation. Van Bo then said he would report in detail to Hanoi. He then concluded the session by saying that he would be available to see us at any time in the future.

It perhaps should be noted that only toward the conclusion of this conversation was the NLF mentioned by Van Bo. This was injected into the conversation without any attempt to state a condition for future conversation that would necessarily involve participation by the NLF. We avoided raising the question deliberately, and it is fair to say that it arose only most incidentally in the body of these conversations.

Our reception at the State Department when we came in to report on the Paris meeting was not unlike that accorded us by Van Bo—correct, but not notably enthusiastic. There were, of course, still open wounds on both sides from the recent *Pacem in Terris* encounters in Geneva, and these produced a pervasive impression that the Department would be greatly relieved if we retired from the field. While the principals maintained a surface cordiality, one of Governor Harriman's underlings certified our declining status by sneering openly when we suggested that there might be some significance in the fact that we could still be received by Mai Van Bo. "Hell," he said, "he even sees Quakers."

There was a faint flickering of interest in the proposal we had made to Van Bo—that both parties might meet secretly and agree on an agenda for a conference which would not be initiated until the bombing stopped. Katzenbach admitted this was something new. Bundy seemed interested. But the idea sank into the absorbing bureaucracy and we didn't hear of it again until just before our second journey to Hanoi, when Bundy said the proposition had been "kicked around" in the Department and he thought it would be useful for us to resurrect it in our talks with the DRV. It was, of course, Phase A–B, without the label.

There was no response to the message we sent to Hanoi through Van Bo, and toward the end of the summer we asked General Said Uddin Khan, who had joined the faculty at Claremont Graduate Center as a visiting professor, to take a swing through Southeast Asia and see if there were any prospects of action on the proposed regional conference. He returned to report that the idea was still strongly supported in every one of the capitals, and that there was an increasing sense of urgency.

However, General Khan had been unable to get any agreement for North Vietnamese participation; the DRV and NLF representatives he talked with were not disposed to give such a meeting priority while the fighting continued to intensify in South Vietnam. All parties in Southeast Asia agreed that there was no point in bringing the other countries together without the DRV and the NLF. The general was confident there would soon be a thaw, but for now the prospect of movement on the regional front was frozen.

In the United States the continued stalemate was beginning to produce frayed political nerves. As organized protest in the streets mounted against the Vietnam war, and was supported by increasingly stringent criticism in high places, Lyndon Johnson decided upon a characteristic countermaneuver. On November 10, under the banner head JOHNSON REBUKES WAR CRITICS the *Washington Evening Star* reported from Fort Benning, Georgia:

The President launched an offensive against dissenters with a speech in New York last night, then flew here today with an impassioned call for national unity to back the Vietnam war effort. The trip opened a two-day, coast-to-coast tour of military installations in connection with the observance of Veterans Day tomorrow. . . .

It was evident that Mr. Johnson had something more in mind than the discharge of a ceremonial duty to cheer the brave and the true. As he proceeded westward to salute the Air Force in Kansas, the Marines in California, and the Navy aboard an aircraft carrier at sea, the political commentators in his trailing press and television retinue observed that the President had wrapped himself in the flag in response to urgent political developments.

On the basis of soundings taken in late October, the public opinion polls had recorded Mr. Johnson's popularity at dangerously low ebb. Louis Harris reported: "Public confidence in President Johnson personally, and in his handling of the war, has reached an all-time low of 23 per cent as views about American policy in Vietnam have polarized away from the Administration's 'middle ground.'" George Gallup concurred.

Moreover, the generals and admirals in the Pentagon and in the field had been shaken by increasing Congressional restiveness on Vietnam war policy, and required some public reassurance that the President was not going soft on a negotiated settlement as opposed to a hard-line military resolution. And, finally, the President needed a headline-making maneuver to blanket the impending announcement that in the Democratic primaries he would face a direct challenge on Vietnam from a senior and respected member of his own party, Senator Eugene McCarthy of Minnesota.

It could be argued, as Mr. Johnson's supporters did argue, that every President at one time or another had thus used dramatic license to rally the public behind his policies, employing the star-spangled symbols of his office in the name of national unity. In the same vein, administration spokesmen rallied round to fill the air with optimistic reports of developments in Vietnam bearing the official imprimatur of the senior officers and diplomats at the front. General William Westmoreland and Ambassador Ellsworth Bunker were summoned home from Saigon for a highly publicized display of confidence in the commander-in-chief.

As the new year began, the formula was working as before. The President's popularity rating was back up to 48 percent on the Gallup scale, and the polls again indicated that he would win the coming Presidential election against any Republican or Democratic challenger then in sight. But it also was becoming evident that a price was attached to the Presidential technique of answering his critics by changing the subject. The march of events continued to bring into question the administration's sanguine estimates of our Vietnamese allies' ability to gain popular support for the new government we had created in Saigon, and of our Vietnamese enemies' presumably declining capacity to stand off the half-million-man United States expeditionary force.

It was not the political debate Mr. Johnson deplored as divisive, but published and broadcast factual reports by correspondents at the Vietnamese front that introduced the term "credibility gap" into the language. On Mr. Johnson's call Americans, as always, continued to rally around their President in time of crisis. But the opinion polls that measured the President's fluctuating popularity also implied that most of those who supported him no longer believed him.

Mr. Johnson had always been plagued by serious critics of his Vietnam policies. These included some of the best-informed members of the Senate, such leading newspapers as *The New York Times,* and a preponderance of the country's Asian scholars and specialists. With it all, however, he had enjoyed a generally favorable press. Most of the newspaper proprietors, television commentators, and editorial writers, like the public at large, tended to swallow their doubts about the distant war and follow the flag when the President chose to wave it.

However, as American fighting forces had grown in Vietnam, so had the strength and quality of the attending press corps. The jungle fighting provided the stuff of the first "television war" and, even though on an erratically selective basis, Americans were seeing for themselves some of the horror, casual brutality, and incredible waste of a modern military campaign.

Early in the new year, explosive events in South Vietnam drew an unmistakable contrast between these eyewitness reports and the official representation of what was going on there. This was no longer a matter of differences of interpretation, niceties of language, or diplomatic nuances. The issue now turned on claimed facts and figures relating to the military effort and the supporting programs of economic aid and social and political reform.

A considerable majority of the correspondents on the ground had concluded that the massive military operations in South Vietnam, and the aerial campaign of attrition in the North, had failed to effectively reduce the fighting capacity of the NLF and North Vietnam. They further reported that control of the countryside by American military and South Vietnamese forces remained tenuous at best; that the pacification program had been a disastrous failure; and that behind the democratic façade erected in the 1967 elections the Thieu-Ky junta maintained a military dictatorship incapable of, and probably disinterested in, basic reforms. Finally, most charged that the combination of an inept, unpopular South Vietnamese government with the presence of the huge, affluent American military and civilian establishment had produced gross corruption throughout the country.

The nation-wide guerrilla offensive in February, which sent NLF combat units all the way into the United States Embassy compound in Saigon, provided much shocking evidence to sustain this bill of indictment. Yet, official statements in Saigon and Washington continued to insist that there was no dimming of the "light at the end of the tunnel"—and a propaganda counteroffensive was mounted on the basis of claims that the punishing raids would prove to be the last gasp of a desperate enemy in the face of impending collapse. At a time when the staid, cautious Associated Press was reporting that "attack and counterattack widened devastation across Vietnam, with large sections of Saigon and Hue left in smouldering ruins," James Reston observed in *The New York Times* that the official line in Washington continued to be that everything happens for the best. "The communiqués sound more and more like a TV singing commercial," he wrote. " 'We are winning, we are winning,' they cry."

Such attacks on the credibility of official pronouncements on Vietnam became routine, not only in liberal journals but in the most conservative newspapers, and particularly in network television reports from the front. This phenomenon was explored by four highly respected correspondents in a National Educational Television broadcast from Saigon: Robert Shaplen of *The New Yorker,* Peter Arnett of the Associated Press, William Tuohy of the Los Angeles *Times,* and R. W. Apple Jr. of *The New York Times.* Apple summed up their collective view:

Well, no responsible reporter is making up quotes, making up statistics to back up a view he has presented. We get it, in fact, from majors, captains, sergeants, middle-level civilian officials, both American and Vietnamese. We don't get it from Hanoi Hannah. We don't get it from a Ouija board. We get it from the same people who are sending information up through the long complex channel toward Washington. I would argue that often the information that starts out with the captain or the major doesn't make it to Washington.

It's worth mentioning that this is not a very homogeneous group of people—these reporters in Saigon . . . If you went around this room right now, you would find that some of us think we shouldn't have been here in the first place, some of us think we definitely should have been . . .

To try to paint this as some kind of monolithic group, opposed to the government—opposed to what our government is trying to do—unpatriotic, the friend of the dissenters in the United States—is silly. There is a large group which tends to identify with the administration it is covering. They want to be part of the Establishment . . .

It is worth pondering why so many different people with different [intellectual] backgrounds and different professional motivations seem to come up with the same answer.

After the February resurgence of the NLF guerrilla campaign, the increasing tension between the Johnson administration and the press became a news story in its own right. Stewart Hensley of United Press International reported from Washington that a "third front" had opened up against the reporters, and a few days later *The Wall Street Journal* identified the source of a sensational off-the-record outburst cited by Hensley as Dean Rusk. In response to questions about the obvious lack of preparations in Saigon for the NLF assault, the normally imperturbable Rusk had replied:

There gets to be a point where the question is: Whose side are you on? Now I'm Secretary of State and I'm on our side. None of your papers or your broadcasting apparatuses are worth a damn unless the United States succeeds. They are trivial compared to that question, so I don't know why, to win a Pulitzer Prize, people have to go probing for the things one can bitch about when there are 2,000 stories on the same day about things that are more constructive in character.

"More and more," James Reston wrote, "the President and his principal aides, particularly Secretary of State Rusk, have been falling into the habit of self-pity which occasionally borders on self-delusion." And Reston's colleague, Tom Wicker, the *Times* Washington bureau chief, bluntly pointed out the consequences of the long period of protracted double-talk on negotiations backed by unduly rosy reports on American operations in the field:

Last November, Ambassador Bunker and General Westmoreland came home from Saigon to convince the American people that the war in Vietnam was being won. It now can be seen that what they had to say represented poor judgment, gross overstatement, or worse. . . .

. . . while the Administration has publicly insisted that it is fighting only for the freedom and self-determination of the Vietnamese people, at their request, it has privately had in mind an American political goal of maintaining a line in Asia against both Communism and Chinese nationalism. . . .

It has pretended to be doing one thing while doing another, and from that kind of deception "in the national interest" it is an easy step to the shabby employment of generals and ambassadors in the propagandizing of the American people.

This kind of reporting and commentary took an inevitable toll. By mid-February the Gallup reading on approval of the President's war strategy was back down to 35 percent. "This marks one of the sharpest declines over a period of three to four weeks yet recorded for President Johnson," Gallup noted, "and ends a three-month's upward trend of his popularity rating." The signs and portents were gathering that would lead Lyndon Johnson six weeks later to astound the world with the announcement that he had decided not to seek reelection.

9

THE SECOND ROUND

Lyndon Johnson announced his decision to stand down from the Presidency on Sunday evening, March 31, in the course of what had been expected to be a routine speech angled to the voters of Wisconsin, where he was entered in the Democratic primary the following Tuesday. We heard of it in a place where its surprise content probably attracted as intense interest as could be found on the face of the globe—the lobby of Reunification House in Hanoi.

There, on the far side of the international date line, the speech bounced in via short-wave relay from Manila at 9:30 a.m., Monday, April 1. We had returned to Hanoi on the ICC flight the Friday before, and taken up our private meetings with Hoang Tung at the editorial offices of *Nham Dan* about where they left off fourteen months earlier. The Johnson address did not seem to us of sufficient importance to justify interrupting the schedule to hear it. Mary McCarthy and Franz Schurmann, who had arrived ten days ahead of us as guests of the Peace Committee, planned to listen in on a Japanese correspondent's short-wave radio, and we arranged to get a summary from them at lunch.

When we came into the hotel lobby shortly before noon, the excitement was electric and visible. Miss McCarthy delivered the startling news along with a celebratory embrace, and we were thus launched upon an exercise that would for many months occupy many millions of people of many races—trying to figure out what Lyndon Johnson really meant by what he had just said and done.

Although the Johnson pronouncement turned out to be even more Delphian than usual, at first hearing it seemed straightforward enough. The President restated his deep dedication to peace, invited Ho Chi Minh to respond in kind, and announced a new restriction on the bombing of North Vietnam:

We are prepared to move immediately toward peace through negotiations.

So, tonight, in the hope that this action will lead to early talks, I am taking the first step to de-escalate the conflict. We are reducing—substantially reducing—the present level of hostilities.

And we are doing so unilaterally, and at once.

Tonight, I have ordered our aircraft and our naval vessels to make no attacks on North Vietnam, except in the area north of the demilitarized zone where the continuing enemy build-up directly threatens allied forward positions and where the movement of their troops and supplies are clearly related to that threat.

The area in which we are stopping our attacks includes almost 90 per cent of North Vietnam's population, and most of its territory. And there will be no attacks around the principal populated areas, or in the food-producing areas of North Vietnam. . . .

Now, as in the past, the United States is ready to send its representatives to any forum, at any time, to discuss the means of bringing this ugly war to an end.

I am designating one of our most distinguished Americans, Ambassador Averell Harriman, as my personal representative for such talks. In addition, I have asked Ambassador Llewellyn Thompson, who returned from Moscow for consultation, to be available to join Ambassador Harriman at Geneva or any other suitable place—just as soon as Hanoi agrees to a conference.

I call upon President Ho Chi Minh to respond positively, and favorably, to this new step toward peace.

On its face this sounded very much as though President Johnson had virtually met the DRV's demand that the bombing be halted so that talks could begin. The Vietnamese, made skeptical by both ancient and recent history, waited for supporting evidence—and when it came it seemed to indicate that the President once again was playing his familiar game, waving an olive branch in one hand while using the other to lay about him with a broadsword.

For several days after Mr. Johnson announced that he had limited the American assault to enemy movement that "directly threatens allied forward positions," the bombing continued in an area extending more than 200 miles north of the demilitarized zone. The administration then acknowledged that the new Presidential order permitted bombing all the way up to the 20th parallel, just 70 miles south of Hanoi. According to the nearest atlas, this exposed territory contains about four and one-half million Vietnamese, which figures out to 27 percent of the population rather than the 10 percent Mr. Johnson mentioned.

By April 3, only three days after the dramatic peace offer, Vietnamese press monitors would be encountering reports like this in *The Wall Street Journal:*

Without announcing it to the world, the President is shaking a big stick at Hanoi . . . Officials say privately that word has been passed to Hanoi that a sword hangs over them—that North Vietnam can be smashed in ways not hitherto attempted. The calculation here is that Hanoi might not find such escalatory threats at all possible coming from a U.S. President seeking re-election from war-weary voters but they might be thoroughly credible coming from a non-candidate.

The *Journal* went on to describe the kind of escalation the President presumably had in mind—mining Haiphong Harbor, massive bombing of population centers, the breaking of dikes to flood agricultural areas—and added, "Invoking visions of such assaults, it is observed, is intended to make Hanoi face up to tough decisions, even make top Reds worry about their personal safety."

If this could be dismissed as only newspaper speculation, possibly promoted for propaganda purposes, there were also overt manifestations of the hard line. The day after the Johnson speech the 13,500 "support troops" he had mentioned as being on their way to South Vietnam were revealed by official Pentagon reckoning to be closer to 50,000. And in the South the U.S. and Vietnamese forces launched a new joint offensive with the highly unpacific title "Operation Complete Victory." Soon the Washington *Post* would report that Khe Sanh, the beleagured outpost near the demilitarized zone, "is being transformed from a fortress to a springboard under a plan just approved by General Westmoreland. The April 15th air attack on North Vietnam was the heaviest since early January, and Hanoi radio charges the bombing has been doubled since the President's peace offensive and that the bombing sites included populated areas and crop lands."

The administration did seek to reduce the tangible evidence that President Johnson had once again indulged in what White House correspondents have come to call rhetorical overkill. The bomb line was pulled down from the 20th to the 19th parallel to bring the affected zone more in conformity with Mr. Johnson's 10 percent population estimate. But the administration's own figures indicated that while the bombed area had been contracted, the number and frequency of strikes, and the bomb tonnage dropped, had actually escalated.*

* On May 28, testifying before the House Appropriations Committee, Defense Secretary Clark Clifford said: "The restriction of the bombing . . . has not done us much damage. We are concentrating our forces on a much smaller area . . . We are increasing the number of missions over that area very substantially." Deputy Defense Secretary Paul H. Nitze testified that the number of sorties over North Vietnam since April 1 "has not decreased because we have increased the rate of bombing."

For three days after receipt of the Johnson speech the upper echelons of the DRV government largely disappeared from view, having gone into a huddle to figure out how to respond. During this time the people of Hanoi and the northern provinces had only rumor to explain the sudden emptiness of the skies; the press and radio carried no word of the President's speech or of the suspension of bombing over most of the country.

All of this had a profound impact on what had started out to be a leisurely discussion with Hoang Tung of some possible variation of the Phase A–Phase B formula to get private talks under way while the bombing continued. We had discovered upon arrival the previous Friday night, March 29, that the social and propaganda trimmings of our previous visit had been pared away and that what the DRV had in mind was a protracted exploration of the mechanics of opening negotiations. It was, indeed, a sort of preliminary test run of Phase A–Phase B—and to be sure that there was nothing that could be construed as official contact, Tung, an ostensible private person, would stand between us and the actual government officials concerned in any binding decision that might be reached.

The pattern, as it evolved on Saturday, our first full day together, provided for three hours of free-style give-and-take, which concluded with Tung's request that we summarize our understanding of the DRV position on the matters we had discussed. He would then discuss these points further with his principals—never formally identified but clearly the decision-makers in the government and party structure—during the interval before our next session and return with whatever modifications or new ideas the DRV desired to put up for consideration.

On our side, we had returned to Hanoi equipped, as before, with an extensive briefing by William Bundy and his State Department Vietnam experts. We were acting in response to our own decision to make another try at breaking the impasse under the formulation we had passed on to Hanoi through Mai Van Bo—a decision we had reached in early March when all indications were that unless some break came soon, the administration response to the successful DRV Tet offensive would be another massive escalation of the war effort.

The catalyst of our second journey was *The New York Times* report that President Johnson had decided to accede to General Westmoreland's request for an additional 206,000 troops, even though this meant calling up the reserves and would require something like full wartime mobilization. The *Times* article, which gave off vibrations of a White House trial balloon, was generally regarded in Washington as a move to test the public reaction to an all-out effort that accepted the risk of World War III.

By this time we had become involved in the political maneuvering within the Democratic Party as it splintered in reaction to the administration's course in Vietnam. Ashmore, as chairman of the Advisory Committee of the California Democratic Party, in November had been informed by Senator Eugene McCarthy of his decision to enter the primaries in a direct challenge to President Johnson. This led to a discussion of our Hanoi mission with Senator Robert F. Kennedy, who by now had emerged as one of the leading proponents of a negotiated settlement of the Southeast Asian conflict.

Kennedy had indicated that he wanted to see us when we first returned from Hanoi in January 1967, but we had avoided the meeting on the ground that President Johnson's animosity to the New York Senator was such that any contact between us might disrupt what we then believed was a sincere administration effort to get talks going with Hanoi. Kennedy agreed that this was probably the case. Our meeting almost a year later was arranged primarily to sound out his intentions regarding the California primary—a matter of practical moment to Ashmore, who had already made a commitment to support

McCarthy and was in the middle of the disintegration of the California party organization. Baggs was an identified supporter of the Kennedy faction in the Democratic Party, and had a particular interest in the Florida primary. At that time Kennedy told us that his decision still was that he would not run in 1968, but he spoke with an edge of desperation when he referred to the Vietnam war.

The young Senator's book, *To Seek a Better World,* had just been published, and in it he had made some revelations of his own about the background of the contradictory letters to Hanoi dispatched from Washington the previous January. At about the time we were drafting our reply to Ho Chi Minh in the State Department, Kennedy had been in Paris, where he received indications through the DRV representative, Mai Van Bo, that Hanoi was prepared to move toward negotiations. Upon his return to Washington, however, he found that administration policy had hardened markedly, and he bluntly charged in his book that disruption of the open channel to Hanoi was a deliberate act on the part of the President.

At that point, with a false scent of victory leading us on, the United States cast away what may well have been the last, best chance to go to the negotiating table on terms we clearly would have accepted before. . . . In the winter of 1966–67 important United States officials felt we were on the brink of a military victory, that our position was considerably stronger, and that of our adversary considerably weaker than had been true a year before. Therefore they thought we could afford to stiffen our position. And we did.

In the early months of 1968 we consulted regularly with Senators Kennedy, Fulbright, George McGovern of South Dakota and others in Washington who were in a position to appraise the administration's reaction to the alarming course of events in South Vietnam. All of these were convinced that the situation was building to another acute crisis, and that President Johnson would have to take some major action in response. The form chart indicated that it would probably be still more escalation.

On March 11 Ashmore cabled Hoang Tung:

CONTINUING EFFORT CENTER STUDY DEMOCRATIC INSTITUTIONS TO CLARIFY ISSUES PROLONGING WAR MAKE IT IMPERATIVE WILLIAM BAGGS AND I RETURN HANOI FOR FURTHER CONVERSATION WITH YOU.

On March 19 Hoang Tung replied that he was available and had arranged our entry visas at Phnom Penh. Bundy, informed that we had again been cleared by Hanoi and proposed to return forthwith, indicated interest in the re-opened channel and suggested that we ought to be brought up to date on what he referred to as "the current level of the bidding." Baggs came through Washington on March 24 on his way to join Ashmore in Los Angeles for the flight to Phnom Penh and met with Bundy and his aides at the State Department. He also had an extended telephone conversation with Averell Harriman, who was vacationing in Hobe Sound, Florida. The briefing developed seven points, summarized as follows in a memorandum we dictated in the State Department on April 10:

Baggs met with Bundy, [Heywood] Isham and [Frank] Sieverts. The following seven points were developed:

1. Sieverts briefed Baggs on the American prisoners now being held in DRV territory. He said our intelligence indicated some of these prisoners were ill. He gave Baggs a 3-page résumé of the US views on the question of prisoners, and on the desirability of a Red Cross agency to facilitate mail between the American prisoners and their relatives. Sieverts, with Bundy contributing occasional comments, asked Baggs to make certain inquiries in Hanoi to determine if an enlarged exchange of prisoners might be arranged. Bundy said that our government was willing to exchange DRV prisoners in the South for captured American airmen in the North on any fair basis and suggested we probe to see if we could get a reaction to such an offer from the appropriate parties in the DRV. Bundy said he was persuaded that an ex-

change of prisoners might lead to cooperation in other regards.

2. . . . Bundy suggested that we might explore the idea of a Red Cross agency from any Scandinavian country, or Switzerland, or France, and point out that the agency could be established both in the North and in the South, again on an equitable basis, to handle the basic needs of both American and DRV prisoners.

3. Bundy said it would be useful in our discussions in Hanoi if we reminded the North Vietnamese of the statement by Clark Clifford, on January 25, which suggested that "a normal infiltration" of troops and matériel south from the DRV during any talks would not be considered objectionable by the USA, or at least would be anticipated.

4. Bundy also pointed out that the private position of the US on the National Liberation Front was the same as the public position. Our government was prepared at any meeting to hear the views of the NLF, or representatives of the NLF.

5. Then discussed was the idea which Ashmore and Baggs brought back after the talk with Mai Van Bo last summer in Paris. The proposal was that the DRV and the USA, only, meet privately and agree informally on an agenda, with the understanding that no official conference would be convened until after the bombing of DRV territory stopped. Bundy said the idea had been discussed around the State Department and suggested that we test the reactions of appropriate parties in the DRV to the idea. He pointed out that the President had indicated, time and again, that the US was willing to talk to the DRV at any place.

6. Bundy said we should also inform the DRV that our government was prepared to deescalate the war in the South if the DRV were prepared to match the deescalation.

7. It was considered inevitable that we had to discuss the possible influence of domestic politics on the question of the Vietnam war. Bundy pointed out that not one candidate for the presidency, either a presumed or admitted candidate, had advocated a unilateral withdrawal of US troops from South Vietnam, and, indeed, certain of the candidates, if elected to the presidency, might inaugurate a more harsh war policy than the present one of Mr. Johnson. All of this, Bundy told Baggs, should be made known to the Hanoi leaders.

Thus, despite all the public and private recriminations of the past, we were recast in our ambivalent role as demi-unofficial emissaries—too important a contact with Hanoi to be dismissed, and too demonstrably independent and recalcitrant to be entrusted with any mission that required absolute fealty to State Department policy.

Bundy's office made the usual demi-diplomatic arrangements, alerting the U.S. ambassadors to Thailand and Laos of our status in case we needed to use their channels to communicate with Washington. During the pause at Vientiane outward bound, we were met by Robert Hurwitch, counselor of the embassy there, who had handled negotiations with the Vietnamese that resulted in the first minimal prisoner exchange. Three captured North Vietnamese sailors were being loaded aboard the ICC flight in return for three released U.S. fliers, and he suggested that we might use the coincidence to establish our association with the prisoner-exchange effort. The embassy would be standing by for messages, he said, and he would be on hand to meet us when we came out a week hence.

We arose early on our first morning in Hanoi, after a night interrupted by three air raids, one close enough to propel Baggs from the rare luxury of a hot bath. At dinner the night before, we had been given our first appointment, and a car was waiting to drive us across downtown Hanoi for our 8 a.m. session with Hoang Tung. It was our first daylight view of the city, and we saw no signs of bomb damage along the route.

The early-rising Vietnamese were in full stir, and Tung was waiting outside the old villa to greet us. He ushered us upstairs to his editorial office, where the windows overlooking the lake were still missing and a fresh breeze was blowing through the spacious room.

Baggs pointed to the empty window frames and said, "But McNamara's no longer in the Defense Department."

"I know," Hoang Tung replied, with an exaggerated shrug. "This is Westmoreland's calling card."

We got down to business straightaway. The talk was relayed through a thoroughly competent interpreter we had not seen before, Nguyen Phuong, who would become a familiar figure to American television viewers when he turned up in Paris to translate the press briefings staged on behalf of the Vietnamese delegation by Hoang Tung's chief deputy, Nguyen Thanh Le. There was also a silent male assistant who made extensive notes in Vietnamese. Otherwise we were alone, as we would be through all our subsequent meetings with Tung.

We followed the sequence of proposals pretty much as the State Department had set them forth, ticking off the essential points in order. Hoang Tung disposed of the first two politely but firmly. His government would be prepared to talk later about prisoner exchange and the Red Cross, and anything else we wanted to discuss. But the first priority ought to be on ways and means of getting talks started. "If we can figure out a way to end this war," he said, "the exchange of all prisoners, the role of the Red Cross, all of these matters can be taken care of."

He dismissed the Clifford modification of the President's San Antonio formula as irrelevant. "It means nothing to speak of normal resupply and reinforcement of the fighting men in the South," he said. "As you can see we have been able to supply the South adequately while the bombing goes on. We will continue to do so without the bombing—until the shooting stops."

This pretty much precluded any discussion of other forms of mutual deescalation. As Bundy had suggested, we probed in several directions, cautiously preceding the probe with the phrase "We know our government is interested . . ." But we ran into a palpable stiffening at any suggestion of formal reciprocity.

As the morning wore on, it became clear that so far as Hoang Tung was concerned we already were engaged in

Phase A of the two-part negotiating formula—that is, we were meeting privately to discuss procedural questions while the bombing continued, as it did dramatically, with three raids in the afternoon, one close enough to prompt our host to take us to the lower floor near the entrance to the shelter, and to bring on the sharp crack of fire from nearby anti-aircraft emplacements.

Here is the summary of the two three-hour sessions we held with Tung on Saturday, as dictated in the April 10 State Department briefing memorandum:

Hoang Tung said he would like to give us the position of his government as it related to talks.

First, he said, the US simply must stop the bombing of DRV territory without condition. He said this was the one inflexible position of his government. We asked if this insistence included the territory of South Vietnam. No, Hoang Tung responded. His government considered US acts of war against DRV territory unilateral and indefensible. On the contrary, there was fighting between two parties in the South. And, anyway, he emphasized, both sides must realize that the peace could only be made step by step.

He continued by saying that, if the US wished to test the good will of the DRV, then the US should stop the bombing. He added that the DRV was prepared at any time to sit down with the US to find "sensible solutions." At this point, Hoang Tung said he would like to emphasize the procedure for meeting from the DRV view:

1. Halt the bombing without condition. He emphasized that the bombing was really the important ingredient; however, he used the phrase, "all acts of war against DRV territory," specifying that this includes the naval bombardment, and the artillery barrage across the DMZ.

2. After the bombing has stopped, Hoang Tung said, the DRV *will* meet promptly with the US. "It will be a matter of days," he said.

He suggested that his government thought the first meeting should be "a contact" between a representative of any level, high or low, and that this contact should determine three matters:

   a.   The timing of a conference between the two countries.
   b.   The place of a conference.
   c.   The level of representation at the conference.

He said the DRV would meet any place mutually agreeable with the US. At this point, Hoang Tung said the first contact should be procedural. He made it clear under our questioning that he visualized that the first contact would not engage in any substantive discussion, even of agenda. These matters would be postponed until the first meeting that would follow this "first contact." The position was later significantly modified after President Johnson's speech.

He asked us to state our understanding of what he had said and we repeatedly went over point by point our interpretation of what he had said, and he indicated concurrence that it was the correct understanding. At one point we pressed very hard on the question of whether the old issue of "would" and "could" could be raised in connection with what he was now saying. He said emphatically that he was saying that the meeting *will* take place and added that he had so stated previously in a letter to us that was never received.

We said that immediate questions were raised by the DRV's position as he stated it. What would be the basis for the talks? Would the DRV insist that the Geneva Accords of 1954, the 4 points of the DRV, and the position statement of the NLF be the basis for talks? No, he said. These adequately set forth the general views of his government, but the actual basis for talks would be determined by the DRV and the US. He added that he understood that the talks could not be limited to points raised by the DRV. In answer to questions, Hoang Tung said the interests of the NLF and the Saigon government would have to be discussed by the DRV and the US. In sum, he concluded, the agenda would be composed of anything the DRV and the US wished to talk about.

What assurances, we asked, were there that such an open-ended agenda would not lead to the development of the kind of endless marathon the USA had endured at Panmunjom in Korea? Well, there were two eventualities, Hoang Tung replied. The talks could end the war, or the talks could fail and all the fighting would resume. We probed on the previous DRV insistence that the US withdraw its troops. He said this undoubtedly would be discussed at a conference, but he said that he could not imagine an agreement to withdraw that would result in 500,000 Americans pulling out the next day. We interpreted this as acceptance of a phased withdrawal of troops, with some flexibility on timing. We used this phrase, "phased withdrawal," subsequently and it was never objected to.

What of a future government in the South? Hoang Tung said his government believed that a coalition government would evolve in the South, but procedures to establish the government there would have to be discussed in the conference when the DRV and the US get down to how they would bring the NLF and Saigon into the conversations.

We inquired again about a cessation of bombing as the signal for talks to begin. Would some formal statement by the US be necessary? No, he said. His government would accept the simple act of just stopping the bombing.

In this regard, speaking to the point of the initial contact, Hoang Tung said the DRV wouldn't care who moved first after the bombing stops. The DRV would make the call to establish the contact, if desired. He said his government would want only to be assured that the bombing had stopped by the time that the contact began.

We broke the morning conversation at 11 a.m. and returned at 3 p.m. It was obvious that during the interval Hoang Tung had been reviewing our conversation with official parties. He said as much, and we thought we could see some indication of shifting positions between morning and afternoon. We began by summarizing our understanding of the views he had expressed in the morning.

We emphasized that, while we had no authority to negotiate in any sense on any of these procedural details, we did think that as much specific detail as possible should be included and transmitted by the DRV to our government. We said that we thought that, if his proposals could be refined so as to name places, suggest time, state intervals, this would be evidence of good faith, and should avoid the kind of confusion on which some previous contacts had foundered. He seemed to agree that this was advisable and constantly talked to the point of making definite determination of such matters. However, he always seemed in this and subsequent conversations to want the initial motion for, say, designating a place of contact to come from the US.

We concluded our talks late in the afternoon. We agreed to meet again on Monday. Hoang Tung asked if we would summarize in writing our understanding of what he had said. We agreed to give him such a summary of what he had said when we met again on Monday.

We diligently put together the written summary Hoang Tung had requested, and had it waiting when we saw him again early Monday afternoon. But by that time Lyndon Johnson had spoken, and as the obviously harried editor pointed out, everything that had been said on Saturday had to be reviewed in this new light. He must, he said, get back to an important meeting and would be in touch with us again as soon as possible. But, he added at the door, he and his colleagues would be interested in the reaction of two loyal, if critical, Americans to Mr. Johnson's announcement.

Mr. Johnson had surprised us as much as he had anyone else in Hanoi, we said, but in our view the importance of the announcement could not be overestimated. We took it to be Lyndon Johnson's way of certifying the sincerity of this new move toward peace—perhaps the only method left to him to do so in view of the steady erosion of confidence in his pronouncements at home and abroad. For a man of the President's temperament and ambition the decision not to run again had to be regarded as an act of political self-immolation. We thought it urgently important that the DRV take the new offer to negotiate seriously and respond in kind.

This, Tung said, was what we now needed to talk about, and he would be in touch with us as early as possible on Tuesday.

In the late afternoon we walked down the broad avenue to the Indonesian Embassy to return the social call we had had earlier from our friend Ambassador Nugroho, and to ask him to transmit by coded radio a message for the U.S. Embassy at Vientiane:

PLEASE SEND URGENT WILLIAM BUNDY WASHINGTON STOP EX-
TENDED DISCUSSION OF PROPOSALS REVIEWED WITH YOU HAVE
PRODUCED TENTATIVE AGREEMENT ON PROCEDURE FOR MEET-
ING BETWEEN DRV AND USA ONLY STOP STATEMENT BY PRESI-
DENT JOHNSON MAY REMOVE LAST OBSTACLE STOP FORMAL
OFFICIAL RESPONSE EXPECTED TOMORROW STOP WE CAN BE
REACHED THIS CHANNEL STOP

10

WAITING FOR THE WORD

Our prediction to Bundy that we might have an official response from the DRV within twenty-four hours turned out to be unrealistic. It would come, but only after four more cliff-hanging days. There was, first of all, Hoang Tung's obvious distraction, which, we began to understand, was occasioned by a division within the government over the correct response to President Johnson's overture.

One faction, with which Tung was evidently identified, wanted to accept the new restriction on bombing as sufficient to justify at least an initial contact with the United States at the official level. Others regarded the juggling of the bomb line a mere trick, and the tangible evidence was on their side. In the first thirty-six hours after the President's speech there were twelve heavy air raids against DRV territory, some of these as much as 350 kilometers north of the demilitarized zone.

The dialogue within the government continued through Tuesday and most of Wednesday, while Washington and the world waited for some official reaction from Hanoi. At our one extended meeting with Hoang Tung during this period, at dinner on Tuesday evening, he grimly handed us a detailed list of the air raids that had taken place since the President's speech. By this time Tung knew that we had opened a communications channel to Washington via Vientiane, and he clearly wanted word passed as to the possible consequences of this apparent contradiction of the newly announced bombing policy.

In a message to Bundy sent through the Indonesian Embassy we transmitted the list of twelve bomb strikes located by town name and coordinates, adding our own view that "Washington must recognize that these cancel conciliatory effect of Johnson speech so far as DRV is concerned if continued."

Meanwhile, we continued our effort to supply Tung with ammunition for advocating a softer line in his discussions with the DRV inner circle. The compelling fact, we insisted, was Lyndon Johnson's announcement that he was withdrawing from the Presidential contest. From our own fairly considerable experience with Democratic Party politics, we could attest that his was an irrevocable decision. Thus his decision not to run again had to be regarded as his own peculiar testimony of faith, intended to slam a hard period at the end of his statement that he was severely restricting the bombing. We pointed out to Tung that even if the President should later have second thoughts, he had already unleashed restive leaders of his party at a critical moment and put into motion political forces he could no longer control.

Without the Presidential withdrawal, we conceded, the juggling of the bomb line could hardly be accepted by Hanoi as evidence of good faith. In the context, however, it had to be seen as a genuine move toward negotiation —a turning of the Presidential back on those in the administration who had sold Mr. Johnson on the disastrous theory that he could bring the Vietnamese war to a close on his own terms by applying military pressure on the North.

The best test of our thesis, we suggested, lay in the general public reaction to the speech in the United States. Although we were sealed away from the news, it would be our expectation that Mr. Johnson's gesture had been widely hailed as a genuine move toward a negotiated settlement—and as such had received overwhelming public support in almost all quarters. Tung could check his own monitored radio reports from the United States, and the summaries of American press reaction available to him, and see if our long-distance guessing was correct. If so, we argued, a decision by Hanoi to reject the President's overture certainly would have a tremendously adverse effect on American public opinion—might, indeed, restore the credibility of the hard-liners who had been arguing all along that the DRV was not really willing to enter into peace talks but was using the prospect of negotiations as a ruse to weaken the American military effort in the South.

Tung indicated that he would put these arguments to the Vietnamese leaders who, somewhere beyond our ken, were wrestling with the fateful problem. At his request we reduced the case for negotiations to a written summary he could use as essential background in the course of the arguments that would continue until the official DRV response to President Johnson was issued late Wednesday.

If the President's speech had increased the nervous tension and hopelessly disrupted our original schedule of meetings with Hoang Tung, our physical situation at least had been vastly improved. Early on Tuesday morning a small entourage came to remove us from our two bedrooms on the top floor of Reunification House and establish us in a walled villa on the edge of the embassy district. Hoang Tung, we were informed, was faced with the problem of meeting with us on a very irregular basis and felt the need of more privacy than the hotel or his office afforded.

The stucco villa, apparently maintained by the government as a VIP guest house, was a modest but comfortable establishment—an ample sitting room, bedroom and bath upstairs, with a dining room and service facilities on the ground floor. It was fully staffed with a chef, housekeeper, and maids—five servants altogether, and these were clearly peasants well versed in their duties as opposed to the lady intellectuals who had poured tea for us at *Nham Dan*. Although the cool, rainy weather gave us no need for it, there was a late-model Frigidaire air-conditioning unit in the bedroom window, and among the delicacies laid out on the coffee table was a vacuum tin of peanuts packed in San Francisco. We took this as evidence that there must be two-way traffic on the Ho Chi Minh Trail.

The respite in the comfortable villa was particularly welcome, since Ashmore had become one of the walking wounded before we even arrived in the combat zone. Coming into Vientiane the ICC plane had been unable to lower its landing gear, an event so commonplace that the French captain had not bothered to make an announcement or turn on the seat-belt sign when he dispatched the co-pilot to open a hatch in the floor of the passenger compartment and go below to crank the wheels down by hand. Ashmore had walked into this unexpected opening in the aisle, laying open a considerable gash in his shin and acquiring a rainbow of bruises all the way up to his rib cage.

A French doctor in Vientiane installed three stitches and a large dose of penicillin, and in Hanoi Ashmore had passed to the care of DRV medics—who came regularly in surgical garb and face masks to check for infection, change the dressing on the open wound, and make comforting if unintelligible sounds as they surveyed the great purple areas of bruised thigh and chest. We tried to impress upon our hosts that it would be much more economical of the doctor's valuable time if Ashmore went by a hospital for these ministrations, but it appeared the house calls had somehow become mandatory.

All we could do was apologize to the surgeon and his

gentle-fingered nurse for diverting them from more serious duties. "Yes, we are busy," he said, "but in a war you learn to make out. In our service we figure every person must do the work of two." The team's field surgical equipment had seen much service but seemed in good shape, and the bandages and medicines were of the standard kind. We asked if there were any serious medical shortages. "We need some things we do not have," the doctor replied, "but there is no real shortage of the essential supplies. We are making out."

At dinner at the villa on Tuesday evening Hoang Tung, with the manner of a distracted host, suggested that in view of the uncertainty of his own schedule we might want to take a look at the countryside next day. We were anxious to do so, and it was arranged that we would head south over the route we had traveled before in January 1967. The expedition was laid on for 10 a.m. Wednesday morning, which would allow time to complete the written summary of our views Tung had requested.

On Sunday we had been driven around Hanoi proper, and had seen some bomb damage in the random pattern of our first visit. Coming in from the airport this time we had to cross the Red River on the one-way pontoon bridge which now parallels the remains of the bombed-out Long Bien Bridge. Even in the dark we had a strong impression of the ruins that lay beyond the city proper, and of the great increase in vehicular traffic that marked this new phase of the war.

Baggs was committed to a series of articles for *The Miami News* immediately upon his return, and with this in mind his office had insisted on equipping him with what his chief photographer asserted was a camera so simple it could be worked even by a multi-thumbed wordsmith who had never taken a picture in his life. Baggs proved him wrong at the end of the first film cartridge, putting the camera so hopelessly out of commission that even the professional Japanese photographer at

Reunification House returned it, unrepaired, with an awed expression. So we added to our party a staff photographer from *Nham Dan,* and set out in a modest convoy of two fairly new Russian command cars with their curtains up against the steady, soaking rain.

The following descriptive notes and impressions of the journey are taken from the joint log in which we both made entries as time and energy permitted:

En Route

We have acquired a new interpreter, Nguyen Hap, a *Nham Dan* photographer, Thinh Hai, and we are again in the hands of our old escort from the first trip, Vu Qhoc Thanh, who wears an insistent grin.

We followed Route One, the main highway from Hanoi to Saigon. At the edge of the city the bomb damage begins in earnest, and for as far as we could see on both sides of the highway hardly a house larger than a straw-thatched mud hut had been missed.

The great irony of this is that the movement of goods seems to have increased in proportion to the bombing of the transportation route.

At Phu Ly there has been no effort to rebuild the totally destroyed town, so now after fourteen months vines and creepers are taking over the ruins—but while we were walking around in the debris a long train passed through on the narrow-gauge track, and a switch engine was busy on a siding. Everywhere you see this kind of instant patchwork of bombed-out road and railroad.

Along the way down we saw no more than a dozen vehicles knocked out by bombs—one locomotive, a few railroad cars, perhaps eight trucks gutted by fire or wrecked by blast. This must be the whole of the recent crop, since it is unlikely that the Vietnamese would have done more than shove a wreck to the side of the road—where all kinds of debris and supplies—steel plates, reels of wire, reinforcing rods—are left standing in the open.

The impression recorded earlier of a great increase in quantity and quality of rolling stock was reinforced. Most of the trucks look new, are in the two-and-a-half-ton class, and we are told proudly and repeatedly that the Socialist countries have greatly stepped up the supply of equipment. We saw one concentration of about 30 big fuel tank trucks gathered under trees near the road, presumably halted until dark. At another place similarly situated there were twelve to fifteen long trailers awaiting prime movers. These bore what could only have been portable rocket launchers. This was the only combat equipment we saw on the way down except for three full-tracked personnel carriers which bore no visible armament.

Comment

We are struck by the frequency with which we sight church spires on both sides of the road. When the actual churches are visible they are elaborate structures—19th-century French style—and it is shocking that in this poverty-stricken countryside they should be so grand and so numerous. In many cases we sight one tall spire on one side of the road, while we can still see another on the other side—this on a day of driving rain when the visibility must be less than two miles. But perhaps even more shocking is the fact that—with one exception out of perhaps 20 sighted—these churchly symbols of the Western occupation are about the only things in sight that haven't been bombed. In Phu Ly the church—of cathedral scale—is literally the only building standing largely intact.

My Trung, Nam Ha Province

We had understood that we would go directly to Nam Dinh, the battered textile town we had visited before. Because of the President's announcement that bombing would be confined to the area just north of the demilitarized zone it was now presumed safe to stay overnight in the city proper, and arrangements had been made for us to meet there with some of the local committeemen we had seen on the first trip.

However, as we drove into the edge of the city the two cars suddenly halted and we were ordered out. An air alert had sounded, although we hadn't heard it, and our driver had noticed the local citizens standing alongside the shelters that lined the street. We were led to a concrete bunker with at least two feet of rain water in the bottom, and about 30 Vietnamese ranged within diving distance of the entrance. It would have been a new high in damp togetherness if we had had to use it—but the all-clear sounded before we heard a plane or a bomb.

The best guess is that the alert was touched off by a reconnaissance mission—but even so it is indicative of the futility of LBJ's grandstand gestures. Nam Dinh is only 90 km. below Hanoi—more than 600 km. above the DMZ. If U.S. planes are still kicking off alerts here, who can believe 90 percent?

The alert was enough to cause Thanh, our wagon master, to divert to the country village of My Trung—with its guest house in the midst of the rice paddies where we had put up in 1967 when there was no doubt that the American bombing crews enjoyed open season over Nam Dinh.

The long, low building, a former schoolhouse and community hall, was locked and deserted when we arrived. There followed a period of utter, arm-waving confusion, which sounds even more so in Vietnamese. In the midst of this one of the command cars was dispatched across the perilous, deeply rutted mud road that runs along the dikes between flooded paddies. Someone got the door to the main room open. There are no electric lights here, no running water, no plumbing. The building is unchanged except that capacious holes for bomb protection have been sunk in the concrete floor, and the long tables replaced over them.

We took a nap in the chairs lined along the sides of the dim room, and after about an hour the command car returned with the man and woman who run the place and a big basketful of cold lunch. So far as we can determine we stay here tonight.

My Trung, 4:20 p.m.

A lovely sight and sound: Across the flooded paddy, splashing down the muddy dike that serves as a road, come the school children, all sizes below about 12 years old. Most wear the conical hat of the countryside and loose blue denim overalls. There must be two score, at least, and the sound of the lilting, high voices is happy—even against this rainswept, war-pocked landscape.

Comment

We used up some of the slack time having Hap translate

the headlines and lead stories in today's *Nham Dan*—four pages, quite smartly made up, and well-printed. Here the Communist line emerges sharp and clear. All accounts of the fighting are in the polemic style—"imperialist invaders" and "capitalist bandits" versus "stalwart defenders" and "victorious comrades." Their factual exaggerations are probably no worse than ours—for example those ten-to-one casualty figures from Saigon—but the good-and-evil adjectives make them sound so. The mirror theory of political discourse is sharply demonstrated by the fact these constant polemicists are themselves so bitterly resentful of American use of such relatively mild terms as "Red" or "Cong." In our most casual conversation we are at pains to remember that it's DRV and NLF.

Perhaps one-fourth of *Nham Dan* was news matter—accounts of the fighting, governmental reports of food production (good) and the like. There were a few official text items —i.e., Ho Chi Minh's letter of congratulations to the new Czech president. Most of the rest of the newspaper was given over to lengthy exhortations to the co-ops to increase farm production, "good" and "bad" examples from the field, citations for outstanding service, etc.

The rigidity of the bureaucracy shows through the printed matter like a skeleton. It shows, too, in the set limits of all the conversations we have at the level of the functionaries accompanying us on this trip. On matters where there is an official line—bomb damage, agricultural production, history (everyone tells the Genghis Khan story)—the replies come fast and glib. Once you go outside a man's stated competence, however, a great vagueness sets in. Even though the matter is obviously a routine one, questions are greeted by a polite but firm refusal to answer at all, and the interpreters' English begins to go to hell. Baggs, who is always pressing for statistics—how many bicycles in Hanoi? how many one-man bomb shelters?—usually bats zero. When he stubbornly keeps up his inquisition past the obvious point of no return the final defense is that they will put him in touch with someone who can answer. They never do.

At the level of Hoang Tung it is markedly different. The impression is one of sophistication and frankness—and of enough authority to make promises and carry them out, and even to waive certain inhibitions and conventions. Limits show up here, too, however—as in the current case where all the policy questions Hoang Tung was prepared to discuss were suddenly reopened after the Johnson speech. It seems clear now that we are in the country because Tung needs time to get the line straight for our next talks.

My Trung, 9:00 p.m.

Nguyen Viet Ca, a representative of the province administration whom we had met on the first trip, suddenly appeared out of the rainy night while we were getting ready for bed. He is a lusty, loud-voiced Chamber of Commerce type with whom Baggs did most of the talking—about the rice crop (good but a little late) and about their respective children (all are thriving). It was arranged that we will leave early in the morning for Nam Dinh, which Viet Ca says is now more than 50 percent evacuated and has suffered double the damage we saw. The city was bombed last on the previous Friday. Two alerts today, but no actual attacks.

All of this conversation has been conducted in an atmosphere of some embarrassment, the reason for which becomes clear when it is explained that the formal welcome that had been arranged for us had been called off because there had been a message that the trip planned for two Americans had been canceled. This had caused great confusion, and has genuinely pained our hosts and attendants. Courtesy is no casual act with the Vietnamese.

Hanoi, April 4

We were awakened at about 12:30 a.m. in My Trung with the intelligence that Hoang Tung had ordered us returned to Hanoi forthwith. This, it appeared, was the real source of the confusion. The message had been received by wire at 8:30 p.m., but because of our wagon-master's horseback decision to divert to My Trung after the air alert in Nam Dinh the province headquarters couldn't locate us. Finally, someone had thought to try the guest house in the paddies and a messenger had made his way out on foot.

We headed back through Phu Ly in the rain—a long, jolting journey that frequently reminded Ashmore that he still had a sore rib cage.

We passed one south-bound train—combination passenger and freight—but there was surprisingly little road traffic. Trucks were fairly numerous, but most were pulled to the side of the road and parked.

The concentration of 30 tank trucks was still where we saw it on the way down; also the trailers with the rocket launchers. Between Phu Ly and Hanoi we passed four truck-drawn heavy artillery pieces on four-wheel mounts. They were hooded and we could not identify but would estimate that they are something on the order of a 106-mm. rifle.

We got back to the villa at 3:45 a.m., to find the DRV official statement of April 3 waiting for us. The "however" paragraph apparently agreeing to open negotiations told us why Tung had been searching for us.

It had been a long night, and it would be a long day. At 6 a.m. one of our outriders came back to the villa to report that Hoang Tung was expecting us at the newspaper office at 7:30 a.m. Before we left we telephoned the Indonesian Embassy to ask that a car be sent to pick up this message to Bundy:

EXPECT IN A FEW HOURS THE DETAILS AND PROCEDURES OF DRV COUNTERPROPOSAL TO MEET WITH USA STOP WILL FILE PROMPTLY STOP

Hoang Tung was ready to get down to cases all right, and he made it clear that the way was open for direct contact between the two governments. However, he said, the problem now was to make certain that it was understood that the substantive discussion at the meeting could not begin until the bombing actually had been halted. This was the point that would provide the main peg of controversy all through the opening weeks of the Paris negotiations.

Here is the summary of our Thursday, April 4, session as we dictated it in the briefing memorandum for Ambassador Harriman at the State Department on April 10:

When he met us Hoang Tung was obviously extremely

pleased with the official DRV statement in response to President Johnson. He pointed out the "however" paragraph and indicated that this represented a conciliatory gesture of real magnitude. He grinned and said: "They went further than I thought they would." We told him that our reading of the message agreed with that interpretation and that we felt that this might well make way for the beginning of the contact he had discussed earlier.

Then, at his suggestion, we began to go over the papers we had sent him, including our previous summaries, step by step. This was the most detailed discussion yet, devoted almost entirely to attempting to get a precise understanding of what the DRV expected to actually happen at the first contact, and so far as possible, what was expected, in procedural terms, to follow at the conference proper.

Hoang Tung would illustrate his replies by moving objects around on the table and saying such things as, "The two come together and shake hands,"—"The USA representative announces total cessation of the bombing."—"DRV representative says he knows this is so because no bombs have fallen."—"Then they have a talk about the time and place of the conference."

We pursued this in flyspecking detail because, as we told Hoang Tung, we felt that the official statement in its English version might be subject to misinterpretation. It was not possible, we suggested, to tell precisely what the DRV expected in regard to a guarantee that the bombing had halted. It was possible, we said, to read the statement to mean the DRV is prepared to meet with the bombing still going on, on the assumption that at that point this could be a matter settled promptly, but this could mean bombing was still subject to discussion.

Hoang Tung said that the language of the reference "with a view to determining with the American side the unconditional cessation of US bombing raids" meant that the bombing raids should be halted by the time the representatives of the US and the DRV met. We pointed out that this was certainly not plain to us and that again, if the DRV really wanted talks to end the war, then it should be more specific on this point and immediately transmit this information to our government. Hoang Tung agreed.

There apparently was some shift in Hoang Tung's previous position, which we had understood made a very clear and sharp distinction between procedural matters to be dealt with at the first contact, and more substantive questions, which were to be delayed until the conference proper. At this stage, in order to try to establish the distinction between contact and conference, he began referring to the "Harriman conference"—meaning the high-level meeting, and not necessarily the point of first contact. We took this to mean that the procedure was still for a first exchange at the ambassadorial level which would take care of determining the facts of the halting of the bombing, and the details of the following separate meeting. However, Hoang Tung never quite agreed that this was an accurate statement—always leaving open what appeared to be the possibility of talking of "other things" at the initial contact. He finally asked that we write down, again, the clearest possible interpretation in English, by the numbers, of our understanding of what his position was as based on our discussion of the April 3 DRV statement. He said he would have this approved, amended, or rejected, in whole or in part, as soon as possible by his government—maybe today, certainly tomorrow. He said again, when we pointed out that time was running out, that we could be assured that he could give us "a piece of paper" before we left Hanoi.

The following six points were drafted in Hoang Tung's office while he and the interpreter stood by, except for one departure for Hoang Tung's private phone booth where presumably he reported he was bringing over another piece of paper.

The six points, as understood by us, from our detailed conversations with Hoang Tung, were thus put down on paper:

"The following is presented as setting forth the official position of the DRV on acceptable procedure for arranging contact with USA.

"1.   USA representative will be prepared to inform DRV representative that the bombing of all DRV territory has been halted without condition.

"2.   Total cessation of bombing will have been in effect for at least 24 hours prior to contact between DRV and US representatives.

"3. Initial contact will be at ambassadorial level in Moscow, or at any other site where both countries maintain diplomatic missions.

"4. The initial contact will deal with questions of procedure to arrange a conference. These questions include:

"a. Time of conference.

"b. Place of conference.

"c. Level of representation at conference.

"5. Upon agreement on procedural matters, DRV and USA will announce simultaneously the time and place of the conference.

"6. Representation of conference would consist initially of DRV and US. All substantive questions raised by both countries will be open for discussion."

Hoang Tung took the paper and promised again an official response by his government.

(The inclusion of Moscow as the site for the conference resulted from repeated statements by Hoang Tung that any one of a number of capitals would be suitable. We suggested that he should designate if possible what the DRV first choice would be. In the course of the conversation he seemed at that point to think that Moscow was the most likely capital mentioned. We asked if, in writing down the summary, he wanted us to write down Moscow or leave it out. He said go ahead and write it in; it is your summary—but it may be changed. We took this to mean that he did not at the point have final information as to what the selection of the city would be.)

We would like to emphasize again that this sequence of papers written by us and handed to Hoang Tung for consideration by his government were entirely responsive in nature. In each instance we were responding to his request to summarize our understanding of what Hoang Tung had said. Nothing included should be construed as representing a procedural or substantive suggestion from us.

We wound up our session with Hoang Tung shortly after 10 a.m. and went straight to the Indonesian Embassy to dispatch this message to Bundy:

DRV NOW CONSIDERING SIX POINTS ON PROCEDURE ON CON-

TACT AND SUBSEQUENT CONFERENCE STOP EXPECT DECISION
TODAY STOP

Our estimate of when we would receive the "piece of paper" again proved to be unduly optimistic. We had wound up our session with Hoang Tung in mid-morning, but we would not hear from him again until 7 p.m. Then the message was only that he would come to the villa for lunch the next day at noon. We responded with a note pointing out that Washington was waiting for a message from us indicating when the DRV reply might be expected, and that we did not like to leave the situation in suspense overnight. Our log notes that Hoang Tung's reply came at 9 p.m., and adds, "It was calculated to ruin another night's sleep."

On the 11 p.m. transmission to Vientiane from the Indonesian Embassy we sent the following to Bundy:

REFERENCE OUR LAST CABLE DRV WRITTEN RESPONSE AT
2100 THURSDAY HANOI TIME FOLLOWS IN ENTIRETY QUOTE
WILL ANSWER ALL QUESTIONS TOMORROW STOP WE ARE IN-
FORMED THAT TODAY U.S. PLANES HAVE BOMBED A LOCALITY
IN LAI CHAU ONE OF OUR PROVINCES ON THE VIETNAM-CHINA
BORDER UNQUOTE.

11

THE PIECE OF PAPER

Our last day in Hanoi was beset by manifestations of time running out. Late the previous
afternoon the forehanded bureaucracy required that all
ICC passengers pack their luggage and deliver it to a
downtown depot, which left us living out of brief cases
and flight bags for the next twenty-four hours. Added to
this mild irritation was our virtual confinement to the
villa, chained as we were to the telephone and to the messengers who clacked away in Vietnamese in the down-
stairs common room.

Hoang Tung arrived shortly after noon for our luncheon date, but only to report that the "piece of paper"
was still in process and would not be available until 3:30
p.m. Five minutes before the appointed hour we arrived
at *Nham Dan* to find Tung waiting outside, smiling
broadly, and waving a large brown envelope. We gathered around the coffee table in his office, and Hoang
passed the papers across to Nguyen Thuong, the interpreter, observing as he did so that we would not be
pleased at some of the things we were about to hear, but
there were other things we would like.

We leaned forward and strained to catch each word as
Thuong solemnly read through the document the DRV
had designated an *aide mémoire*. We were shaken by the

opening references to prisoner exchange; these by now
seemed almost irrelevant, until we realized that the Vietnamese were simply responding to the propositions we
had advanced earlier in the week on behalf of the State
Department in the order we had set them forth. The log
entry notes:

As the interpreter rounded onto page two—and he is an eloquent, rabbinical reader—we realized that we had been
through the usual polemical preamble and were coming now
to the essence of the message. The obvious importance was
naming the place—Phnom Penh—and giving enough procedural detail to provide substance to the offer. As Hoang Tung
had said, it wasn't all we had hoped for—but what was left
after the whittling and nit-picking and record-making was
surely enough to indicate serious purpose. At our opening
meeting the Saturday before, Tung had promised that before
we left Hanoi he would produce what he called "trump
cards." It wasn't the hand we would have chosen, but he had
delivered.

After the reading we were handed the *aide mémoire* in
the original Vietnamese, along with an official DRV
translation in English. It was dated April 5, 1968, and
follows in full:

1. The Government of the Democratic Republic of Viet
Nam has repeatedly protested against the U.S. action in illegally laying hold of civilians and military personnel on board
fishing boats and freighters even in the territorial waters of
the Democratic Republic of Viet Nam. The Government of
the Democratic Republic of Viet Nam demands that the
United States stop all its arrogant acts, respect the sovereignty,
territory, and security of the Democratic Republic of Viet
Nam, and release immediately, unconditionally and without
any need for an agreement between the two parties, all citizens of the Democratic Republic of Viet Nam now being
illegally detained.

As for the captured American pilots, they are regarded by
the Government of the Democratic Republic of Viet Nam as
guilty to the Vietnamese people. Acting upon orders from the

U.S. Government, they have bombed the Democratic Republic of Viet Nam, an independent and sovereign country, killing civilians and destroying the property of the Vietnamese people. However, in accordance with the humane and lenient policy of the Government of the Democratic Republic of Viet Nam, they have enjoyed good treatment. On the occasion of the last Tet festival, for the 1st time, three of the captured U.S. pilots were released in view of their correct attitude during their detention.

2. With regard to the "limited bombing" of North Viet Nam announced by President Johnson, the Government of the Democratic Republic of Viet Nam made clear its view in its April 3, 1968, statement.

The U.S. Government has not seriously and fully met the legitimate demands of the Government of the Democratic Republic of Viet Nam, of progressive American opinion and of world opinion. However, for its part, the Government of the Democratic Republic of Viet Nam declared its readiness to appoint its representative to contact the U.S. representative with a view to determining with the American side the unconditional cessation of the U.S. bombing raids and all other acts of war against the Democratic Republic of Viet Nam, so that the talks may start.

Details about the contact between the representatives of the Democratic Republic of Viet Nam and the United States may be as follows:

—The representative with ambassadorial rank of the Government of the Democratic Republic of Viet Nam is ready to contact the representative of the U.S. Government.

—The place of contact may be Phnom Penh or another place to be mutually agreed upon.

—In the course of the contact, the U.S. side will specify the date when the unconditional cessation of the U.S. bombing raids and all other acts of war against the Democratic Republic of Viet Nam will become effective; then the two parties will reach agreement on the time, place and level of the talks.

3. Any interpretation of the point of view of the Government of the Democratic Republic of Viet Nam at variance with the content of this *aide mémoire* is null and void.

The designation of Phnom Penh as the suggested point of initial contact would figure large in the news for the next several weeks. It was offered here as the initial response of the DRV to the opening gambit by President Johnson, who had proposed Geneva in his speech. The Swiss site, we were to learn upon our return to Washington, also had been formally tendered through diplomatic channels in Vientiane. It could be taken that the President had disposed of some other matters we had wrestled with earlier, such as the level of representation, when he announced that he would send as his personal representatives the very senior Ambassadors Harriman and Thompson. But there were still urgent questions left unanswered.

Hoang Tung impressed upon us that the *aide mémoire* was his government's formal reply to President Johnson's speech, to be treated as a secret document and delivered only to our government. We indicated that we would deliver it by hand to Ambassador Sullivan in Vientiane that night, rather than trust it to radio transmission. He nodded agreement, observing that he had already checked and had found that the ICC flight would be departing on schedule at 8 p.m. From the log entry:

We were by this time seriously squeezed for time—which Tung sensed, too, for he cut through Baggs' usual rolling farewell to get us on the way. We pressed for as much clarification as we could get on whether substitution of Phnom Penh for Moscow, as mentioned in our previous exchange, had serious political meaning. We pointed out that the United States had no diplomatic relations with Cambodia, which meant that a contact there, while possible, would be far more difficult than in other capitals. Secrecy, if this was a factor, would be especially difficult since Prince Sihanouk hardly has a reputation for reticence. Tung listened to this with careful attention—but his only response was, all right, the rest of the sentence proposing Phnom Penh invites the United States to propose an alternative—there is nothing final about this.

Impression: There is no way to be sure whether original insistence on "step by step" approach has been abandoned, but it would appear that it has at least been modified. Implied acceptance of negotiation at "Harriman level" seemed to indicate that the prior sharp distinction between "contact" and "meeting" has been blurred. Statement in *aide mémoire* that U.S. must specify date of cessation of bombing is less vague than reference in official statement on April 3. Tung would not amplify except to say that it would be helpful if word of the bombing halt were sent before contact is made, adding that this is not a condition. Finally, we leaned hard on Tung on the question of communication. The *aide mémoire* obviously required a reply, possibly an exchange, on the question of whether Phnom Penh was acceptable to the U.S. How did they want this? What channel? Directly from embassy to embassy? He agreed that this was critical, and said he would give us the answer when he came to the airport to see us off.

Our concern over the exact wording of the stipulation concerning cessation of bombing proved to be unhappily well-founded. After weeks of skirmishing over a site for the meeting finally ended with agreement on Paris, this became the principal debater's point behind which both sides concealed their real negotiating positions and ultimate purposes. Almost two months after our conversation with Hoang Tung, the senior DRV representative at Paris, Xuan Thuy, addressed the American delegation at the fifth deadlocked negotiating session:

"I am waiting, gentlemen, for a reply to this question: When will the United States cease unconditionally its bombing and all other acts of war on the whole territory of the Democratic Republic of Vietnam, in order to allow the discussions to proceed then to other questions of interest to the two countries?"

And Ambassador Harriman replied on behalf of the United States:

"We reject the suggestion now being urged by you that the only reason for our meetings is to give the hour and date of the cessation of bombing." All of Hanoi's communications, starting with the note of April 3 agreeing to the talks, Harriman insisted, "indicated you were prepared to enter into discussions which could lead up to a cessation of bombing. We are, and have consistently stated we are, ready to discuss the question of cessation of bombing. But we have pointed out that it is necessary to discuss at the same time related matters on the basis of the President's speech."

By the time we reached Tokyo en route to Washington we would discover that the State Department was already laying theoretical groundwork for the Harriman position by insisting upon a rigid distinction between official and unofficial communication intended to denigrate the *aide mémoire,* and any other contradictory information brought out of Hanoi by its bearers. But on this dwindling Friday afternoon we accepted the message we had been given at its face value, and briefly believed the ultimate recipients in Washington would too—and turned our thoughts to the numbing news from home Hoang Tung had brought us at lunch.

He could give us no details, only the stark fact that Martin Luther King had been shot down by a white sniper in Memphis, and that racial disorders were erupting across the United States. We were, in that dim dining room with its awkward, French bourgeois furnishing, literally on the other side of the globe from the scene of the gentle King's death, and it felt as though we were on the far side of the moon.

We had both known King well, from the days when he came out of the obscurity of his Alabama pastorate to lead the Negro protest against discrimination on Montgomery's buses—a matter of only a few years ago on the temporal scale, but already a fading event left over from another historical epoch. We could remember the young preacher's fatalistic, imperturbable courage on occasions when mobs howled outside. And we could hear him again at *Pacem in Terris* in Geneva, proclaiming in his measured, prophetic tones, "I criticize America because I love her, and because I want to see her stand as the moral example of the world." He went on to indict his country for launching a war in Vietnam that "has exacerbated the hatred between continents and, worse still, between races." And at Geneva he had concluded with words singularly fitting for this place on this day:

"Now this is not to overlook the ambiguity of the total situation and the need for collective solution to the tragedy of Vietnam. Neither is it an attempt to make North Vietnam and/or the National Liberation Front paragons of virtue, and it is not to overlook the role they must play in a successful resolution of the problem. While they may have understandable reasons to be suspicious, life and history give eloquent testimony to the fact that conflicts are never resolved without trustful give-and-take on both sides."

We recounted some of these thrusting memories to Hoang Tung and Nguyen Thuong, and they listened with grave courtesy. They were, in fact, models of tact throughout the painful opening minutes of our luncheon meeting, holding to the role of sympathetic bearers of bad tidings, putting down any human temptation to gloat over the discomfiture the assassination of a distinguished colored sympathizer with the Vietnamese cause was bound to inflict upon their enemies.

Perhaps to ease the tension, or perhaps only because he knew this would be his last opportunity to talk freely and informally with his round-eyed contemporaries, Hoang Tung for the first time in our acquaintance allowed the conversation to flow into wholly personal channels. Always before he had politely deflected questions about his own history and private life, but now he told us his age, 49, as preface to asking our own and establishing that we were of the same generation. He had left childhood behind as a teen-age revolutionary destined to spend a total of six years in French prisons where, he explained, he had mastered the French language and completed his education. From the log:

Hoang Tung spoke quite emotionally of riding a bicycle down Route One to Nam Dinh in 1945—and how the roadside was littered all the way with the bodies of children who had starved in the famine brought on when the occupying Japanese stepped up rice shipments to their beleaguered troops and simply wrote off the Vietnamese civilian population as inadvertent war casualties.

He made a number of personal references to his son in the army by way of establishing his deep, personal desire to see an end to a war which, in one form or another, has been going on almost as long as he can remember. Then he pointedly added that despite this he would never abandon the things he had invested his life in—the long fight for freedom and independence. "If we have to, we will fight on to victory —you must never doubt that." This was doubtless intended, in part at least, as an autobiographical warning not to mistake the DRV's willingness to negotiate for a sign of weakness.

Once Baggs quoted from *Dr. Zhivago* to make a point, and Tung came back on his first opportunity to observe that of course he did not agree with the philosophy expressed in the book—one of the few times in this conversation when he sounded party-line doctrinaire.

He asked us to tell him frankly what our impressions were after a second visit behind the "bamboo curtain," using the phrase with conscious irony. Ashmore used the opportunity to do a little testing on attitudes toward China—remarking that while he was not a socialist, he could see how socialism adapted well to the peculiar economic needs of Vietnam; that the system seemed to him tolerable so long as it was run by humane men of demonstrated integrity like Ho Chi Minh; but that where the system involved wholesale repression, as in China, he could not accept it. Tung heard this out impassively, although there were small flickers of expression that indicated understanding if not sympathy.

It is not possible to appraise where the line comes between propaganda and sincere statement of conviction in a conversation such as this—which no doubt is just as true on his side as on ours. He jokes about this, his face breaking up into his wonderful grin when he says something like, "Now I make a little propaganda . . ." He is an ironist, and the sharp wit comes through the interpretation—indeed the accomplished Thuong often breaks up himself before he can deliver the barb, as when Hoang Tung responded to a question as to whether he had ever been in Geneva: "No, but I know that John Foster Dulles."

His candor has limits, and when pressed he goes mute—retreating into vagueness or promising to get an answer later. But he makes a great point that nothing is barred from our conversation. He now uses as a standard phrase "on the table"—meaning speaking without inhibition—and also, when the going gets stuffy, he indicates, sometimes with gestures, that we should take off our diplomat's hats and put on our journalist's hats.

He responds warmly to our satirical comments about "diplomats" and "bureaucrats" and, whether it is real or an affectation laid on for the occasion, he obviously enjoys the assumption of professional freemasonry among journalists. When Baggs offers to make up the inside pages of *Nham Dan* so Tung can take the night off, he mockingly replies that he can't consider accepting such a generous favor until he can come to Miami and return it.

Yet he is meticulous in making the distinction between what is official—i.e., the certified, flyspecked word, in writing if possible—and what is "personal" opinion. But he is quite candid, by implication at least, in letting us know that we should never assume that he would express an opinion he did not believe to be that of his government.

Summary Impression: A genuinely first-class mind; a surprising sophistication, diluted only by the circumstance that it comes largely from reading and reflects a second-hand view of the great world; a streak of romanticism which occasionally softens the usually dominant intellectual toughness; a powerful sense of presence and authority reflected in the more than necessary deference he gets from his extensive and, so far as we could judge, well qualified staff, and in his ability to get response from the government. If he were a Western type he would have to be called a gentleman.

Somewhere in the course of this strained, unraveled luncheon, we discovered that we had come to think of this little Vietnamese editor as a friend, not in the limited sense Americans give the term when they apply it to anyone with whom they have civil and sustained contact, but in the special way one makes a place in memory for those with whom he has shared a crisis. We could not assume that we had entirely spanned the void between our cultures, or achieved anything approximating a complete understanding. There were too many mental cul-de-sacs on both sides, too many occasions when the conversation went blank, not because either party was dissembling but because painfully groping minds found no common referents.

We had no such sustained exposure to any of the other Vietnamese we saw and dealt with in these two visits behind the enemy lines. Scores would touch us in casual contact and slide away into the past, leaving us with the generally warm and pleasant feeling that we had been dealing with decent, thoughtful people who bore us no malice. This may have been due in part to the circumstances, in which we were ordinarily certified in advance as honored strangers, but we could recall no similar junket in which we encountered so few churls.

We were in a distant place, as distant as the globe's geography permits, under circumstances that could modestly be described as bizarre. Yet there is surprisingly little that intrudes upon the memory that might be termed exotic. Perhaps this is due to the heavy, pervasive overlay of French culture on the physical environment, and the Western-style trappings that are now necessary for all men at war. Or perhaps it is just the industrious Vietnamese themselves, surely on their way into the contemporary technological society, more by dint of their own curiosity and enterprise than by any Marxist formulation that could possibly have filtered down from some distant ideological peak.

These are surface impressions we set down here, uncheckable under the circumstances by any of the reportorial techniques we would ordinarily employ. We did get around a bit on this second visit, singly for the most part, one of us going out to poke around the town while the other stood by for messages at the villa. Thus we were able to patch together a sketchy appraisal of the current scene in North Vietnam based on our own observation, checked against the limited secondary sources available to us among the diplomatic corps and the handful of correspondents.

The prevailing view in these circles is that Hanoi genuinely wants a settlement of the war and has established a position between the Russians and the Chinese which makes some degree of maneuver possible. The question is how much Hanoi is willing to pay for the end of overt hostilities. It is our view that the price may very well be lower today than it would have been a year and a half ago, since the physical bolstering by the Socialist allies appears to have left the Vietnamese far better equipped to go the distance than they were when we first wandered through these streets in January 1967. Whatever the price may be, we found no one here who believes that it is likely to involve a settlement that can be construed as having been paid for by capitulation to the bombing.

It is not that the Vietnamese have not been hurt by the attacks from the air and the attrition of the fierce campaigns in the South. It is common knowledge that Hanoi has had to accept the assistance of Chinese work battalions to keep the supply routes open. These are unarmed, nonmilitary formations, but they are still Chinese, and guesses as to their strength run to more than 100,000. Historically, there could be no more sharp incentive to get the war over in order to get these ostensibly friendly invaders back north of the border.

The Vietnamese look healthy, and the conclusion must be that the diet is adequate. There is no starvation here, no beggars, no signs of the reduced energy brought on by malnutrition. There are some food shortages, indicated by the increased proportion of imported cereals to rice in the standard ration, which runs to 14 kilograms for office workers and 22 kg. for laborers. There also are figures, gleaned from published planning reports, that indicate a total reduction in rice acreage in 1968 by some 200,000 hectares, which by rough measure might cut production by as much as a million tons. Meat is rationed to a portion a week, as is fresh fish, but salt or dried fish is usually available on the off days. Vegetables are plentiful until July. Since the Vietnamese reduce everything to a kind of thick soup this would seem to provide a tolerable base diet. The consensus is that there is poverty here, but little privation. The worst burden may be the sheer monotony of a long war which has stripped away the most modest of nonessential creature comforts.

The diplomats in Hanoi are professional Communist-watchers; indeed, those from the non-Communist bloc countries, which provide little of the goods and technical support to keep the war going, have very little else to do. There are not many travel visas issued these days, or trade agreements negotiated. The game here is to keep book on the real governing hierarchy that operates behind the façade of government ministries and party structure.

It is generally accepted that Ho Chi Minh still functions as the court of last resort, but he is not seen much any more, and the prevailing view is that he is increasingly removing himself from day-to-day affairs. Beneath him, in order, the diplomats rank Le Duan, secretary-general of the Communist Party; Truong Chinh, chairman of the National Assembly; Pham Van Dong, the prime minister; Vo Nguyen Giap, defense minister and commander-in-chief; and Nguyen Trinh, foreign minister. The only significant changes recorded on the form chart recently came when Truong Chinh, reputedly the only pro-Mao member of the hierarchy, moved down from No. 2 to No. 3.

Shortly before we came to Hanoi there was an announcement in *Nham Dan* about a threatened crackdown on saboteurs and fifth columnists. This caused quite a stir in the Western press, which always quivers with excitement at any intimation that the CIA may be riding again. A diplomat who considers himself a neutralist, although he is publicly branded counterrevolutionary by the refusal of the Chinese ambassador to shake his hand at embassy receptions, thinks there was no such threat and that the public pronouncement was a political gambit—probably intended to reassure the Chinese that the Hanoi regime isn't going soft on the revolution. His own government not long ago inexplicably came under sharp attack in the Vietnamese press; and when he went discreetly padding around the ministries to see what might be done to smooth things over, he was told not to worry. In a short time the attacks faded away, and the diplomat concluded that for some reason having to do with high international Communist politics Hanoi had thought it useful to give his country what he called a whack for the record.

To the casual eye there are no visible signs of police-state repression. The Catholic church, although deeply affected by the traumatic aftermath of the great exodus to the South, is still very much alive. A Catholic foreigner to whom we talked estimates that there are probably about 350,000 Vietnamese still on the church rolls. The foreign hierarchy is now completely replaced by native clergy, and there are no Catholic schools. But at Christmastime, he said, the cathedral in Hanoi was full to overflowing, and the parishioners appeared to be of all ages. Mass was said in five languages: Vietnamese, Chinese, French, German, and English.

In our own limited observation it appeared that the pagodas showed more signs of desuetude than did the parish churches, and others who reside in North Vietnam confirmed the impression. Buddhism apparently had only a light hold on North Vietnamese urbanites, and under the influence of the worldly Marxists the pagodas are being given over to cobwebs and the ministrations of a dwindling tribe of old women. It may be different in the villages, but in Hanoi we didn't catch sight of a single Buddhist monk.

One Westerner of sociological bent has been much interested in what is happening to the family under the impact of the long war. He characterizes the Vietnamese as charming and courteous in their dealings with strangers, but he thinks they are not a particularly gregarious people, and that they tend to turn inward toward the family unit, Mandarin-style. Still, as he observes the actual experience of the few Vietnamese with whom he has close personal dealings, he wonders how the traditional family pattern can stand the profound dislocations of the time. He cited the example of his French teacher, a woman who is still in Hanoi, while her husband, a doctor, is permanently stationed in the provinces; their children are in school somewhere in the countryside. It was, he thought, a typical pattern of dispersion affecting all classes.

There are no available figures on divorce, and the subject is not mentioned. The heavy hand of Communist puritanism shoves such vice as there may be out of sight. Our demi-sociologist acquaintance suspects that there is probably a scant amount of free-lance prostitution in the working-class quarters to meet the hit-and-run needs of soldiers and sailors on leave. He notes that there is much more freedom of association among the young than is allowed in most traditional Oriental societies, and on warm days the young lovers are a splendid sight strolling hand in hand through Hanoi's generous lakeside parks. He thinks there may very well be a bit of hanky-panky in the bushes.

These observations, whether first- or second-hand,

ought, as we say, to be leavened with the realization that on our journeys to Hanoi, and particularly the second one, we have functioned as principals in a scenario that had the jerky characteristics, and unnerving suspense, of a Pearl White serial. Journalism became our spare-time occupation, to be pursued in the interstices of our demi-diplomacy, and some idea of the working conditions may be gleaned from the final log entry covering our departure from Hanoi. It was scrawled by Ashmore on the ICC flight to Vientiane, and it is offered here untouched, complete with its glaze of fatigue.

Hoang Tung came to the villa with two of the old Russian Volga sedans, one of which contained two flower girls, complete with bouquets. The girls, us, one of the more inept of the interpreters, and our hand luggage—including two of the pointy-top straw hats—completely filled the car. Tung and company went ahead, leading the way across the ersatz Long Bien Bridge, through the bombed-flat industrial district, past the check-point, to the airport.

The two flower girls were in full regalia, and radiantly beautiful. Baggs was in lapse, so I took up the diplomatic chore of filling in the long pauses in the middle of the pontoon bridge, where the traffic inevitably clogged. I tried the gambit of suggesting that my daughter at Vassar—which I translated into "university" to cut down the confusion—would have some personal questions about these young ladies—such as, what occasions did they consider proper for make-up, which they were obviously wearing?

As I suspected it might, this took us into forbidden territory—which the interpreter staked out by saying he did not have the words for "lipstick," "rouge" and "eyeshadow"—all of which were in evidence in neon shades.

It then turned out that the girls worked at the newspaper, as typists, and doubled as Hoang Tung's greeters. The one in the back seat said she was 20 years old and hoped to go to the university after the war. I went into an avuncular bit about marriage and how so beautiful a pair of maidens could not escape it, and the interpreter seemed to be riding along with this very well. Then it turned out that the girl in the front seat was very much married, to a soldier, and had a five-year-old daughter. To my round eye she looked even younger than the 20-year-old.

In desperation I told the interpreter to tell the girls to ask me any questions they might have in mind. He said they were shy—which may have been true of the little mother but certainly was not the case with Miss Back Seat, who promptly launched into a series of abrasive, doctrinaire questions in a suffragette manner that would have entitled her to an honorary degree from my daughter's alma mater.

She wanted to know how the capitalist warmongers could justify their position to the peace-loving young people of the USA, and things like that. I did the best I could, while lurching across a pontoon bridge with the gladiolas in her bouquet tickling my chins. Baggs rested in his corner of the seat, and occasionally laughed out loud.

At the airport Hoang Tung and our outriders assembled in a more or less private alcove off the cold, austere, aggregate-floored formal waiting room—around an ell from the restaurant-bar where the departing ICC hands and other less favored people were living it up in the conventional way of travelers about to become airborne.

Mary McCarthy and Franz Schurmann were in the opposite alcove, a good 50 feet away, with their own ceremonial bearers. We were all up to our elbows in flowers. Remarkably enough, these alcoves are furnished with Boston-style rocking chairs.

Hoang Tung had one final piece of business—the word he had promised to bring us as to the best means of communicating the U.S. reply to the DRV *aide mémoire*. It could be done directly, ambassador to ambassador, at any point of contact where both countries had legations, without prior notice. And he, of course, would always be available if we had anything we wanted to communicate directly to him.

We lurched out to the old Boeing with our handbags, rice-paddy hats, flowers, and corrugated memories, and went off to Laos.

12

THE LONG VOYAGE HOME

It was pleasant, for the brief time it lasted, to bask in a cloud of euphoria and to enjoy VIP handling by the United States foreign service. Counselor Hurwitch was at planeside at Vientiane, as promised, and we were hand-carried past customs and immigration and borne off to the ambassador's residence in a black car with a sheathed flag on the fender. There was even a royal touch; Princess Moune Souvanna Phouma, a compatriot from Geneva, was on hand to greet Mary McCarthy and we paused on the ramp for a small, regal reunion.

Hurwitch inquired if we thought it advisable to bring Charles Collingwood, the CBS correspondent, along to the residence. We said we thought not, since we had an official document to hand to the ambassador and this would doubtless lead to private conversation. We had, in fact, been sparring with Collingwood ever since we joined up with him at the Phnom Penh airport on the way out, cutting up old touches and exchanging trivial pieces of public-domain information in the usual manner of competitive correspondents.

We had an idea, too, that Collingwood might fancy himself as operating on the demi-diplomatic circuit. We recalled that some years ago he had been Averell Harriman's information officer during the governor's first tour in the State Department. And his sudden recall from a year's leave in Mexico for this coveted assignment as the first American television correspondent to break the North Vietnamese barrier was a considerable surprise. We had been expecting to see his senior CBS colleague, Walter Cronkite, whom we knew had been cleared by Hanoi after protracted negotiations.

Whatever his mission, Collingwood drew the second shift in Vientiane, breakfast with the ambassador next morning, while we proceeded forthwith to the residence to turn over the *aide mémoire* and give Sullivan a preliminary briefing for transmission to Washington. The word at that point was that President Johnson still planned to come to Honolulu for a scheduled meeting with the leaders of the Southeast Asian countries supporting the U.S. in Vietnam, presumably to fill them in on the impending negotiations. Sullivan, a brisk, handsome, JFK-style career man, accepted our report with apparent enthusiasm and suggested that we plan to stop in Hawaii to meet Bundy, who would be with the Presidential party. We welcomed the thought of lopping a few thousand miles off the return trip, and left it to the embassy to juggle our reservations while we slept out what was left of the night in the disintegrating modern hotel the Laotian expatriate colony refers to as the CIA Hilton.

Both Ambassador Sullivan and Hurwitch spent a good deal of time trying to lay to rest the report of a bombing raid on Lai Chau province up where the Vietnam-China border coincides with that of Laos. We had relayed this through the embassy the night before, and our own best guess was that a strike so far outside the usual pattern must have been an overshot by strayed overt or covert U.S. bombers supporting Laotian troops. A thorough check of all planes aloft from Laos on any mission had been made, Sullivan said, and it could not have been one of ours. He offered his personal speculation that the bombing might have been done by the Chinese in order to disrupt the pending negotiations. Whatever merit this notion had, it was easy to see how a man could come by it if he lived for long in Vientiane, where the atmosphere is so saturated by the spy business that it takes on the coloration of a cloak-and-dagger supermarket.

By next morning the Presidential trip to Honolulu was in serious doubt, and we were advised to go on to Tokyo and check in with Ambassador Alexis Johnson. We were also asked to continue under wraps and to be prepared to join Bundy, wherever he wound up, as soon as possible. We agreed, and took off on the wearying loop south to Phnom Penh, east to Hong Kong, and north to Tokyo, which avoids China's air space by adding more than a thousand miles to the trip.

We regrouped with Mary McCarthy, Schurmann and Collingwood for what we all felt was a disembodied journey through the Asian skies. Only fragments of news from the States reached us in the steaming airport at Phnom Penh where we shifted from the old Boeing to an Air France jet. In the transient passenger lounge at Hong Kong nothing was available except a local English-style tabloid which, incredibly enough, gave the aftermath of the Martin Luther King assassination four paragraphs on page eight—possibly on the theory that Hong Kong was no place to be talking up race riots.

In Tokyo our VIP status was still holding firm. The kind of amiable middle-aged type who usually winds up as week-end duty officer was on hand with an embassy car and hauled us off to The New Imperial. It was now definite that the Honolulu meeting was off, and the word here was that we were to go straight through to Washington the next day. We subsided gratefully into the solid comfort of the Japanese hotel, but it was to be another chopped-up interval, and one that would drain away the optimism we had brought out of Hanoi. From the log:

A call from Ambassador Johnson at 2 a.m. He said he had

been asked by Washington to talk with us as soon as possible, and asked if we would prefer to get at it immediately or wait until early next morning. We took the option, and it was agreed that he would send a car at 7:30 a.m.

At 6:30 a.m. Johnson telephoned to report that the Department was sending him a list of questions to be put to us and it now looked as though he would not have these in hand until at least 10:30 a.m.—and we might as well go back to sleep until further notice. We didn't. The clock had now worked around to the point where it was feasible to get on the overseas telephone to our heirs, assigns and associates in the United States.

First-hand reports of the Martin Luther King aftermath only compounded the preposterous quality of the event. Verdict from the calm ones: the actual killing and looting was not extensive, but the political/psychological implications were immense. The summary view is that the pressure generated by the reaction to the King assassination cumulatively pushes LBJ toward settlement in Vietnam. Therefore we should be high priority at the State Department.

There had been only passing mention of our presence in Hanoi in the papers, but the good reporters were on the trail and panting. Ben Bradlee of the Washington *Post* had been working on Baggs' secretary, and Harrison Salisbury of *The New York Times*, who had cabled us in Hanoi, was working on Ashmore's. He had even tried to loosen her up with the come-on statement that we had obviously written the "however" paragraph in the official DRV statement—a rumor that has more substance than most. Sander Vanocur of NBC is haunting both our wives. We told the secretaries and wives to keep stalling until further notice.

A little before 11 a.m. the call came from the embassy. We were delivered to the ambassador's office, and left to cool for a half-hour. It turned out that this time Collingwood had had first call, and Johnson had been with him while he prepared to go on the air via satellite for a direct broadcast to the United States—in which he dropped the news, received from Foreign Minister Nguyen Trinh in Hanoi, that Phnom Penh had been proposed as the site for negotiations. Collingwood also suggested opaquely that he had been the "missing link" required to bring the parties together.

Johnson read us a message from Bundy urging that we not consider that the Collingwood broadcast released us from our obligation to stay out of print until after we had talked with him and his colleagues. We agreed. Johnson then handed us a copy of a statement just released by the White House which may have been prompted by the Collingwood broadcast but which sounded as though it were intended to reject the official *aide mémoire*. The burden of this was the complaint that Washington had made a formal proposal of Geneva as a site, transmitted by Sullivan to his DRV opposite number in Vientiane, and had still received no official reply.

We reacted with some profanity. We told the ambassador the North Vietnamese would have every reason to read this as a rejection of their Phnom Penh proposal, which we had handed to Sullivan in writing more than 36 hours ago. We proposed sending a holding cable in the hope of offsetting the damage and he replied that this was our business, but that he had no objection.

We sent a cable to Hoang Tung through the DRV representation in Phnom Penh telling him that the *aide mémoire* was being transmitted to our government and that we were ourselves en route to Washington. We sent a copy of this to the embassy with the request that it be forwarded to the State Department along with an adequate representation of our view that this is a hell of a way to run a peace negotiation.

We flew nonstop to San Francisco, where a State Department emissary transshipped us with only an hour on the ground, and landed at Dulles International at 5 o'clock on Sunday afternoon—only a few hours after we departed Tokyo, the calendar said, what with the great gouge taken out of the clock by the unreeling time zones. A State Department man was waiting to detour us around the terminal and the possibility of waiting reporters, and on a warm, bright spring afternoon we entered the nation's capital to confront an eerie spectacle no American had seen since our Confederate forebears rode across the Potomac with Jeb Stewart to find that the besieged federal government had decamped. Stewart's cavalrymen, fearing ambush, rode right back out again, but we would stay another five days in a city partially paralyzed by the curfew that provided an ironic memorial for an apostle of nonviolence.

We rolled in awed silence down the broad avenues, past the White House, up 16th street to our hotel in the heart of the downtown district. An occasional police car prowled past, or a military personnel carrier with armed troops, but nothing else moved. Down the whole length of 16th, from Lafayette Square to Scott Circle, past the grand hotels, the Soviet Embassy, the University Club, only one pedestrian was in sight, a single defiant Negro with no one to accost and, until a patrol car came by, no one to accost him.

Our hotel, the blessed Jefferson, was without servants since the curfew kept the colored staff confined to their homes across the city. But the doughty ladies who run the place managed somehow to scrape together supper for their guests, who were themselves barred from the streets and cut off from sustenance. The telephone plucked us back from this strange, unnerving tranquillity. It was Bundy, arranging to see us the next morning, enjoining us to silence, and already, it seemed to us, laying the groundwork to discredit the *aide mémoire* and any other inconvenient information we might have brought back.

Apparently acting on the principle that the best defense is a good offense, Bundy stiffly suggested that we had exceeded our instructions—which Baggs in his turn suggested it was impossible for Bundy to know since he had not yet heard what we had done. It was clear, at any rate, that our message from Tokyo had been received. Baggs put through a call to Katzenbach suggesting that it might be well if he attended our conference next morning, in case there was need for a referee.

We were picked up on Monday morning by Dan Davidson, an able young assistant to Harriman, and borne off to Bundy's suite in the State Department. The pleasantries in the car quickly turned brittle when we suggested that we couldn't understand the White House statement complaining that there had been no reply to the offer of Geneva as a meeting site when we had handed over a written counterproposal at the first State Department outpost we had come to. Surely, Davidson replied, we couldn't consider any message we delivered *official;* no offer to meet in Phnom Penh could be accepted as a response from the DRV until it was formally tendered to Ambassador Sullivan by the chief of the DRV mission in Vientiane.

If this was so, Baggs replied, then we surely had been jobbed, since we had been asked by the Department to treat the *aide mémoire* as a secret diplomatic document, and had done so even while Charles Collingwood was partially scooping Baggs with his broadcast from Tokyo —all of which would make an interesting second-day lead for *The Miami News* now that he was apparently free to write it. "There you go, threatening us already," Davidson said. Baggs said he thought his statement might more accurately be considered a promise, or possibly a summation of the situation as we now understood it.

We waited some fifteen minutes alone in Bundy's office while Davidson went off to brief his superiors on the truculent mood of the returned emissaries. When the conference assembled, it included Katzenbach, Harriman, Bundy, Davidson, and Robert Holbrook of Katzenbach's staff. There was some stiffness, but it was obvious that placation was the order of the day.

When Bundy again complained that it appeared that we had exceeded our instructions—which now became "understanding"—Katzenbach broke in to say that this was all water over the dam, since the point at issue had been resolved. Ambassador Sullivan now had received a formal offer of Phnom Penh from the DRV chargé d'affaires and so all was tidy and official. Governor Harriman followed up by suggesting that, since it now seemed possible negotiation could come at any time, we proceed to a briefing on all pertinent details of our meeting in Hanoi.

For a couple of hours we went over our conversations with Hoang Tung, noting point by point the shift in procedural considerations after the President's speech. There was, we said in summary, apparently a good deal of flexibility on procedure except for one point on which Tung's principals had never yielded an inch—that there must be a total cessation of the bombing before the DRV would pass on to discuss any substantive matters. The position had not changed since we first heard it directly from Ho Chi Minh, fourteen months earlier. "There is no possibility of a conversation with the U.S. until the bombing of our country stops," he said to us, and we found no one who spoke with authority who would move one centimeter from this basic position. It was possible, but hardly likely, that the State Department had received a contrary view through some other channel, but we could only reiterate what we had heard and sensed. The DRV position was that agreement to meet under the partial limitation of the bombing constituted a major concession on their part, and they would not consider any further acts of reciprocity until the bombing had stopped—at which point everything was open for consideration including mutual deescalation of the fighting in South Vietnam.

If there was to be bargaining, we said, it would have to be done on the other side of total bombing cessation; then, as we judged it, there would be considerable room for maneuver if the United States was now willing to accept some form of coalition government in Saigon embracing the NLF. This, we reported, was the essence we had distilled out of many hours of direct talk and background probing.

At that point it seemed as though Governor Harriman turned off his hearing aid, and the others in the room began to gaze at the ceiling. The optimistic assumption was that this studied lack of reaction simply reflected our interrogator's unwillingness to give such untrustworthy characters any indication of their negotiating strategy. An alternative assumption, bolstered by our past experience, was that the administration was on the point of blundering into a negotiation with the DRV without having prepared a coherent position on the kind and degree of compromise it was willing to accept as the price of settlement. The gloomy assumption, soon to be borne out by events, was that Harriman, as chief negotiator, was going to proceed on the basis that total bombing cessation was still negotiable, and stand on the old demand for a guarantee of military reciprocity.

We wound up the session with an agreement to dictate a complete briefing memorandum for the use of Harriman and the others involved in the pending negotiations. This ran to 27 single-spaced pages, and is the memorandum dated April 10 from which we have quoted frequently in the foregoing. We put this together on Tuesday, and had our final session with Harriman, Bundy, Davidson and Holbrook on Wednesday.

By this time the protracted quibbling over the site of the initial contact was already well launched and the tentative aura of hope and good will that had followed the Johnson speech and the DRV response was rapidly being dissipated. Our own waning optimism went down to zero when Harriman simply rejected our contention that the North Vietnamese had made it quite clear that while they would make contact while the bombing went on, they would not begin to negotiate seriously until it had been halted. "That is simply not possible," Harriman said. "They can't expect us to stop the bombing without getting some concession from them to protect our troops near the DMZ."

Before we closed out our dealings in Foggy Bottom we were treated to another laboratory example of the kind of schizophrenic activity we had previously cited as evidence of the existence of two frequently conflicting State Departments. Early Thursday morning the wire services relayed a Tass report from Moscow that Hanoi had accepted Washington's rejection of Phnom Penh as a meeting site and was now offering Warsaw.

This news was received in the State Department with relief, and even with a touch of jubilation, since it seemed to mean that the North Vietnamese were willing to move into Moscow's orbit even at the risk of incurring Peking's displeasure. Acceptance of Warsaw clearly was considered only a formality, and we were told that a plane to bear the negotiatiors to Poland had already been put on standby. Before the day was over Warsaw was indignantly rejected by the White House. Here is the account of the day's events by Bernard Gwertzman in the Washington *Star:*

By 9 a.m. the official proposal from Hanoi was received in Washington, and a high State Department official confided to one reporter: "Warsaw's okay."

He said John Grounouski, U.S. Ambassador to Warsaw, is a veteran of the Vietnam diplomatic wars, that U.S. negotiator Ambassador W. Averell Harriman is an old acquaintance of Polish Communist boss Wladyslaw Gomulka, and that even the Red Chinese could not object to talks there since they meet with the United States periodically in the Polish capital.

The State Department official, however, failed to take into account the sensibilities of President Johnson.

The fact that Hanoi let its proposal be "leaked" to the world by Tass apparently infuriated Johnson. He felt that the Communists were trying to gain propaganda points. He recalled that Poland had supplied aid to North Vietnam. And what about the U.S. proposals for "neutral sites—Jakarta, Vientiane, New Delhi, or Rangoon?

As he mulled the matter over with his aides, the wire services, the radio, and *The Star* were reporting that Warsaw "was expected" to be the site of the talks.

Christian's normal 11 a.m. briefing for reporters was postponed, building up an air of expectancy around the White House. At noon, Ambassador Dobrynin made an unscheduled appearance at the State Department, summoned by Acting Secretary of State Nicholas Katzenbach, on White House orders.

Katzenbach told Dobrynin that the United States regarded the Tass story as a breach of diplomatic protocol since if the Communists were serious about the talks, they should use conventional diplomatic channels for their proposals and not publicize them.

About 1 p.m., Christian read this statement to reporters:

"We learned this morning from reading a Tass dispatch that the North Vietnamese government has proposed Warsaw as a possible location for contacts. This was later confirmed by a message received through our embassy at Vientiane, Laos.

"The U.S. government has proposed a number of neutral countries as possible sites for contacts and we have not yet had any response to this proposal.

"On serious matters of this kind it is important to conduct talks under a neutral atmosphere, fair to both sides.

"The selection of an appropriate site in neutral territory with adequate communications facilities should be achieved promptly through mutual agreement, and those acting in good faith will not seek to make this a matter of propaganda."

The newsmen were surprised; they had expected an announcement accepting Warsaw. Questions were turned aside by Christian, including the anticipated one: "What about the President's promise to go anywhere?"

Thus, a new Johnson doctrine was proclaimed: The site must be neutral and have adequate communications.

State Department officials, who a half hour earlier were extolling the virtues of Warsaw as a site, now pointed out such pitfalls of holding talks in a Communist capital, the problems of visas, and Communist-staged demonstrations.

It was possible to have some human sympathy for the State Department hands who had to bite the bullet and put the new line into effect—particularly for Katzenbach, whose preposterous protest to the Soviet Ambassador set that gentleman up to observe to the American wire services that the complaint, as he understood it, was that Tass had some enterprising correspondents. That was true, he conceded, and they had a particularly good man in Hanoi.*

There had been, as we warned Hoang Tung when the Cambodian capital was first broached, good and sufficient reason for objecting to Phnom Penh. But now the President had made a travesty of the whole site controversy. He had clearly abrogated his own unrestricted offer, so often reiterated by him and by Secretary Rusk. This was spelled out again in his San Antonio speech of September 29, cited as the basic statement of the American position on negotiations: "I am ready to send a trusted representative of America to any spot on this earth to talk in public or private with a spokesman of Hanoi."

Moreover, the President had even contradicted his own previous offers. He now complained that Warsaw was not a neutral capital, but in 1966 the United States had accepted a Polish invitation to meet the North Vietnamese there. And in the February 1967 letter to Ho Chi Minh he had proposed a meeting in Moscow, which would have to be considered far more objectionable than the Polish capital on any of the grounds now cited.

But the worst was yet to come. On April 18 the Presi-

---

* The Washington flap produced still another tragi-comic scene in a sensitive foreign capital. Fred Warner Neal found that in Warsaw the acting foreign minister of Poland, Josef Winiewicz, had received an urgent message from U.S. Ambassador John Gronouski informing him that Warsaw had been chosen as the site for the U.S.-DRV negotiations and that the first contingent of Americans would be en route momentarily. Winiewicz alerted his foreign office staff, canceled all week-end leaves, and took off in the company of the U.S. ambassador in search of suitable quarters for the American delegation. They found an adequate site, too—just before Ambassador Gronouski received word that it was now his painful duty to inform the Poles that the White House considered their capital unsuitable.

dent ordered a stoic but obviously embarrassed Dean Rusk to announce that ten additional sites had been formally proposed to Hanoi, bringing the total put forward by the United States to 15. Such remote and improbable capitals as those of Laos, Burma, Parkistan, Nepal and Ceylon were now listed as presumably meeting the Johnson criteria of providing adequate communications, accommodations, and related facilities for the world's press. Conspicuously not included was Paris, the site most insiders had believed from the beginning to be so obviously desirable as to be inevitable, as it turned out to be.

The most paranoid touch to this whole charade was the indignant insistence in all the White House statements that Hanoi was guilty of making propaganda with its site bids—a line that would run with mounting intensity through all the President's comments on the DRV's refusal at Paris to halt the fighting and talk peace until the bombing stopped. The implications went far beyond the immediate subjects of controversy. The syndicated columnists Rowland Evans and Robert Novak wrote that Mr. Johnson regarded the fact that the Warsaw proposal came in by press ticker before the official offer was relayed from Laos as a deliberate attempt to humiliate him:

Mr. Johnson's immediate reaction was fury . . . It was President Johnson alone, backed by only two of his top level advisors, who privately rejected the Hanoi proposal to start talks with the U.S. in Warsaw . . . This is just one example of how tight the LBJ rein is on the Washington-Hanoi negotiations . . .
No one around Mr. Johnson really knows what decisions he will make from one day to the next. Thus, if Mr. Johnson decides that Ho Chi Minh is cashing in on the partial bombing halt, he might well react by full resumption of bombing —and without worry about public opinion.

We quickly found that we were, as before, firmly and irrevocably outside the wall the President has erected between himself and those who dissent from his Vietnam policies. Dean Rusk, finally making an appearance before the Senate Foreign Relations Committee on the Thursday morning of the Warsaw flap, was asked if he had seen Ashmore and Baggs since their return from Hanoi. He said he had not, and did not intend to.

The Secretary was equally brusque when senior members of the Committee urged him—as they knew we had urged Katzenbach, Harriman and Bundy—not to make the mistake of trying to negotiate with the Vietnamese on the bombing cessation unless the administration was prepared to go all the way and propose a full cease-fire as a prelude to discussions of political settlement. "That's an interesting idea," he said, and left it hanging.

As we had told the State Department at the outset we were going to do, we also appeared that afternoon in executive session before three members of the Foreign Relations Committee—Chairman Fulbright, and Senators John Sherman Cooper of Kentucky and Karl Mundt of North Dakota. We gave them for the record a summary version of the information and conclusions we had passed on in our briefing memorandum for Governor Harriman. The air of discouragement left behind by the adamant Rusk seemed to have affected all the members and staff present, even the redoubtable Mundt, who is usually considered the Committee's most steadfast defender of the hard line in Vietnam.

Throughout the week in Washington we had avoided press interviews for the record, which was no great feat with the diversion caused by Martin Luther King's state funeral in Atlanta. We had, however, had a number of frank talks with some of our colleagues among the senior political writers. Most of these were convinced that the President had been sincere in making his dramatic bid for negotiations, but that since his surprise speech he had again come under extreme pressure from the hard-liners. There could be no doubt that these were exploiting the strange quirks in his massive ego in an effort to convince him that the wily Reds in Hanoi were stalling him with phony diplomatic maneuvers while they exploited his generosity to build up the forces they were hurling against hapless American boys.

Harrison Salisbury of *The New York Times* was particularly convinced that this was the likeliest explanation of the apparent contradictions between the conciliatory stance Mr. Johnson had assumed on March 31, and the saber-rattling he seemed to be indulging in only ten days later. Salisbury also had been sealed away from the White House when he returned from Hanoi in January 1967, and he thought it was extremely important that we somehow get directly to Mr. Johnson with a first-hand report of what we had seen and heard. We told him we were willing, but that some very high-level personages had already tried to arrange for us to see Mr. Johnson, or someone in the inner circle who could be presumed to speak frankly with him, and had failed so far in three notable instances.

Salisbury insisted on trying his own resources, and on Friday morning he succeeded in setting up a private appointment for Ashmore with one of the half-dozen persons in Washington still reputed to have instant personal access to the President. By the time Ashmore arrived the President's confidant obviously had taken a reading at the White House and found the temperature much too low to risk intervention even by indirection. He declined even to read the summary memorandum Ashmore offered, with the suggestion that he make his own decision as to whether it contained anything Mr. Johnson ought to know.

That, clearly, brought us to the end of the string. We closed out the log by recording the valedictory cable sent to Hoang Tung from Washington on Friday, August 12:

DIPLOMATS HAVE TAKEN OVER STOP LET US HOPE FOR THE BEST STOP NOW YOU AND WE CAN PUT ON OUR JOURNALISTS HATS STOP MANY THANKS AND BEST REGARDS STOP

Post-Mortem

THE END OF PRECEDENT

The most consistent complaint Lyndon Johnson has voiced throughout his long public career is that he is not understood. There can be no doubt that he has suffered much personal injustice, particularly at the hands of the sentimental sophisticates who adored his urbane predecessor, John F. Kennedy, and were blinded to Mr. Johnson's considerable deeds by their abiding distaste for his personal style. He has always been hypersensitive to the demonstrable fact that he is one of those southern politicians who, as the late A. J. Leibling observed, travel badly, like sweet corn, becoming overripe by the time they reach the great cities of the nation, and offending delicate northern palates.

Being of the Confederate persuasion and largely immune to such offense, we have never objected to Mr. Johnson's style and, in some of its raunchy, private manifestations, we have often found it highly effective and vastly amusing. We have observed him at fairly close range for a good many years, and have done some political business with him on occasion, and we had at least as many high hopes as we did misgivings when he assumed the Presidency in his own right in 1965.

The blind spot, if there was one, would be on foreign policy; there simply was no way to appraise Lyndon

Johnson's capacities in this field because there had been no occasion for him to display them in his great Senatorial years. For the most part he had functioned uncritically within a concept of bipartisanship that left responsibility for shaping the country's course abroad in the hands of the executive.

The form chart did provide some hope that the new President would enjoy considerable immunity from military influence on his foreign policy. His notable lack of humility seemed likely to provide a shield and buckler. One of his closest Senate colleagues once observed, "Lyndon's been looking over these generals and admirals ever since they were junior officers and he sees them naked, without those brass-bound uniforms. He's never found one yet he thought was half as smart as Lyndon Johnson—or more than two-thirds as smart as Bob McNamara."

In this regard Mr. Johnson also had the benefit of the recent and painfully pertinent experience of Jack Kennedy. The late President's most intimate biographers, Theodore Sorensen and Arthur Schlesinger, agree that he was overwhelmed by the presumed authority and beribboned prestige of the generals and admirals when he approved the abortive Bay of Pigs invasion of Cuba. He is recorded as having later decried his own stupidity and weakness, and having vowed never to make the same mistake again. As Vice-President Mr. Johnson was surely close enough to have seen that this, however, was exactly what President Kennedy did when he assigned the nagging Vietnam dilemma to a senior army general for resolution. Maxwell Taylor may be a man of parts, but his professional career and published works left little doubt that he would push for a policy of increased, if still limited, application of American military might by ground and air.

There is evidence that Mr. Johnson did have a premonition, at least, of the fateful nature of the sticky little

Vietnamese war he inherited along with his office. We had breakfast with Adlai Stevenson at his UN ambassadorial residence a few weeks before his death, and the talk turned to the fundamental policy problems facing the United States in dealing with frenetic peoples suddenly released from the broken patterns of colonialism. With his usual, eloquent precision Stevenson said: "The first lesson is that no white army will ever win another war in Asia or Africa." He was asked if he ever argued that case in the White House. He did, he said, frequently, and with all the force he could command. But President Johnson only stared at him glumly and replied, "Of course, Adlai. You're absolutely right. But the question is, what do I do now?"

It is clear that Lyndon Johnson never found the answer. He refused to face up to the alternative of cutting his losses and pulling out, which he probably could have done in the early days, with only minimum political exposure. Ego appears to be the block here; in all the dark hours he has repeated to those around him that he does not intend to be the first American President to lose a war. So he turned to a Texas-style effort to wheel and deal the United States out of Vietnam on terms at least equivalent to those President Eisenhower obtained in Korea, using the leverage of increased military pressure to try to bring his Vietnamese adversaries and their Communist supporters to the conference table, where he promised to deliver peace and plenty for all. If he could just whip 'em a little bit, and make 'em admit it, he would guarantee he would be generous in the settlement.

This was, after all, the way he had been taught to handle any uppity troublemakers who might populate the periphery of his major concerns. In his perceptive book, *JFK and LBJ,* Tom Wicker of *The New York Times* recounts a revealing private comment by Mr. Johnson not long after he became President: "I grew up with Mexicans. They'll come right up in your front yard, and take it over if you let them. And the next day they'll be right up on your porch, barefoot and weighing one hundred and thirty pounds, and they'll take that too. But if you say to 'em right at the start, 'hold on, just a minute,' they'll know they are dealing with somebody who'll stand up. And after that you can get along fine."

As Wicker notes, the Vietnamese also arrive barefoot and weigh in at around one hundred and thirty pounds. Moreover, translated from the Pedernales vernacular, Mr. Johnson's formula for peace on the home place is nothing more nor less than the domino theory—the simplistic strategic concept that a break in the line of containment in Vietnam would open the way for Communist Chinese aggression and topple all the nations of Southeast Asia one after the other.

It cannot be said that Mr. Johnson significantly altered American foreign policy. Rather, he turned away from those within the administration who were warning that the old policy of containment had led to a dead end, and undertook in his heavy-handed way to sell the American people on the idea that their front yard extends all the way to the far side of the China Sea. Over the years the President employed endless personal briefings of Congressmen, editors, businessmen, governors, mayors and assorted White House passersby to gain support for a tricky and inconclusive Vietnam strategy. His standard peroration at these circus-style gatherings was revealing. Pointing to Defense Secretary McNamara he would say, "There's the fellow who has got to keep me in Vietnam." Pointing to Secretary of State Rusk, he would conclude, "And there's the fellow who has got to get me out."

Most of Lyndon Johnson's intellectual critics, and particularly those who view him from abroad, have tried to endow him with a conscious ideology, an uncritical dedication to some extreme theory of Communist containment inherited from John Foster Dulles and translated into a commitment to *Pax Americana*. It is our own guess that the President sees himself in a much simpler, but by his lights much more romantic, role.

He is very probably saying precisely what he believes in those painfully earnest television addresses in which he portrays himself as a sort of international Texas Ranger approaching a local riot with his six-shooter in one hand, waving a white handkerchief in the other, fully prepared to ride off into the sunset as soon as folks have settled down and shown him they are capable of handling their own affairs. He is, we believe, honestly puzzled by the suggestion that he could be sufficiently concerned about control of the means of production and the market economy of Vietnam to shed American blood and squander American gold in those remote jungles to hold back the rising tide of world Socialism. If he sometimes sounds that way it is only because he uses the going rhetoric— and the clichés of our foreign policy are in fact inheritances from the era of John Foster Dulles.

The simplest and most obvious explanation of Lyndon Johnson is the one he makes himself, and it may in fact be the only one that is adequate: he is a man who would like to be friendly with his neighbors, but, failing that, is willing to leave them alone on the minimum condition that they stop shooting at his family and friends. That, unfortunately, only translates into half a foreign policy. The symbolic Johnson family circle is prosperous and well-fed, and it takes in the whole of the white race, including even the feuding cousins in the USSR. But now it is surrounded by another family in an increasingly crowded neighborhood, one united by bonds of color, common misery, and bitter tribal memories of exploitation and degradation at the hands of Lyndon Johnson's family and friends. To ask men in this condition to simply stop shooting is to ask them to accept a patently unacceptable *status quo;* to subjugate them by force is not only inhuman, it is proving to be impracticable. If we are unable to lick them, and unwilling to join them in revolutionary enterprises that involve rolling a good many of our own family's heads, the nation is clearly in need of something entirely new in the way of a foreign policy.

It was precisely on this need that Lyndon Johnson's grand design for a Great Society foundered. He knew what he wanted to do at home, but Vietnam kept diverting him, pushing him past the limits of his demonstrated political competence. Here he had to venture into areas where the forces that shape the ultimate decisions were beyond his control, and apparently beyond his understanding.

In the old America, where the President grew up and knew his way around by instinct, it was generally held that politics stopped at the water's edge, and since the oceans were then wide and deep, politicians could leave foreign affairs to diplomats on the assumption that if anything went wrong it would happen a long way off. If things got so bad the President had to take a hand, as in the case of Franklin Roosevelt and Harry Truman, the chief executive responded by becoming commander-in-chief, and Americans rallied to the flag. Lyndon Johnson found that this formula no longer was valid, and here was the source of his mounting frustration and his ultimate personal defeat.

If the southern eye falls more tolerantly upon Mr. Johnson than does that of the norm of his critics, the vision is no less true. It is not an accident that the President's earliest, most persistent, and probably most effective critic on foreign policy is a regional neighbor and once close political associate, even a friend by the loose standards of contemporary camaraderie: J. William Fulbright of Arkansas. The antecedents and blood lines are similar, the cultural compulsions are not significantly different, and the two have passed through the same epoch in the House and Senate, moving side by side to the front rank of their political party as they came finally to a historic confrontation over Vietnam.

The difference between the two men could not be said to be ideological in the strict sense; on the usual scale, based on performance, Johnson would come out mildly liberal, Fulbright mildly conservative, but the spread would not be great. The great philosophical cleavage turns on their individual concepts of power and its uses and, above all, its limits. In these terms Fulbright would argue that there really wasn't any difference between the Dominican Republic and Vietnam, and Lyndon Johnson simply would not understand what he was talking about.

Tom Wicker, himself of the southern blood, has written what could stand as the Texan's political epitaph:

"The bombing began because Lyndon Johnson, in the ebullience of his power and in the fatal grip of an irrelevant experience, wanted to strike and thought he needed to strike—the result was the fourth bloodiest war in American history."

Whatever deficiencies, delusions, or aberrations may be attributed to Lyndon Johnson, and however high an estimate one may accept as to his political prowess, it is not possible to make an adequate appraisal of his Vietnam policy in terms of the President's personal views and ambitions. To run the course he followed, he had to carry the whole of the executive branch with him, and to bulldoze the Congress into backing escalation of an obviously unpopular war. It could never be said that he had a true popular mandate. His electoral majority was of historic dimensions, but it was essentially negative; it included perhaps as many votes against Barry Goldwater as it did for Lyndon Johnson, and these reluctant constituents for the most part had supported him because they thought he had promised to do in Vietnam the exact opposite of what he actually did.

He could, of course, count on the support of the military, since the application of force is its business and this was the instrument that was to become the President's primary reliance in Vietnam. Yet it is by no means certain that the escalation can be recorded as a triumph for the latest bête noire of the intellectuals, the military-industrial complex. It is well established that the civilian defense chief, Robert McNamara, was a restraining influence, at least in the closing years of his long tenure; and it is our own belief that when the wraps finally come off, it will be revealed that there were substantial tactical and strategic reservations about the Johnson course in the professional ranks.

But there was a *quid pro quo* working here that the protestants had little chance of overcoming. The prevailing military planners offered the President the kind of simplistic, neatly mathematical answers he likes: the addition of x troops supported by aerial interdiction of enemy reinforcement from the North would enable American search-and-destroy forces to clear x provinces in x months. Moreover, going the military's way gave the President a powerful patriotic appeal in selling his policy to the public.

In their turn the military men got an opportunity to test their theories and their new hardware under battlefield conditions, and to perfect the techniques of application—and in personal terms to replace the boredom and frustration of peacetime garrison duty with the excitement and opportunity of war, which, after all, is what their profession is about.

We were often reminded of a conversation we had in Geneva with N. N. Inozemtsev, the astute Soviet academician who had been an editor of *Pravda,* in which he warned that one practical danger in the continued conflict in Vietnam was the restiveness of Soviet professional military men. "All generals are the same," Inozemtsev said. "Ours see yours working out developments like your new airborne cavalry in South Vietnam, and they aren't even allowed to send observers into the field with the NLF. They keep reminding us how the Germans used Spain as a proving ground. Believe me, our best officers of all ranks are potential volunteers for Vietnam on a purely professional basis. It wouldn't take any political finagling to set up such a corps."

The same considerations applied in some degree in the State Department, at the top levels at least, and in the field in Vietnam, where the desperate efforts of United States foreign service teams to prop up failing Saigon and provincial regimes could be expected to generate a defensive dedication to the policies with which they were identified. Mr. Johnson had inherited a Secretary of State who had long since made his own emotional commitment to the doctrine of military containment in Asia—so much so that he had been largely bypassed when his original patron, John Kennedy, made fitful efforts to alter the country's international stance by taking policy-making back into the White House. There was no need for Lyndon Johnson to adopt a similar course. In the Georgian, Dean Rusk, he found an intelligent, dedicated, experienced bureaucratic practitioner who shared his fundamental view of the sanctity of the American front porch, and of the best means of protecting it.

It has been observed that the entrenched State Department bureaucracy has a richly deserved reputation for frustrating the new foreign policy brooms that occasionally appear in Washington. Dean Rusk, of course, had no such problem. He did not want to change the direction of American policy, only to follow the general lines that had fallen into place two decades ago after the tremendous explosion of World War II destroyed all the old power arrangements. He is preeminently the Cold Warrior, and Lyndon Johnson found him congenial because he offered an identifiable enemy, and brought a kind of moral certitude to an inner council that would soon include only those who could accept the President's devious pragmatism.

There would be occasions when Lyndon Johnson's hobnailed handling of the most exalted of his subordinates would roil even Dean Rusk, but he has remained a paragon among the bullet-biters. Gossip-mongering reached a new high in the Johnson years, but we can recall no instance when the Secretary of State by word or deed was thought to have indicated any dissent from, or reservation about, even the most bodacious of the President's pronouncements on Vietnam. There were, on the other hand, many occasions when the Secretary stepped in to repair the breach after the President, sentimentally carried away while playing his role as apostle of peace, seemed to imply that he was ready to make major concessions in order to get a settlement in Vietnam.

After the preliminary sparring was out of the way in Paris, one of the most respected of American diplomatic correspondents, Chalmers M. Roberts of the Washington *Post,* wrote:

The United States is prepared to accept a role for the Communists in the political life of South Vietnam—and to accept it regardless of the protests of the Thieu-Ky government and the generals who provide the power base for the Saigon regime.

This was being acknowledged high within the administration as discussions between the United States and North Vietnam unfold in Paris.

It is a decision that flows logically from President Johnson's determination to reject General William C. Westmoreland's call for more troops—a commitment that Mr. Johnson concluded to be a bottomless pit.

The military decision to halt further escalation is as close to irreversible as such a decision can be. Only a major new influence, such as a surprise military initiative by Hanoi, or Peking's entry into the war, is likely to alter the President's decision against escalation . . .

The political decision, by contrast, has murky aspects. A

central fact, however, is clear: Washington has concluded it has been far too easy on Saigon. That period is over; tough talk to Saigon is the new order of the day.

Secretary Rusk came right back on the rebound with a specific and indignant personal denial of the Roberts report:

There is a press story this morning which suggests that the United States attitude on a Communist role in the political life of Vietnam has been changed and that the United States is prepared to impose a Communist role upon the South Vietnamese government and people regardless of their views.

Such a suggestion is mischievous and false. The position of the U.S. government is unchanged and has been publicly stated and restated many times—for example the joint statement issued by President Johnson and President Thieu at Canberra last December 21 and more recently in President Johnson's March 31 speech.

False reports of this kind are most unfortunate, particularly at this time, because they mislead Hanoi into thinking that their propaganda can divide the United States and its allies.

Under some circumstances, such solicitude for the sensibilities of a nervous ally might be construed as the ordinary business of the State Department, and the occasion for justifiable diplomatic dissembling. But what was at issue here was a fundamental question of policy. There was a total contradiction between the Roberts report— which was undoubtedly solidly grounded in sources at least as high in the Johnson administration as Mr. Rusk —and the Secretary's petulant denial. This meant either that the issue was still unresolved on the desirability of a negotiated settlement, or that it was believed that to tip the negotiators' hand by any intimation that a Saigon coalition could be considered was so dangerous as to justify outright lying by the Secretary of State.

We ran into a variation on this theme when we returned from Hanoi the second time. At one point in our conversation with Katzenbach, Harriman and Bundy, we suggested that the North Vietnamese would be reassured about the pacific intentions of the United States if the negotiating team included someone who was known to be favorable to a nonmilitary settlement.

"Your friend Fulbright has publicly proposed Mike Mansfield or Ed Reichauer," Katzenbach replied. "Do you know what would happen if we announced we were putting either one of those on the delegation? It would collapse the government in Saigon."

We refrained from observing that this was an extraordinary manifestation that cleavage existed in Washington as well as Saigon, considering that the Under Secretary was talking about the Democratic majority leader in the Senate and a distinguished former ambassador to Japan. We did note that it seemed to us collapse of the Saigon regime—or at least the removal of General Thieu and Marshal Ky from its top positions—is apt to be a minimum consideration for a negotiated settlement. Preparing for this eventuality in Saigon would, of course, be a delicate piece of diplomatic business, but we were left with the dismal feeling that there simply had been no anticipation of the need, or even serious thought given to it, before Mr. Johnson made his startling pronouncement on March 31.

There can be no doubt that the President's obsession with secrecy has hampered State Department operations. David Kraslow and Stuart H. Loory, in their Los Angeles *Times* series on *The Secret Search for Peace,* revealed that any time a diplomatic maneuver aimed at a Vietnam settlement began to seem promising, the President personally ordered the distribution list for pertinent documents progressively limited until many of those ordinarily concerned with Vietnamese affairs were bound to be left in the dark. The shrinkage was illustrated by their report on the fate of a special State Department task force set up to coordinate military and diplomatic efforts in South Vietnam: "The 10-man group, which was conceived as a kind of 'country desk' staffed by experts with all the facts and figures at their command, has become in large part a speaker's bureau and public relations agency for the Johnson administration . . ."

Loory also has revealed that Mr. Johnson went completely outside his official circle when he came to the ultimate decision to partially deescalate the war. Concerned over the discrepancy between the rose-colored intelligence reports he received through military and State Department channels, and the much less sanguine estimates of developments in Vietnam by the CIA, the President called in nine ranking members of the eastern establishment to examine all the evidence and give him a recommendation. Reversing the position they had taken as late as December, when they urged continuation of the military effort, the nine-man jury returned this verdict: "Continued escalation of the war—intensification of bombing of North Vietnam and increased American troop strength in the South—would do no good. Forget about seeking a battlefield solution to the problem and instead intensify efforts to seek a political solution at the negotiating table."

Loory lists the nine as George Ball, former Under Secretary of State and soon to be appointed to succeed Goldberg at the UN; Arthur Dean, a prominent Republican New York lawyer who was a Korean truce negotiator; Dean Acheson, Secretary of State under President Truman; General Matthew B. Ridgeway, retired commander in Korea; General Maxwell D. Taylor, former chairman of the Joint Chiefs of Staff; Cyrus R. Vance, former Deputy Defense Secretary; McGeorge Bundy, Ford Foundation president who has been foreign policy adviser to both Kennedy and Johnson; Douglas Dillon, former Secretary of the Treasury; and General Omar N. Bradley, the World War II field commander in Europe. There is only one reputed "dove" here, George Ball. The mere listing of these names made familiar by the Cold War is evidence of the manner in which Lyndon Johnson has given hostages to the past.

The transformation within the once-proud foreign service epitomizes Lyndon Johnson's approach to foreign policy. He has pulled decision-making inward to fit his preconceived notions and to minimize dissent within the administration, and at the same time he has relentlessly employed the professionals from the Washington bureaus in his Madison Avenue-style effort to manipulate public opinion. Even Joseph Alsop, the President's most passionate supporter among the Washington columnists, has conceded that Mr. Johnson has undertaken "attempts at news control much more aggressive, comprehensive, and, one must add, repugnant to American tradition, than any such attempts by other presidents."

We found in the course of our own experience that the most compelling characteristic of this massive stultification of the foreign policy-making process is an almost total absence of both villains and heroes. In the last year or so, many prominent figures at the top level of the administration, and an increasing number in the second tier, have quietly disappeared from the Washington scene. It was quite clear that most of these were disaffected with the President's policies and priorities—and no matter where they started, the discontent led back to the expensive, inconclusive fighting in Vietnam. But not a single one of these resigned on principle and raised his voice in public protest when it might have helped rally the growing popular movement that finally brought down the Johnson regime on the issue of Vietnam.

Secretary McNamara even suffered without comment the humiliation of having his basic policy recommendation against further escalation in Vietnam abruptly and publicly refuted by the White House; Secretary of Health,

Education and Welfare John Gardner limited the explanation of his surprise resignation to the implication that the war did not leave adequate resources for the essential domestic job; and the distinguished UN Ambassador, Arthur Goldberg, swallowed his evident disappointment and stepped aside when he was frozen out of the Vietnamese negotiations for which, among other things, he had sacrificed his judicial career.

As good an explanation as any for this extraordinary process has been provided by one of the scores of bright young career men who have departed Washington. James C. Thomson Jr. at 36 has served as a special assistant to William Bundy in the State Department, and to Mc-George Bundy, when he was White House foreign affairs chief. Now a professor of history at Harvard, Thomson has appraised the futility of his career as a tame "dove" in an article in the *Atlantic*.

He finds that "domestication of dissenters" has been raised to a high art by the sometimes subtle, sometimes brutal manipulation of the human desire to be "in" with the sources of power. Under the prevailing pragmatic ethic, Thomson says, "the most ominous complaint that can be whispered of a bureaucrat is: 'I'm afraid Charlie's beginning to lose his effectiveness.'" Thus the easy rationalization that to speak out in public policy protest, or to resign on principle, is to sacrifice the possibility of being "effective" on the other, even more critical issues that are bound to be coming along.

Continued indulgence in this dispiriting exercise undoubtedly contributes much to the "executive fatigue" which most commentators find so marked in Washington. And as he buys time at the price of pride and self-respect the bureaucrat in some inverse ratio increases what Thomson calls his "human ego investment"—a personal stake in proving that his past decisions were right which precludes his supporting any policy change that might repudiate his own judgment.

All of this, of course, has been endemic in Washington for many years, as it is in most seats of public and private power. However, it has been accentuated by the communications revolution and the attendant headlong rush of history, a process that in turn is colored by what may be Lyndon Johnson's only distinct personal contribution to the era. This is what Thomson calls the "rhetorical escalation" or "oversell" commonly employed to persuade public, press and Congress that a given policy is sacrosanct. "Once you have *said* that the American experiment itself stands or falls on the Vietnam outcome," Thomson points out, "you have created a national stake far beyond earlier stakes."

This is a process that inevitably has cast even the mildest critics of the Vietnam war in a dissenter's role, and forced them outside official circles if they were to be effective. It can be said for the communications media that they did not prevent these from being heard and, with their insatiable appetite for controversy, may even have contributed to Mr. Johnson's downfall by overblowing the extent of his opposition when it was largely limited to the desperate and the shrill. The heroes of press and broadcasting were reporters for the most part, and particularly those at the front in Vietnam who steadily widened the credibility gap with their eyewitness accounts. There were exceptions among the political writers and commentators, some of whom are cited in the foregoing, but for the most part the Washington journalistic gentry floated with the tide.

Most White House correspondents accepted Lyndon Johnson's rhetorical overkill at face value and passed it on without effective qualification or demurrer. Even when they were personally disaffected by the thin-skinned bully with whom they had to deal, they rarely questioned his effectiveness as a political leader. It is a rare irony, doubtless particularly pleasing to that inveterate correspondent-baiter, Lyndon Johnson, that he calculated his own political demise long before these presumedly detached observers saw his opposition as anything but a kind of whimsical protest movement, and caught them all flat-footed when he announced it. The Washington press corps, no less than the bureaucracy with which it is intertwined, wants to be "in," and now that it enjoys the kudos and rewards of the establishment, few of its members could bear to sink into that limbo from which a cabinet officer will not accept a personal telephone call.

Journalists acquire their own vested interests in their sources, and to maintain them they tend to identify with the policies these purveyors of news matter espouse. Some go well beyond this, acquiring what amounts to a proprietary interest in a public issue. Perhaps the most notable contemporary instance of this tendency is provided by Joseph Alsop. The columnist treats the Vietnamese war as though he invented it, and he has long since become the most consistent conduit of the unabashed military hard line. In return he has acquired an inexhaustible supply of military intelligence estimates, captured enemy documents, exclusive prisoner interviews and the like. The short and unhappy life enjoyed by such Alsop exclusives as his report of several years ago that the North Vietnamese were about to be brought down by famine does not diminish his ardor, discourage his military suppliers, or infringe upon his elliptical and original views.

Alsop also has a pointed, and doubtless effective, way of playing upon the Presidential ego when Mr. Johnson displays signs of going soft on the columnist's personal design for total victory. Here is a fair sample, in which Alsop takes off from his own proclamation that Hanoi is counting on the effects in South Vietnam of a "paralyzed American president who is powerless to deal with a more and more sanguinary war." This, Alsop assures millions of his readers (including, surely, that primary one in the White House), is ludicrous, for "Lyndon Johnson did not make his great renunciation in order to arrange a concealed surrender. He made it, rather, to free his hands, to gain room for maneuver, to shed almost all of his concerns save those of commander-in-chief. As commander-in-chief no one can say him nay until he lays down his office next January; and he is certainly not going to lay down his office as the first American president who ever lost a war."

This calculated effort to galvanize Mr. Johnson into renewed military action might be understandable if it stemmed from some deep, ideological passion on the part of the author—a commitment to the notion that godless Communism must be stayed wherever it raises its head. But as veteran readers, and sometime pressroom companions of the columnist, we can't escape the feeling that to Alsop, as to the great majority of hard-liners in the press, and indeed to Mr. Johnson himself, Vietnam has somehow become an end in itself, a test of strength, not of rectitude. Here is a telling appraisal by Edward Engberg in *The Center Magazine:*

Alsop's is a world in which "granite" men (his adjective for a Marine officer in Vietnam) make war as if it were a poker game taking place on a square-rigger sailing to Byzantium. War is a game of gambles and raises, showdowns and crunches, harsh facts and stern measures. The war in Vietnam specifically appears to be a drawn-out game of seven-card stud, in which each card dealt creates a new phase; and each deal makes for a whole new war. All kibitzers, including other journalistic prospectors and speculators, are as suspect as the old man in the green eye shade at the north end of the table.

If Alsop is the most spectacular practitioner of this kind of journalistic gamesmanship, he is certainly not the only one. Indeed, it can be said that the run of the Washington reporting and commentary is presented as the record of a continuing contest between individuals, and the prize of status seemingly is awarded almost exclusively for coming out ahead. For example, the running controversy between Dean Rusk and the Senate Foreign Relations Committee has been reported virtually as if it were an Indian wrestling match between the Secretary of State and the Committee chairman. When Rusk appeared for televised hearings after refusing for many months to subject himself to public interrogation on Vietnam policy, the question emphasized in most accounts was whether Senator Fulbright or the Secretary led on points. Rusk, it was noted, kept his cool, but Fulbright made a record that the administration now considered itself empowered to take any military action it saw fit in Vietnam without the traditional advice and consent of the Senate. The confrontation was generally rated a draw—and almost nobody went past the personalities to deal adequately with the fateful constitutional issue Fulbright had tried to raise.

More, we believe, than any of his predecessors, Lyndon Johnson has managed to reduce high government policy to the first person singular. James Reston of *The New York Times* has written of the Great Society's prevailing mood: "In this subjective atmosphere all problems are seen as personal problems. The question becomes not where the cities stand today but where the President stands; not where the nation is but where Lyndon Johnson is, not what the facts of the problem are but what the politics of the problem are."

Again, Lyndon Johnson cannot be said to be the creator of the mood. In one sense he was the beneficiary of the increasing national tendency to reduce all issues to some kind of personal equation; as the outsize incumbent in an outsize office it seemed for a while that in his hamhanded way he would be able to spread around enough of the national bounty to meet most of the immediate personal demands of most disaffected Americans. But the demands of the dispossessed were escalating as well as the war, and they moved past material goods to such intangibles as human dignity—and in the moving struck a responsive chord in the young and restive. In the end Lyndon Johnson became a victim of the cult of personalization; the demand grew for an image of probity and integrity, and the old wheeler-dealer simply could not project it.

The great question now is whether this condition passes with Lyndon Johnson. Is the demand really for another policy, or only for another person, one who somehow projects charismatic vibrations more in tune with the volatile national mood? The evidence is not encouraging. From the nadir of his popularity the President managed to deflate the Vietnam issue, not by changing his stance but by altering his rhetoric and diverting his critics. In early June, two months after he removed himself as a primary political target, *The New York Times* White House correspondent, Max Frankel, wrote:

It was primarily to buy time at home to keep waging the war's military and diplomatic battles abroad that Johnson accepted the dovish counsel of at least a partial halt in the bombing on March 31 and threw in his own retirement for good measure.

So far, the tactic has worked better than he dared to hope. The bitter controversy has abated and the political candidates have been muted. And, unexpectedly, Hanoi came to the conference table, essentially on the President's terms.

Frankel's final statement is correct only if the President's terms are substantially different from those he has repeatedly stated, and charged Averell Harriman with standing on in Paris. Hanoi's response to Mr. Johnson's partial bombing halt was clearly and specifically an agreement to come and discuss substantive issues only on the agreement that all the bombing would be halted. The effort of Harriman to trade out for some kind of reciprocal military restraint is a clear whittling of the understanding—as the Vietnamese have repeated on every occasion when Harriman has attempted the ploy.

The Vietnamese may very well be stubborn and unrealistic in their refusal to yield on the point, but they are not in any sense departing from the letter and spirit of every public exchange between the two governments—or of those critical private exchanges to which we were privy when the meeting was being arranged.

Yet the President, who quite blatantly kept changing his own ground rules in the course of the haggling over a meeting site, now constantly complains that the Vietnamese are abusing his tolerance and good faith. One of those White House pipeline dispatches by Evans and Novak was accurately summarized in the headline the Los Angeles *Times* gave it: HANOI'S DUPLICITY MAY FORCE END OF WAR'S DE-ESCALATION. Mr. Johnson professes to be outraged because Hanoi is guilty of continuing to fight until it sees some evidence of good faith in the negotiations. Yet the reliable Keyes Beech of the *Chicago Daily News* reported from Saigon at the end of May:

A top-secret directive has gone to all U.S. field commanders in South Vietnam telling them to win the war within the next three months.

The timing of the bluntly worded directive indicated the U.S. objective was to break the current military stalemate and give the Americans a decisive voice at the Paris peace conference.

Lyndon Johnson, of course, cannot thus play fast and loose with his Vietnamese adversaries without subjecting his own people to the same kind of double-dealing. Yet this seems to produce only sporadic cries of moral outrage, and even more infrequent complaints of insult to the intelligence. A substantial number of Americans continue to applaud this kind of calculated deceit, even when they are themselves taken in by it, on the ground that the only way to deal with the Communists is to trick them before they trick you.

In the State Department there is a cult of professional negotiators who do regular obeisance to the memory of the late Admiral C. Turner Joy, who wrote in summary of his experiences with the North Koreans at Panmunjom: "When dealing with Communists, one would be reckless indeed to assume good faith on their part." It is difficult to see how this principle permits any negotiation at all, unless one is willing to lie a little in his own right to get the conversation going. The Turner Joy doctrine seems closely akin to the dictum that the only good Indian is a dead Indian—which may be useful in fighting a war of extermination, but is of very little help in dealing with a live adversary if your policy is to let him stay that way.

Somewhere in the Asian skies we fell to discussing these and assorted philosophical matters with Mary McCarthy, who has emerged as perhaps the most uncompromising moralist among the intellectuals who have elected to double as war correspondents. In her brief book, *Vietnam,* which recounted her explorations in the South, she took the stand that the issue was first and last a moral one and must not be treated as subject to any degree of compromise. American intellectuals, she proclaimed, should follow the lead of their compatriots in France at the time of Algiers. The only answer for America was to get out of Vietnam; it is not the business of intellectuals to figure out *how* this is to be done, or whose face is to be saved; the practical matter of disengagement is the tawdry business of generals and politicians. In her hortatory mood, Miss McCarthy had dismissed with contempt those who had opposed the Vietnam war but had fiddled with formulas for ending it by negotiation—the likes of Fulbright among the politicians, and Kenneth Galbraith and Arthur Schlesinger among the intelligentsia, and, of course, ourselves.

Now, emotionally spent after more than two weeks behind the lines, she was indulging in second thoughts. Perhaps she had been too hard on Fulbright and the others; they had, after all, fought the good and lonely fight; and because they had done so, Lyndon Johnson was now removing himself from the scene and allowing hope to blossom again across the troubled planet. We, in our turn, were suffering from premonitions of more double-dealing to come, and we found ourselves urging Miss McCarthy and her cohorts to stick to their guns. We could count ourselves among the compromisers, and we could quote with approbation Galbraith's explanation of his own role: "My instinct is to express myself within the framework of the political process. I haven't marched; I don't carry signs. I have a certain asymmetric effect on a parade." But there were other ways of expression, and, God knew, in the days ahead the country would need them all.

We fell to playing a kind of weary word game as the plane swung north toward Tokyo. The missing quality in the excessively personalized age into which we have been catapulted, we decided, might be defined as disinterest. Our society seemed to have lost the distinction between a disinterested and an uninterested man; one was assumed to be in on the action for what it could do for him, or he wasn't expected to be in it at all; and Dr. Freud has taught us that rewards can be emotional as well as material, so that even the martyrs are not beyond suspicion.

In the unwinding of the long journey, it seemed to us that disinterested men, without undue commitment to the past or excessive passion for change, were surely our nation's greatest need if we are to face up to the new world foreshadowed by the agony of Vietnam—a world in which the arrangements of power cannot yet be dismissed, and the traditional instruments of power no longer work.

A CHRONOLOGY
OF AMERICAN INVOLVEMENT IN VIETNAM

Part I: The Postwar Years, 1945-1954
Part II: The Decade of Limited Involvement, 1954-1964
Part III: The Significant Year, 1964
Part IV: Escalation, 1965-1968

INTRODUCTION

The turmoil in Southeast Asia today has its roots deep in the history not only of that region but of all Asia, a history of local ethnic rivalry, outside conquest, and colonial exploitation. The immediate conflict in Indochina, now called the war in Vietnam, erupted after the Allied victory in World War II. Japan's rapid advance through Asia and across the Pacific early in that war had severed Britain, France, and the Netherlands from their colonial holdings. When World War II ended in Japan's defeat, these European powers expected their colonies back. In every case the expectations proved vain.

By negotiated withdrawal, or defeat at arms, or both, the old hegemony in Southeast Asia crumbled under the pressures of grass-roots nationalism and anti-colonialism. These movements have drawn inspiration from both the American and Bolshevik Revolutions, and they have fed upon bitter resentment of Western exploitation. Local insurgent movements were under way in some areas well before World War II abruptly shattered the traditional hold of the colonial empires. In Indochina, the most successful of the revolutionary nationalists were known as the Vietminh, and the Communist-trained Ho Chi Minh was their leader.

In all the prewar colonial period, the United States had hardly a token interest in Indochina. Yet today, little more than twenty years later, the United States has an army of more than a half million in combat in Vietnam at a cost in excess of a billion dollars per month. The chronology that follows is the story of that sudden, deep involvement.

Confusion has attended this conflict from its inception. The places, the names, the rapidly rotating Vietnamese regimes, the many faces of the enemy, the alternating official optimism and gloom—all have bewildered Americans and added to their concern.

At the time it all began, President Roosevelt was still speaking out for the right of every national group, as soon as it was ready, to govern itself according to its own will. Yet his Democratic successor, and the Republican who followed, aligned the economic might and international stature of this country behind the efforts of a colonial nation to recapture its supremacy in Indochina.

Year after year, four Presidents in succession have affirmed that this is a Vietnamese conflict, to be resolved by Vietnamese for Vietnamese. And yet American troops bear the brunt of the fighting on the ground, and more bombs than were dropped on either Germany or Japan in World War II have rained on Vietnam from American planes.

The colonial powers we supported in their effort at reinstatement in Southeast Asia have one by one withdrawn from its soil, first France, then the Netherlands and Britain. Yet they who are, or have been, our Allies refuse to support our military effort in Vietnam and on occasion even condemn it.

Criticism of our role in this conflict sweeps our own land—hot, rebellious, emotional criticism and serious, concerned, intellectual criticism. It emanates even from men in our government and men of high military rank. Yet it is the government that directs and the military that executes our strategy in Vietnam.

Since the founding of our nation, certain major responsibilities have rested with the Congress as the representative of the people, and among these is the responsibility for declaring war. Yet no Congress in the last twenty years has determined it appropriate to recognize formally the conflict in which we are embroiled in Vietnam. Since 1961, according to the official figures as of July 10, 1968, 25,752 Americans have died and 160,691 have been wounded in a non-war against a non-enemy.

This chronology is an attempt to locate the sources of these confusions. Since 1945, United States policy in Southeast Asia has undergone profound periodic changes. Each section in the account that follows deals with a major alteration in the direction of our policy and the events that stimulated the shift. The narrative has been reduced to bare facts. Each segment of narrative is accompanied by close documentation from the statements of government figures, from public records, and from official broadcasts, supplemented by the accounts of recognized authorities on Vietnam. Statements from foreign sources as well as domestic are included. Editorial comment and subjective interpretation have been excluded. Space has been omitted between items in the documentation to indicate the pairing of items which, in whole or in part, are in sharp contrast or even contradictory to each other.

Besides corroborating essential background facts, the documentation is intended to illuminate events and provide a basis for assessing rapidly changing reports coming now from Vietnam.

In a democracy, crucial commitments cannot come from a single, unified decision of all-powerful government. Congress challenges Presidential policy and often alters it in the course of approving expenditures; the President's own Cabinet appointees differ on the issues and contest for preference; career professionals in the military forces, the diplomatic corps, and the operating agencies overtly and covertly challenge and sometimes subvert the policies of their political superiors. Where such differences of opinion, or contradictions, have marked the public discourse or belied the published facts at any stage, the disparities are recorded in this documentation.

PART I: THE POSTWAR YEARS, 1945-1954

1945

> *On September 2, 1945, the Democratic Republic of Vietnam issued its Declaration of Independence. Encouraged by support received during World War II from the American Office of Strategic Services and by President Roosevelt's interest in the self-determination of colonial people, Ho Chi Minh anticipated Allied support for the Vietminh independence movement.*

"All men are created equal. They are endowed by their Creator with certain inalienable rights, among these are Life, Liberty and the pursuit of Happiness." * (First paragraph, "Declaration of Independence of the Democratic Republic of Vietnam," Ho Chi Minh, *Selected Works,* reprinted in George McT. Kahin and John W. Lewis, *The United States in Vietnam.* Dell: 1967, Appendix 1, p. 345.)

"In my last conference with President Roosevelt . . . I told him that the French, British and Dutch were cooperating to prevent the establishment of a United Nations

---

* Spelling, capitalization, and grammatical style are used in these excerpts as they appeared originally.

trusteeship for Indo-China. . . . The President said that in the coming San Francisco Conference there would be set up a United Nations Trusteeship that would make effective the right of colonial people to choose the form of government under which they will live as soon as in the opinion of the United Nations they are qualified for independence." (Letter from Ambassador Patrick J. Hurley to President Harry S. Truman, May 28, 1945, *Foreign Relations of the United States, Diplomatic Papers, The Conference of Berlin, 1945*. Government Printing Office: 1960, Vol. 1, p. 917.)

"We are convinced that the Allied nations which at Teheran and San Francisco have acknowledged the principles of self-determination and equality of all nations will not refuse to acknowledge the independence of Vietnam." (Ho Chi Minh, in Kahin and Lewis, *op. cit.*, p. 346.)

1945-1946

The Potsdam Agreements of July 1945 stipulated that Vietnam would be occupied in the north by Chiang Kai-shek and in the south by British forces. The assigned mission was to round up Japanese troops and release Allied prisoners. Free France, still reorganizing after the collapse of the collaborationist Vichy government, was temporarily bypassed in the Potsdam arrangements. The British, short of men, used both Japanese and Vichy French troops in carrying out their occupation. The commander of the British Occupation Forces ignored the limitations of the Potsdam mandate, allowing the French to reinstate themselves around Saigon. With the departure of the British and the Chinese, French troops took over in both areas.

"At Potsdam in July, 1945, a precise line of demarcation was defined: south of latitude 16° N., South-East

Asia Command was responsible, and north of that line the Chinese (Document No. 1). Thus a precedent for the partitioning of Indo-China was established." (*Documents Relating to British Involvement in the Indo-China Conflict, 1945-1965,* Cmd. 2834, Miscellaneous No. 25. Her Majesty's Stationery Office: 1965, p. 6.)

"British action was, as agreed at Potsdam, confined to the south of Indo-China. In the north, the Chinese were in occupation and there, under Chinese patronage, the Viet Minh established a firm grip on much of the country." (*Ibid.,* p. 8.)

". . . [A]t Admiral Mountbatten's suggestion a Civil Affairs Agreement was negotiated in Europe between British and French authorities. The agreement recognized that the aim of the British forces in Indo-China was to enforce the surrender and disarmament of Japanese forces and the liberation of prisoners of war and civilian internees." (*Ibid.,* p. 7.)

". . . General Gracey on 21 September issued a proclamation . . . declaring his determination to enforce order in all Indo-China south of 16° N. This step was not part of the duty prescribed by the Chiefs of Staff or by the Civil Affairs agreement with the French, but was in his judgment forced on him by circumstances." (*Ibid.*)

". . . I felt that this proclamation . . . was contrary to the policy of His Majesty's Government; and . . . I warned Major-General Gracey that he should take care to confine operations of British/Indian troops to those limited tasks which he had been set." (*Ibid.,* Document No. 1, p. 49, report by Admiral Louis Mountbatten.)

"If there is anything that makes my blood boil, it is to see our Allies in Indochina and Java deploying Japanese troops to reconquer the little people we promised to liberate. It is the most ignoble kind of betrayal." (General Douglas MacArthur as quoted by Edgar Snow, *The Other Side of the River: Red China Today*. Random House: 1961, p. 686.)

1946-1949

Relations between the French and the Vietminh, uneasy from the beginning, deteriorated into open hostilities by the end of 1946. To attract Vietnamese nationalist support away from the Vietminh, France in 1949 set up an ostensibly autonomous regime with the former Annamese emperor Bao Dai as its head. Real control remained with the French.

"The Government of Vietnam declares itself ready to receive the French army in friendly fashion when, in accord with international agreement, it relieves the Chinese troops." (From translation of *Bulletin Hebdomadaire,* March 18, 1946, in Harold R. Isaacs, *New Cycle in Asia, Selected Documents on Major International Developments in the Far East, 1943-1947*. American Institute for Pacific Affairs: 1947, p. 169.)

". . . [I]t was soon evident that there was no real basis for agreement between the Viet Minh, intent on complete independence for all Viet-Nam under a Communist regime, and the French, determined to retrieve something of their former position. A conference at Fontainebleau in July-August led to no result. On 13 September, however, Ho Chi Minh signed a *modus vivendi* relating mainly to economic and cultural matters but also including an undertaking by both parties to put an end to acts of hostility, for sporadic clashes between French and Viet Minh elements were going on throughout the country. But despite this agreement, conflicts continued, and on 23

November a French bombardment of the port of Hai-phong, whence Viet Minh forces had refused to withdraw, inflicted heavy casualties on the Viet-Namese population. On the night of 19 December the Viet Minh launched a general attack on French posts and French-occupied houses in Hanoi, the capital of northern Viet-Nam, and from that moment a state of general civil war prevailed." *(Documents Relating to British Involvement in the Indo-China Conflict, 1945-1965, Cmd. 2834, pp. 9–10.)*

"H. M. Bao Dai failed to rally moderate nationalist opinion; it was felt in Viet-Namese political circles that the country still lacked true independence, and though many ardent nationalists, including Ngo Dinh Diem, had abandoned the Viet Minh because of its excessive and increasing dependence on the Communist faction, there were still many others who regarded Ho Chi Minh, despite his Communist principles, as the true representative of Viet-Namese nationalism." *(Ibid., p. 11.)*

1950-1951

Meanwhile, in response to Cold War events, and in particular the Korean war, the United States developed a policy of opposition to new Communist regimes and aligned itself behind France's effort to reassert control of Indochina.

"The attack upon Korea makes it plain beyond all doubt that communism has passed beyond the use of subversion to conquer independent nations and will now use armed invasion and war. . . . Accordingly, . . . I have . . . directed acceleration in the furnishing of military assistance to the forces of France and the Associated States in Indochina and the dispatch of a military mission to provide close working relations with those forces." (President Truman, *Department of State Bulletin,* July 3, 1950.)

"In Indochina we have allied ourselves to the desperate effort of the French regime to hang on to the remnants of empire. There is no broad general support of the native (Bao Dai) Vietnam Government among the people of that area." (John F. Kennedy, *The Strategy of Peace.* Harper: 1960, statement in November 1951, p. 60.)

" 'There had been a noticeable lack of French aggressive attitude from a military point of view in Indo-China. The central problem in Indo-China was the fence-sitting by the Population. They would never come down on one side or another until they had a reasonable assurance of who would be the victor and that their interests would be served by the victor.

" 'We are helping France to the extent of carrying between one-third and one-half of the financial burden of the Indo-Chinese war. We have had military discussions between the five powers—the United States, the United Kingdom, France, Australia and New Zealand—which had not been effective in devising agreed military solutions against the contingency of overt Chinese intervention in Indo-China. The French now sought political discussions to carry the matter forward.

" 'This is an urgent matter upon which the new administration must be prepared to act.' " (Secretary of State Dean Acheson, November 1952, quoted in Harry S. Truman, *Memoirs.* Doubleday: 1956, Vol. 2, p. 519.)

Pre-1954

The French, with strong United States backing, fought the Vietminh for control of Vietnam from 1946 to 1954.

"A new foreign aid program of $3,497,000,000, one-third of which would be spent to support anti-Communist forces in Indo-China, was submitted to Congress today. . . ." *

"[Mr. Stassen] . . . disclosed today . . . that the biggest single item in the program was $1,133,000,000 for Indo-China.

"Of this amount $500,000,000 would be for direct support of the anti-Communist fighting forces, allocated through France; $300,000,000 for equipment supplied to the fighting forces; $21,185,000 for economic assistance, and the rest for technical assistance." (*The New York Times,* April 7, 1954.)

"Although the Associated States [of Indochina] are said to be 'independent within the French Union,' the French always have a permanent control in the high council and in the Assembly of the Union and the Government of France guides its actions. . . . Militarily French control is nearly complete. . . . Economically, French control of the country's basic resources, transportation, trade, and economic life in general is extensive. In Vietnam, estimated French control is nearly 100 percent in the field of foreign commerce, international and coastal shipping, and rubber and other export products. . . . All of this flies in the face of repeated assurances to the American people by our own officials that complete independence has been or will be granted." (Senator John F. Kennedy, *Congressional Record,* Senate, April 6, 1954.)

* Ellipsis dots indicate that the sentence quoted is incomplete. Quotation marks at the end of paragraphs preceding the final paragraph from one source indicate that more than a sentence has been omitted.

1954

*In April of 1954, the Eisenhower administra-
tion considered and rejected a plan for immediate United States military intervention to support failing
French forces. The French were decisively defeated at Dien
Bien Phu on May 8, 1954.*

". . . [T]hat Saturday morning [April 3, 1954] eight
members of Congress, five Senators and three Representatives, got the scare of their lives. They had been called
to a secret conference with John Foster Dulles."

"What was wanted, Dulles said, was a joint resolution
by Congress to permit the President to use air and naval
power in Indochina."

"Radford offered the plan he had in mind once Congress passed the joint resolution.

"Some two hundred planes from the thirty-one-thou-
sand-ton U.S. Navy carriers *Essex* and *Boxer,* then in the
South China Sea ostensibly for 'training,' plus land-based
U.S. Air Force planes from bases a thousand miles away
in the Philippines, would be used for a single strike to
save Dien Bien Phu."

"In the end, all eight members of Congress, Republi-
cans and Democrats alike, were agreed that Dulles had
better first go shopping for allies."

"In these [diplomatic] talks Dulles ran into one rock
of opposition—Britain. Messages flashing back and forth
between Washington and London failed to crack the
rock."

"Some of those at the meeting came away with the
feeling that if they had agreed that Saturday to the resolution, planes would have been winging toward Dien Bien
Phu without waiting for a vote of Congress—or without a
word in advance to the American people." (Chalmers M.

Roberts, "The Day We Didn't Go to War," *The Reporter*, September 14, 1954.)

"Mr. MANSFIELD. . . . [T]he administration asked a group of responsible congressional leaders what they thought of the idea of having a resolution passed, which would give to the President of the United States the discretion to use authority as he saw fit in the Southeast Asia area. Those proposals are a matter of record."

"I also wish to make the observation that it will be noted on the list of those who were present that, outside of the Senator from California (Mr. Knowland), who was there in his capacity as majority leader, I am sure there was no one present from the Foreign Relations Committee."

"Mr. SMITH of New Jersey. I am amazed at the statement made by the Senator from Montana that there was apparently a secret meeting.

"Mr. MANSFIELD. It was mentioned in the press.

"Mr. SMITH of New Jersey. I am a member of the Foreign Relations Committee and chairman of the Subcommittee on Far Eastern Affairs.

"Mr. MANSFIELD. The Senator from New Jersey was not present.

"Mr. SMITH of New Jersey. I never heard of any such meeting.

"Mr. MANSFIELD. But the meeting was held. I inform the Senator from New Jersey, although he was not there.

"Mr. SMITH of New Jersey. The Senator from New Jersey was not invited to be there. I think if the meeting concerned such an important problem, I probably would have been invited to it, because I am chairman of the Subcommittee on Far Eastern Affairs of the Committee on Foreign Relations. I had discussed this matter with the Department. I never understood an attempt was made to pass such a resolution as has been mentioned.

"Mr. MANSFIELD. The proposal was made and turned down, thank heaven, by the leadership.

"Mr. SMITH of New Jersey. I know nothing about it. I can confirm what the Senator from Michigan said, that we were not at the meeting."

"Mr. MANSFIELD. That was one of the difficulties I had. Since some of us protested, thanks to the majority leader, there has been better liaison between the State Department, the Defense Department, and the committees." (*Congressional Record,* Senate, July 9, 1954.)

". . . [W]hen the day comes for me to face my Maker and account for my actions, the thing I would be most humbly proud of was the fact that I fought against, and perhaps contributed to preventing, the carrying out of some harebrained tactical schemes which would have cost the lives of thousands of men. To that list of tragic accidents that fortunately never happened I would add the Indo-China intervention." (Matthew B. Ridgway, *Soldier: The Memoirs of Matthew B. Ridgway.* Harper: 1956, p. 278.)

"At the time of the French defeat, it seemed to us military planners that if an effort were made by the United States to secure Vietnam from Chinese military exploitation, and that if force on the scale that we were talking about were to be employed, then the Chinese would very likely reopen the fighting in Korea.

"At the time, General Ridgway thought it prudent to bring this situation directly to the attention of President Eisenhower, pointing out that we should be prepared for a large-scale war if we were to make the initial large-scale commitment to the Hanoi Delta that we were thinking about." (Lt. Gen. James M. Gavin, USA [Ret.], "A Communication on Vietnam," *Harper's Magazine,* February, 1966.

". . . [T]his Administration has been arguing that no Western power can go to Asia militarily, except as one of a concert of powers, which concert must include local Asiatic peoples.

"To contemplate anything else is to lay ourselves open to the charge of imperialism and colonialism or—at the very least—of objectionable paternalism." (From a letter to General Alfred Gruenther at NATO, in Dwight D. Eisenhower, *Mandate for Change*. Doubleday: 1963, p. 352.)

"The United Kingdom Government has been reproached in some unofficial quarters for their failure to support armed intervention to try to save Dien Bien Phu. It was quite true that we were not willing to support such action. This was for three reasons which then seemed to be good and still seem to be good: firstly, we were advised that air action alone could not have been effective; secondly, any such military intervention could have destroyed the chances of a settlement at Geneva; thirdly, it might well have led to a general war in Asia." (Anthony Eden, *Great Britain, 5 Parliamentary Debates* [Commons], Vol. 529, Cols. 434-435.)

1954

In the winter of 1953-1954, the foreign ministers of the United States, the United Kingdom, France, and the Soviet Union worked out plans for a spring conference on Southeast Asia to include the People's Republic of China and other states of the area. This was the Geneva Conference, held from April 26 to July 21, which originally was intended to consider both a political settlement in Korea and a resolution of the Indochina war. Korea presented insoluble difficulties, but the Conference reached two conclusions concerning Vietnam.

"Mr. Molotov had proposed that the [Berlin] Conference should discuss . . . the convening of a five-power conference, including China, to 'seek measures for reducing tension in international relations.' . . . I urged favourable reflection upon the possibility of a five-power conference, provided that the Americans could be brought to consider it."

"[The Americans] are at present strongly opposed to the idea of a five-power conference with China, mainly, I understand, because they are not prepared to admit the right of Communist China to be one of the great powers dealing with world problems." (Anthony Eden, *Full Circle*. Houghton Mifflin: 1960, pp. 97, 98.)

"Mr. Molotov, the Soviet Foreign Minister, lost no time in bringing up his pet proposal for a 'Big Five' conference—to include Communist China. . . . [He] tapered down his demands to make the five-power meeting solely on the problems of Asia. This was still unacceptable to us."

"Since the British and French both were seeking Far East talks, it would be less of a sign of disunity if the United States proposed it formally, and carefully restricted it to that area. In addition, if discussion was inevitable, it was desirable to initiate it prior to any unfavorable developments in the Indochina fighting." (Eisenhower, *op. cit.*, pp. 342-343.)

1954

The first, officially termed the Geneva Agreements but often referred to as the Geneva Accords, were detailed cease-fire arrangements signed only by the two protagonists: the French and the People's Army of Vietnam. This armistice accord attempted to establish the foundations for peaceful resolution of political problems in Indochina through four sets of provisions. A

*provisional, military demarcation line was to permit re-
grouping of forces; each of the parties to the Agreements
would administer its respective zone pending general elections for all of Vietnam; a ban was placed on new military personnel and matériel, new military bases, and the
formation of military alliances; and an International Control Commission was to ensure and supervise the execution of the Agreements. Both signatories signed for themselves and their successors.*

"The signatories of the present Agreement and their
successors in their functions shall be responsible for ensuring the observance and enforcement of the terms and
provisions thereof." (*Geneva Agreements,* Article 27.)

"A provisional military demarcation line shall be fixed,
on either side of which the forces of the two parties shall
be regrouped after their withdrawal. . . ."
". . . [A] demilitarised zone shall be established on either side of the demarcation line . . . to act as a buffer
zone. . . ." (*Ibid.,* Article 1.)

"The Commanders of the Forces on each side . . .
shall order and enforce the complete cessation of all hostilities in Viet Nam. . . ." (*Ibid.,* Article 10.)

"Pending the general elections which will bring about
the unification of Viet Nam, the conduct of civil administration in each regrouping zone shall be in the hands of
the party whose forces are to be regrouped there. . . ."
(*Ibid.,* Article 14(a).)

"With effect from the date of entry into force of the
present Agreement, no military base . . . may be established in the re-grouping zone of either party; the two parties shall ensure that the zones assigned to them do not
adhere to any military alliance and are not used for the

resumption of hostilities or to further an aggressive policy." (*Ibid.*, Article 19.)

"Responsibility for the execution of the agreement on the cessation of hostilities shall rest with the parties." (*Ibid.*, Article 28.)

"An International Commission shall ensure the control and supervision of this execution." (*Ibid.*, Article 29.)

"An International Commission shall be set up for the control and supervision over the application of the provisions of the agreement on the cessation of hostilities in Viet Nam. It shall be composed of representatives of the following States: Canada, India, and Poland.
"It shall be presided over by the Representative of India." (*Ibid.*, Article 34.)

"The recommendations of the International Commission shall be adopted by majority vote. . . . If the votes are divided, the chairman's vote shall be decisive." (*Ibid.*, Article 41.)

"When dealing with questions concerning violations, or threats of violations, which might lead to a resumption of hostilities, namely:—
(a) Refusal by the armed forces of one party to effect the movements provided for in the regroupment plan;
(b) Violation by the armed forces of one of the parties of the regrouping zones, territorial waters, or air space of the other party;
the decisions of the International Commission must be unanimous." (*Ibid.*, Article 42.)

"If one of the parties refuses to put into effect a recommendation of the International Commission, the parties concerned or the Commission itself shall inform the members of the Geneva Conference.

"If the International Commission does not reach unanimity in the cases provided for in Article 42, it shall submit a majority report and one or more minority reports to the members of the Conference." (*Ibid.*, Portions of Article 43.)

1954

There was also a Final Declaration—representing the second area of agreement at Geneva. This was not signed by anyone but was instead endorsed by voice vote. All countries present indicated agreement, except the United States and the State of Vietnam (as the French-controlled Bao Dai government was called). Expressing the sense of the Conference, this Declaration supported the cease-fire arrangements. It reiterated the temporary military character of the demarcation line at the 17th parallel and declared that democratic freedoms and institutions should come about in Vietnam as a result of free general elections by secret ballot. In neither the Agreements nor the Final Declaration was it specified that democratic conditions must exist in advance of these elections.

"The Conference recognises that the essential purpose of the agreement relating to Viet Nam is to settle military questions with a view to ending hostilities and that the military demarcation line is provisional and should not in any way be interpreted as constituting a political or territorial boundary. . . ." (*Final Declaration,* Section 6.)

"The Conference declares that, so far as Viet Nam is concerned, the settlement of political problems, effected on the basis of respect for the principles of independence, unity and territorial integrity, shall permit the Vietnamese people to enjoy the fundamental freedoms, guaranteed by democratic institutions established as a result of free general elections by secret ballot. In order to ensure that sufficient progress in the restoration of peace has been made, and that all the necessary conditions obtain for free expression of the national will, general elections shall be held in July 1956. . . . Consultations will be held on this subject between the competent representative authorities of the two zones from July 20, 1955, onwards." (*Ibid.,* Section 7.)

1954

The United States made a unilateral declaration in lieu of a direct endorsement of the Final Declaration, pledging to refrain from disturbing the Agreements by force and endorsing fair, free elections for all of Vietnam under United Nations supervision.

"The Government of the United States of America
Declares
with regard to the aforesaid Agreements and paragraphs that (i) it will refrain from the threat or the use of force to disturb them . . . and (ii) it would view any renewal of the aggression in violation of the aforesaid Agreements with grave concern and as seriously threatening international peace and security." (Under Secretary of State Walter Bedell Smith, *Unilateral Declaration.*)

"In connection with the statement in the Declaration concerning free elections in Viet Nam, my Government wishes to make clear its position which it has expressed in a Declaration made in Washington on June 29, 1954, as follows:—

" 'In the case of nations now divided against their will, we shall continue to seek to achieve unity through free elections, supervised by the United Nations to ensure that they are conducted fairly.' " (*Ibid.*)

1954

> *For the Vietminh forces under Ho Chi Minh, the Geneva Agreements represented major territorial concessions. Militarily superior, the Vietminh controlled most of Vietnam in the spring of 1954, with prospects of total control within a year.*

"On the Communist side, Ho Chi Minh's forces had come a long way from the badly armed guerrilla bands of the mid-forties. The Viet-Nam People's Army now comprised seven hard-core divisions abundantly equipped with modern American weapons captured by the Chinese in Korea and passed along. The Communist forces, with fewer than 100,000 regulars, 50,000 regional semiregulars and about 225,000 local guerrillas, were numerically inferior to the French Union troops, but in a type of war where experts believe that the defending force must hold a 10-to-1 superiority in order to win . . . the French 1.2-to-1 edge made the military contest—all other factors aside—well-nigh hopeless." (Bernard B. Fall, "How the French Got Out of Vietnam," *The New York Times Magazine*, May 2, 1965.)

" 'Because guerrilla warfare basically derives from the masses and is supported by them, it can neither exist nor flourish if it separates itself from their sympathies and cooperation.' " [Quotation from Mao Tse-tung.]

"The Algerian revolution, the least studied in [the United States] though it comes closest to the Vietnamese situation, had actually been crushed militarily but had won politically when de Gaulle negotiated independence. . . . France faced a sullen Algerian population that it had conquered but could not rule."

" 'These events occur where foreign rule is resented, where acute grievances exist, and institutional channels for ventilating and satisfying them are ineffective.' " [Quotation from Algerian guerrilla chief.]

"Guerrilla use of terror . . . is sociologically and psychologically selective. It strikes those who are popularly identified as the 'enemy of the people'—officials, landlords, and the like.

". . . Since most chiefs are local farmers who command legitimacy and loyalty through tradition and kinship, the militants ideally want to persuade them into the movement. When that fails, it takes painstaking political work to engineer their assassination and to prepare the villagers to accept it." (Eqbal Ahmad, "Revolutionary Warfare," Marvin Gettleman, ed., *Viet Nam*. Fawcett: 1965, pp. 353-357.)

1954

The United States regarded the Geneva Conference as a strategic reversal: Communist China was accorded the status of a Great Power at the Conference; the Democratic Republic of Vietnam achieved recognition as the sole government in northern Vietnam; and the forthcoming elections could be expected to give Ho Chi Minh political as well as military control of all Vietnam.

"It would be an understatement to say that we do not like the terms of the cease-fire agreement just concluded." (Assistant Secretary for Far Eastern Affairs Walter S. Robertson, *Department of State Bulletin*, August 23, 1954.)

". . . [I]n my opinion, the mere fact that the United States agreed with France, Great Britain, and other nations to attend the general conference at Geneva, Switzerland, to which Communist China was invited as an interested state, indicates that a degree of recognition was achieved."

"China now is really a far greater power than she was before the Geneva Conference. This is due, in some small part, at least, to the fact that the United States was a party to the particular agreement to hold a conference after the Berlin Conference." (Senator Mike Mansfield, *Congressional Record,* Senate, July 9, 1954.)

"I have never talked or corresponded with a person knowledgeable in Indochinese affairs who did not agree that had elections been held as of the time of the fighting, possibly 80 per cent of the population would have voted for the Communist Ho Chi Minh as their leader rather than Chief of State Bao Dai." (Eisenhower, *op. cit.,* p. 372.)

SUMMARY

The Geneva Agreements were destined to have far-reaching significance. In the future, all parties to the Vietnam conflict would cite the Geneva Agreements as the basis for settlement.

"The Vietnamese people are deeply aware of the value of these [Geneva] Agreements. Now as in the past they . . . are resolved to have these Agreements implemented in their spirit and letters as all international agreements with full legal validity should be." (Statement by the Central Committee of the National Liberation Front, March 22, 1965, Gettleman, *op. cit.,* p. 411.)

"Pending the peaceful reunification of Vietnam, while Vietnam is still temporarily divided into two zones the military provisions of the 1954 Geneva agreements on Vietnam must be strictly respected."

"The unswerving policy of the DRV [Democratic Republic of Vietnam] Government is to respect strictly the 1954 Geneva agreements on Vietnam and to implement correctly their basic provisions. . . ." (Excerpts from Hanoi's Four Points as given on Hanoi Radio, April 13, 1965, Kahin and Lewis, *op. cit.*, Appendix 14, p. 432.)

". . . [T]he Chinese Government deems it necessary that another Geneva Conference on Indo-China be convened by the Co-Chairman of the Geneva Conference, to discuss the question of implementation of the Geneva Agreements in Viet-Nam. The Chinese Government also holds that the three member countries of the International Commission in Viet-Nam—India, Poland and Canada—should be invited to take part in this conference." (Letter from Premier Chou En-lai to the British Government, January 25, 1956, *Documents Relating to British Involvement in the Indo-China Conflict, 1945-1965*, p. 118.)

"We come out for strict observance of the Geneva agreements. . . ." (Premier Aleksei N. Kosygin at the Guildhall, *The New York Times,* February 9, 1967.)

"What we seek in South Vietnam is to bring about a restoration of the conditions contemplated by the Accords of 1954. We seek, in other words, to restore the integrity of the settlement made between the French government and the Communist forces under Ho Chi Minh—a settlement which was joined in by the United Kingdom, Communist China, the Soviet Union, Laos, and Cambodia. This settlement forms a part of the structure of arrangements that are the key to stability in the present-day world." (Secretary of State Dean Rusk in *The Vietnam Hearings*. Random House: 1966, p. 240.)

"We believe that the Geneva accords of 1954 and

1962 could serve as the central elements of a peaceful settlement." (Speech by President Lyndon B. Johnson before a joint session of the Tennessee State Legislature on March 15, 1967, *Department of State Bulletin,* April 3, 1967.)

PART II: THE DECADE
OF LIMITED INVOLVEMENT, 1954-1964

1954

The Geneva Agreements had no profound effect on United States policy toward Asia, which had been hardened by the Korean war. As before, U.S. objectives were to prevent the spread of Communist power and particularly to counteract the strengthened position of Ho Chi Minh's government. This foreign policy was pursued throughout the Eisenhower administration, although its underlying assumption of a monolithic Asian communism was increasingly challenged.

"The important thing from now on is not to mourn the past but to seize the future opportunity to prevent the loss in northern Viet-Nam from leading to the extension of communism throughout Southeast Asia and the Southwest Pacific." (Secretary of State John Foster Dulles, *Department of State Bulletin,* August 2, 1954.)

"You had a row of dominoes set up, and you knocked over the first one, and what would happen to the last one was the certainty that it would go over very quickly. So you could have a beginning of a disintegration that would have the most profound influences." (President Eisenhower, news conference, *The New York Times,* April 8, 1954.)

"Again, as at the time of Dien Bien Phu, the Joint Chiefs divided. Admiral Radford [the chairman] was emphatically in favor of landing a force in the Hanoi-Haiphong area, even if it meant risking war with Red China. In this he was fully supported by the Chief of Staff of the Air Force and the Chief of Naval Operations. In my opinion such an operation meant a great risk of war. Just southeast of Haiphong harbor is the island of Hainan which is part of Red China. The Navy was unwilling to risk their ships in the Haiphong area without first invading and capturing the island. Admiral Radford and the chiefs of the Navy and Air Force felt that, faced with our overwhelming power, the Red Chinese would not react to this violation of their sovereignty. General Ridgway and I had grave doubts about the validity of this reasoning."

". . . Again, fortunately, the President decided not to commit U.S. forces to Southeast Asia.

"However, there was a compromise. We would not attack North Vietnam, but we would support a South Vietnamese government that we hoped would provide a stable, independent government. . . ." (James M. Gavin, *Crisis Now.* Random House: 1968, pp. 48-49.)

"We have failed sometimes to understand the deeply rooted historic forces at work in Asia—anticolonialism, nationalism, the eagerness to wipe out past humiliations, and the determination to advance rapidly but without losing national identity. Instead we have tended to see Asia in a historic perspective derived from other times or other places. We have, as a consequence, overreacted to images in our own minds and underreacted to the actual historical tides of Asia. Monolithic conspiracy has little future in the soil of Asia's diversity. But rapid change, even upheaval, will continue to be a part of the scene, as Asian countries seek to close the gap between themselves and the advanced nations. We must learn to take such up-heavals in stride, putting aside cold war demonology and using our influence with caution and restraint to help channel these changes toward constructive ends." (Edwin O. Reischauer, former Ambassador to Japan, in U.S. Senate, *Asia, the Pacific, and the United States*, 90th Congress, 1st Session. Government Printing Office: 1967, pp. 10-11.)

1954

Forty-nine days after the Geneva Agreements, Secretary of State Dulles announced the signing of a collective defense pact, known as SEATO, by the United States, Britain, France, Australia, New Zealand, the Philippines, Pakistan, and Thailand. The treaty provided that, in the event of an attack from outside, each nation would respond according to the provisions of its own constitution; in cases of subversion or similar threats, the signatories agreed to consult with one another immediately. The State of Vietnam, still a subsidiary of French control in the south, did not sign the treaty. Neither did any provision of the treaty itself commit the signatories to provide troops or other support to any government or state in southern Vietnam.

"Each Party recognizes that aggression by means of armed attack in the treaty area against any of the Parties or against any State or territory which the Parties by unanimous agreement may hereafter designate, would endanger its own peace and safety, and agrees that it will in that event act to meet the common danger in accordance with its constitutional processes." (*The Southeast Asia Collective Defense Treaty*, Article IV, Section 1.)

"If, in the opinion of any of the Parties, the inviolability or the integrity of the territory or the sovereignty or political independence of any Party . . . is threatened in any way other than by armed attack or is affected or threatened by any fact or situation which might endanger the peace of the area, the Parties shall consult immediately in order to agree on the measures which should be taken for the common defense." (*Ibid.*, Article IV, Section 2.)

1954

An additional protocol to the pact, however, signed unanimously the same day, designated Laos, Cambodia, and "the free territory under the State of Vietnam" as coming under the attack, subversion, and economic aid sections of the treaty. Thus, the treaty recognized the southern zone of Vietnam as a political entity, whereas the Geneva Agreements had specified that the 17th parallel was to be no more than a provisional demarcation line.

"Designation of states and territory as to which provisions of Article IV and Article III are to be applicable:

"The Parties to the Southeast Asia Collective Defense Treaty unanimously designate for the purposes of Article IV of the Treaty the States of Cambodia and Laos and the free territory under the jurisdiction of the State of Vietnam.

"The Parties further agree that the above mentioned states and territory shall be eligible in respect of the economic measures contemplated by Article III." (*Protocol to The Southeast Asia Collective Defense Treaty.*)

"Senator GREEN. Then we are obliged to help put down a revolutionary movement.

"Secretary DULLES. No. If there is a revolutionary movement in Vietnam or in Thailand, we would consult together as to what to do about it, because if that were a subversive movement that was in fact propagated by communism, it would be a very grave threat to us. But we have no undertaking to put it down; all we have is an undertaking to consult together as to what to do about it.

"Senator FERGUSON. In other words, the words 'armed attack' in paragraph 1 of article IV are the ordinary armed attack rather than a subterfuge of penetration or subversion.

"Secretary DULLES. Yes, sir."

". . . [A]rticle IV, paragraph 2, contemplates that if that situation [of subversion] arises or threatens, that we should consult together immediately in order to agree on measures which should be taken. That is an obligation for consultation. It is not an obligation for action." (U.S. Senate, *The Southeast Asia Collective Defense Treaty*, 83rd Congress, 2nd Session. Government Printing Office: 1954, pp. 25, 28, 33.)

"The framers of this treaty [SEATO] deliberately rejected the kind of automatic commitment incorporated in the NATO agreement summarized in the principle 'an attack upon one is an attack upon all,' requiring a military response by all parties to aggression against any signatory.

"Article IV of the Southeast Asia Collective Defense Treaty clearly reserves to each signatory the right to determine the nature of its response to armed aggression and does not commit in advance any signatory to use its armed forces to deal with the aggressor." (House Republican Committee on Planning and Research, "Vietnam: Some Neglected Aspects of the Historical Record," read into the *Congressional Record*, House, August 25, 1965, by Representative Charles E. Goodell of New York.)

". . . [W]e are not acting specifically under the

SEATO treaty." (Secretary Rusk, *The New York Times*, November 27, 1966.)

"[Senator] FULBRIGHT: . . . Does the Southeast Treaty, Southeast Asia Treaty Organization commit us to do what we are now doing in Vietnam?

"[Secretary] RUSK: Yes, sir, I have no doubt that it does. (*The Vietnam Hearings* [January-February, 1966], p. 11.)

"That Treaty [SEATO] stated that aggression by means of armed attack in the treaty area would endanger our own peace and safety and, in that event, 'we would act to meet the common danger.' "

"We are involved because the nation's word has been given that we would be involved." (Secretary Rusk's letter to 100 Student Leaders, January 4, 1967, *Department of State Bulletin,* January 23, 1967.)

"It is a fact that the action we are taking in Vietnam is not under the aegis of any international organization. It is not under the aegis of the United Nations or the Southeast Asia Treaty Organization—SEATO. It is a relationship between us—the United States—and the Government of Vietnam. We were invited by the Government." (Former Ambassador Henry Cabot Lodge, "Go On Fighting in Vietnam?" *U.S. News & World Report,* February 15, 1967.)

"The treaty does not oblige the United States either legally or morally to take any course in southeast Asia than the course it might be expected to take if the treaty did not exist." (Professor W. McMahon Ball, cited by Representative Melvin R. Laird of Wisconsin, *Congressional Record,* House, March 15, 1966.)

"[Senator] GORE: . . . South Vietnam is not a signatory.

"[Secretary] RUSK: It is a protocol state." (*The Vietnam Hearings* [January-February, 1966], p. 43.)

1954

> *Ninety-six days after the Geneva Agreements, President Eisenhower offered Ngo Dinh Diem American aid in building a strong state in southern Vietnam. Diem had been appointed Premier by Bao Dai during the Geneva Conference. Eisenhower's landmark letter to Diem arrived at a time of severe political rivalry in the French zone of Vietnam. Although the French remained in complete authority until January 1, 1955, and in partial control until April 1956, Vietnamese elements within the Bao Dai government were struggling for ascendancy. Following the Eisenhower letter, the United States threw the full weight of its economic assistance and military knowledge behind Diem.*

"We have been exploring ways and means to permit our aid to Vietnam to be more effective and to make a greater contribution to the welfare and stability of the Government of Vietnam. I am, accordingly, instructing the American Ambassador to Vietnam to examine with you in your capacity as Chief of Government, how an intelligent program of American aid given directly to your Government can serve to assist Vietnam in its present hour of trial, provided that your Government is prepared to give assurances as to the standards of performance it would be able to maintain in the event such aid were supplied.

"The purpose of this offer is to assist the Government of Vietnam in developing and maintaining a strong, viable state, capable of resisting attempted subversion or aggression through military means." (Letter from President Eisenhower to Ngo Dinh Diem, Gettleman, *op. cit.*, p. 204.)

"He has a theoretical mandate of full powers from the Chief of State, Bao Dai, who in turn derives his authority from a combination of a French grant and the persistence of the symbolic power of his former rule as Emperor."

"In the event that the Diem government falls . . . the United States should consider an immediate suspension of all aid to Vietnam and the French Union forces there. . . ." (Senator Mansfield, *Congressional Record, Senate*, December 1, 1954.)

"I have come to Vietnam to bring every possible aid to the Government of Diem and to his Government only. It is the legal Government in Vietnam, and the aid which the United States will lend it ought to permit the Government to save the country."

"This American mission will soon take charge of instructing the Vietnam Army in accordance with special American methods which have proved effective in Korea, Greece and Turkey and other parts of the world. . . .

"[T]he mission will work under the supervision of Gen. Paul Ely, who remains the Commander in Chief in Indochina. Details of this program have not been finally settled with the French General Staff and the Vietnam Government. . . . The aim will be, however, to build a completely autonomous Vietnam Army." (General J. Lawton Collins, U.S. Special Ambassador in Vietnam, *The New York Times*, November 18, 1954.)

Post-1954

Meanwhile, both the French Union and the People's Army were regrouping their forces in accordance with the Geneva Agreements. This also was the time of the mass migration of North Vietnamese Catholics to the south.

"If Geneva and what was agreed upon there means anything at all, it means . . . Taps for the buried hopes of freedom in Southeast Asia! . . . Now the devilish techniques of brainwashing, forced confessions and rigged trials have a new locale for their exercise. . . . Communism has a world plan and it has been following a carefully set-up timetable for the achievement of that plan. . . ." (Francis Cardinal Spellman of New York, speech to the American Legion Convention, August 31, 1954, *The New York Times*, September 1, 1954.)

". . . [T]he mass flight [to the South] was admittedly the result of an extremely intensive, well-conducted, and, in terms of its objective, very successful American psychological warfare objective. Propaganda slogans and leaflets appealed to the devout Catholics with such themes as 'Christ has gone to the South' and the 'Virgin Mary has departed from the North.'" (Bernard B. Fall, *The Two Viet-Nams*. Praeger: 1964, pp. 153-154.)

"In the South, it is now admitted (though it was carefully hushed up at the time), perhaps as many as 80,000 local guerrillas and regulars and their dependents, including almost 10,000 mountain tribesmen, went northward.

"Perhaps another 5,000 to 6,000 local hard-core guerrillas—probably the élite of the Viet-Minh's military and political operators in the South—simply went underground. They hid their weapons and radio equipment and became anonymous villagers—at least for a while." (Bernard B. Fall, "How the French Got Out of Vietnam," in Marcus G. Raskin and Bernard B. Fall, eds., *The Viet-Nam Reader*. Random House: 1965, p. 88.)

"On May 16, 1955, that is three days before the time-limit fixed by the Geneva Agreement, the last units of the Vietnam People's Army left South Vietnam to regroup into the North. Simultaneously, the Vietnam People's

Army in the North completed the taking-over of newly
liberated regions and towns, including Haiphong perime-
ter." (General Vo Nguyen Giap's speech at a tea party
on May 17, 1955, organized by the High Command of
the People's Army of Vietnam, Gettleman, *op. cit.,* p.
168.)

Post-1954

*The International Control Commission re-
corded frequent failure by both sides to uphold
the terms of the Agreements.*

"There . . . exist cases in North Vietnam where the
Commission's activities are being hindered. The case of
Mobile Team F-44. . . ."

"The Commission has been unable to conduct reconnaissance and control of . . . airfields in South Vietnam. . . ."

". . . [T]he degree of co-operation given to the Commission by the two parties has not been the same. While
the Commission has experienced difficulties in North
Vietnam, the major part of its difficulties has arisen in
South Vietnam." (*Sixth Interim Report of the International Commission for Supervision and Control in Vietnam* [Vietnam No. 1 (1957), Command Paper 31]:
Great Britain Parliamentary Sessional Papers, Vol. 33,
1956/57.)

Post-1954

*In the north, the Commission noted harass-
ment of refugees, interference with the Commission's fixed and mobile teams, and the transfer of arms
from the north to southern insurgents.*

". . . [T]he High Command of the People's Army of
Vietnam, while they did co-operate with the Commission

and took measures to secure freedom of movement in the case of about 8,000 Phat Diem refugees, have so far done little to develop adequate administrative arrangements, with the result that complaints continue to pour in. . . ." (*First and Second Interim Reports of the International Commission for Supervision and Control in Vietnam* [Vietnam No. 1 (1955), Command Paper 9461]. Great Britain Parliamentary Sessional Papers, Vol. 19, 1954/55.)

". . . [T]he Committee has come to the conclusion that in specific instances there is evidence to show that armed and unarmed personnel, arms, munitions, and other supplies have been sent from the zone in the North to the zone in the South with the object of supporting, organizing, and carrying out hostile activities, including armed attacks, directed against the Armed Forces and Administration of the zone in the South. . . ."

". . . [F]urther, . . . there is evidence to show that the P.A.V. has allowed the zone in the North to be used for inciting, encouraging, and supporting hostile activities in the zone in the South. . . ." (*Special Report, International Commission for Supervision and Control in Vietnam* [Vietnam No. 1 (1962), Command Paper 1755]. Great Britain Parliamentary Sessional Papers, Vol. 39, 1961/62.)

Post-1954

In the south, the Commission reported unauthorized introduction of military personnel, interference with the Commission's inspection teams, failure to cooperate in setting up consultations, and violation of the article prohibiting reprisals.

". . . [O]n fourteen occasions the team actually saw military personnel deplaning at Saigon airfield." (*Sixth*

Interim Report of the International Commission for Supervision and Control in Vietnam. [Vietnam No. 1 (1957).] Great Britain Parliamentary Sessional Papers.)

". . . [T]he Commission recorded a violation under Article 14 (c) [reprisals] . . . and a few violations under Articles 16 and 17 [ban on introduction of troops, munitions, etc.] of the Agreement by the French High Command and the Government of the Republic of South Vietnam, and none by the Democratic Republic of Vietnam." (*Seventh Interim Report of the International Commission for Supervision and Control in Vietnam* [Vietnam No. 2 (1957), Command Paper 325]. Great Britain Parliamentary Sessional Papers, Vol. 30, 1957/58.)

"A major difficulty facing the Commission arises from the failure to hold consultations between the two parties and free nation-wide elections with a view to reunification of Vietnam. . . ." (*Ibid.*)

". . . [T]he Commission concludes that the Republic of Vietnam has violated Articles 16 and 17 of the Geneva Agreement in receiving the increased military aid from the United States. . . . [T]he establishment of a U.S. Military Assistance Command in South Vietnam, as well as the introduction of a large number of U.S. military personnel beyond the stated strength of the MAAG (Military Assistance Advisory Group), amounts to a factual military alliance, which is prohibited under Article 19 of the Geneva Agreement. . . ." (*Special Report, International Commission for Supervision and Control in Vietnam.* [Vietnam No. 1 (1962).] Great Britain Parliamentary Sessional Papers.)

"[Senator] SPARKMAN: . . . When did we first give military assistance to South Vietnam?

"[General] TAYLOR: Almost at once. After this agreement in '54 we established a small mission which gradually grew. For a while the French remained in a training capacity in South Vietnam. Eventually they withdrew that formal participation and we took over the entire training task of the armed forces. At the same time there was economic aid going on. . . ." *The Vietnam Hearings* [January-February, 1966], pp. 180-181.)

"[General] TAYLOR: I would say [regarding the ban on introducing new military personnel] that, one, there was never a cessation of hostilities to begin with. The North Vietnamese left behind five to six thousand men in South Vietnam, and large caches of ammunition. They proceeded almost at once to infiltrate armed men from North Vietnam, so I would say that the whole provision was never effective.

"[Senator] MORSE: But the signatories to the Treaty thought so. They signed it.

"[General] TAYLOR: They didn't know what was going to take place, sir. The ink was not dry on that piece of paper before North Vietnam was violating it.

"[Senator] MORSE: You haven't heard France or the other signatories to the charter take America's position that a course of action in violation of these sections was justified? . . .

"[General] TAYLOR: Well, their objection is not being gored, Senator; ours is.

"[Senator] MORSE: But their treaty is being torn up by us." (*Ibid.*, pp. 188-189.)

1955-1956

The Hanoi government made plans for the upcoming consultations and elections, with negative response from Diem.

"All Vietnamese citizens, whether from the North or from the South have the right to canvass freely throughout the country through conference, leaflets, press, etc. The Government of the North and the authorities of the South should ensure the liberty and the security for all citizens during their activities for elections. . . ." (Ho Chi Minh as quoted in B. S. N. Murti, *Vietnam Divided.* Asia Publishing House: 1964, pp. 182-193.)

" 'Her Majesty's government has always regarded it as desirable that these elections should be held and has advised the Government of the Republic of Vietnam to enter into consultations with the Vietminh authorities in order to insure that all the necessary conditions obtained for a free expression of the national will as a preliminary to holding free general elections by secret ballot. Nevertheless, Her Majesty's government does not agree that (South Vietnam) is legally obliged to follow that course. . . .' " (Representative Goodell of New York quoting from statement by the United Kingdom, May 1956, *Congressional Record,* House, August 25, 1965.)

". . . [T]here can be no question of a conference, even less of negotiations. . . ." (Ngo Dinh Diem, September 21, 1955, *The Times* (London), September 22, 1955.)

"Serving the cause of true democracy the Viet-Nam Government considers the principle of really free elections to be a peaceful and democratic institution, but the conditions of freedom, of life and of the vote must first be satisfied." (Statement by the Government of South Vietnam, *Documents Relating to British Involvement in the Indo-China Conflict, 1945-1965,* p. 110.)

"It was the Communists' calculation that nationwide

elections scheduled in the Accords for 1956 would turn all of Viet-Nam over to them . . . The primary focus of the Communists' activity during the post-Geneva period was on political action . . . The authorities in South Viet-Nam refused to fall into this well-laid trap." (*A Threat to the Peace: North Viet-Nam's Effort to Conquer South Viet-Nam*. Department of State Publication 7308. Government Printing Office: 1961, p. 3.)

". . . [I]t is a travesty on the truth to allege that the present situation was brought about by the failure of the South to carry out the 1954 accords. In fact, it was the North that was not willing to submit itself to the test of free elections under international control." (Deputy Under Secretary for Political Affairs U. Alexis Johnson, *Department of State Bulletin,* April 4, 1966.)

1955-1956

On October 26, 1955, Diem proclaimed the Republic of Vietnam, with himself as President.

One year and three months after the Geneva Agreements, two separate states had emerged in Vietnam. The provisional military demarcation line had been redrawn in permanent form, and the unifying elections had failed to materialize.

"Premier Diem is the best hope that we have in South Vietnam. He is the leader of his people. He deserves and must have the wholehearted support of the American Government and our foreign policy. . . . If we have any comment to make about the leadership in Vietnam let it be directed against Bao Dai. . . . If the Government of South Vietnam has not room for both of these men, it is Bao Dai who must go." (Senator Hubert H. Humphrey, *Congressional Record,* Senate, May 2, 1955.)

1956-1963

*The remainder of the decade that culminated
in the death of President Kennedy saw the
foundations for future major conflict firmly laid in place.
Kennedy's attitude toward Asian communism reflected
some shift of emphasis from combating communism to
teaching democracy. His aim was to help the South Vietnamese achieve a "democratic revolution."*

"What we must offer them is a revolution—a political,
economic, and social revolution far superior to anything
the Communists can offer—far more peaceful, far more
democratic, and far more locally controlled. Such a revolution will require much from the United States and much
from Vietnam. We must supply capital to replace that
drained by centuries of social exploitation. . . . We must
assist the inspiring growth of Vietnamese democracy and
economy . . . (John F. Kennedy, *op. cit.,* p. 64.)

"In accordance with that declaration [the unilateral
declaration at Geneva], and in response to your request,
we are prepared to help the Republic of Vietnam to protect its people and to preserve its independence. We shall
promptly increase our assistance to your defense effort as
well as help relieve the destruction of the floods which
you describe. I have already given the orders to get these
programs underway." (President Kennedy, letter to President Diem, December 14, 1961, Gettleman, *op. cit.,* p.
209.)

1956-1963

*Pursuant to this policy, the United States in-
creased the economic assistance and military
aid initiated under the Eisenhower administration. Not-*

withstanding, dictatorial methods, repression, and finally civil war characterized most of Diem's rule. Diem suppressed political opposition and failed to enforce even minimal land reform measures. In agricultural Vietnam, economic exploitation by a small landowning elite resulted in widespread peasant defection and insurgence. By 1963, Diem had alienated large sectors of the rural population, antagonized the Montagnards of the interior, provoked hostility and revolt among nationalists and Buddhists alike, and was being met by open guerrilla warfare among Vietminh sympathizers.

"In terms of aid, the assumption of this preponderant responsibility has meant U.S. outlays of $1.4 billion for economic assistance during the period of 1955-62. . . . On top of economic aid, there has also been provided large amounts of military equipment and supplies and training for the Vietnamese Army, Navy, and Air Force and for other defense purposes. For the period 1955-62 the total of aid of all kinds to Vietnam stands at more than $2 billion." (Mike Mansfield [Senate Majority Leader], *The Vietnam Conflict: The Substance and the Shadow*. Government Printing Office: 1966, Appendix II, p. 19.)

"In the opinion of the Polish Delegation the [Control] Commission's decision allowing the party to double the strength of the personnel of MAAG [Military Assistance Advisory Group] is contradictory with the letter and spirit of the Geneva Agreement. . . ." (*Eleventh Interim Report of the International Commission for Supervision and Control in Vietnam* [Vietnam No. 1 (1961), Command Paper 1551]. Great Britain Parliamentary Sessional Papers, Vol. 39, 1961/62.)

"Article 1—Sentence of death, and confiscation of the whole or part of his property, with loss of rank in the case of army men, will be imposed on whoever commits or attempts to commit . . . crimes with the aim of sabotage, or of infringing upon the security of the State, or injuring the lives or property of the people. . . ."

"Article 17—The decisions of the special military court are not subject to appeal, and no appeal is allowed to the High Court." (Law 10/59, Republic of Vietnam, May 6, 1959, Gettleman, *op. cit.*, pp. 256-260.)

"Behind a façade of photographs, flags and slogans there is a grim structure of decrees, political prisons, concentration camps, milder 're-education centers,' secret police. Presidential 'Ordinance No. 6' signed and issued by Diem in January, 1956, provides that 'individuals considered dangerous to national defense and common security' may be confined by executive order in 'a concentration camp.' . . . Only known or suspected Communists who have threatened or violated public security since July, 1954, are supposed to be arrested and 're-educated' under these decrees. But many non-Communists have also been detained. The whole machinery of security has been used to discourage active opposition of any kind from any source." (John Osborne, "The Tough Miracle Man of Vietnam," *Life,* May 13, 1957.)

"The Minister of Agrarian Reform was reported as not having 'signed leases with his tenants as provided for by land reform decrees and he is most certainly not interested in land distribution which would divest him of much of his property.' " (J. Price Gittinger, American Agricultural Adviser, *Agrarian Reform Status Report,* quoted in John D. Montgomery, *The Politics of Foreign Aid.* Praeger: 1962, p. 126.)

"Solutions must be found for the resettlement villages which have infringed upon the land of the highland people, and for the highland villages which are surrounded by military camps and consequently do not have enough land to make a living." (Brigadier General Vinh-Loc, *The Thing Called "Autonomy Movement" FULRO* [a Montagnard movement for autonomy], Kahin and Lewis, *op. cit.,* p. 107.)

"[T]he people do not know a better life or more freedom under the republican regime which you have created. A constitution has been established in form only. . . . Continuous arrests fill the jails and prisons to the rafters. . . . Political parties and religious sects have been eliminated. . . . Today the people want freedom." ("Manifesto of the Eighteen" [including businessmen, lawyers, priests, politicians, and educators in South Vietnam], April 26, 1960, Raskin and Fall, *op. cit.,* p. 118.)

1956-1963

Repression dominated the political climate in the north also during 1956 and 1957, resulting in peasant uprisings. For the rest of the period, more moderate reforms, embodied in a Three-Year Plan and a later Five-Year Plan, were decreed for the North. Ho Chi Minh concentrated on trying to build an economically stable state in the north, giving to the Vietminh in the south little more than political encouragement.

"As for the Catholic compatriots, the mistakes committed during the land reform have also infringed upon their religious freedom. The Party, Government and the Front clearly realize these mistakes and are determined to correct them." (Hanoi Radio, November 20, 1956, Kahin and Lewis, *op. cit.,* p. 97.)

"Our policy is: to consolidate the North and to keep in mind the South. To build a good house we must build a good foundation. . . . The North is the foundation, the root of the struggle for complete national liberation and the reunification of the country. . . . Therefore, to work here is the same as struggling in the South. . . ." (President Ho Chi Minh, June 19, 1956, Kahin and Lewis, *op. cit.*, p. 90.)

"Today, the economic construction in the North has become the central task of the Party. Therefore it is necessary to cut down [our] defence budget, adequately reduce our army contingent so as to concentrate manpower and material in economic construction." (Vo Nguyen Giap, Minister of Defense, *Third National Congress of the Viet Nam Workers' Party: Documents, ibid.*, p. 116.)

1956-1963

During this period, the National Liberation Front made its first appearance in South Vietnam. The Front drew its early membership from former Vietminh as well as from Buddhists and other groups having no relation to the Vietminh. The early organization alternately called itself the Voice of Nambo (South) and Resistance Veterans, as well as the Liberation Front. During this period North Vietnam was committed to a political rather than a military strategy for achieving reunification, and therefore the militancy of the early southern insurgent groups was denounced by Hanoi.

"First of all, it must be understood that armed opposition to the Ngo Dinh Diem regime inside South Viet-Nam, in one form or another, had never ceased between Viet-Nam's partition in 1954 and the demise of the Diem regime in November, 1963. Apart from the Communists, there existed in South Viet-Nam a variety of political-religious sects, such as the Hoa-Hao and the Cao-Dai; and at least one well-organized semipiratical band, the Binh-

Xuyên, which never fully surrendered to the South Viet-Nam government."

"In March, 1957, the [Diem] regime openly violated the last restraints placed upon it by the Geneva Agreements with regard to reprisals exercised against 'former resistance members'—that is, ex-guerrillas of the Viet-Minh who had fought against the French, and many of whom were not Communists." (Bernard B. Fall, "Viet-Cong—The Unseen Enemy in Viet-Nam," Raskin and Fall, *op. cit.*, pp. 253-256.)

"If the people take up arms to struggle against terror or to punish blood-thirsty traitors, notorious criminals, faithful valets of the American-Diemists, it is only to defend themselves." ("Declaration of Former Resistance Fighters," Kahin and Lewis, *op. cit.*, p. 114.)

"[Their] words seem to be revolutionary, but in reality they are not aimed at the principal enemies of the revolution. That is why this radio [Nambo] causes a listener who is not vigilant to be frightened, terrified about the revolution, about socialism." (Hanoi Radio Broadcast commenting on the Voice of Nambo statements, July 10, 1958, *ibid.*, p. 112.)

"The [Liberation] front was formed at Hanoi's order in 1960." (*Aggression from the North: The Record of North Viet-Nam's Campaign to Conquer South Viet-Nam*. Department of State Publication No. 7839, Government Printing Office: 1965, p. 2.)

"Every one of the numerous recorded Hanoi broadcasts dealing with the Front attacked it violently. As early as June 28, 1958, the Front was accused of 'using their broadcasts to distort Marxist-Leninist theories.' . . . Front statements . . . were denounced . . . as 'vilest slander and distortion of the truth.' " (Hanoi broadcasts, Kahin and Lewis, *op. cit.*, p. 111.)

1956-1963

Not until 1960 was the National Liberation Front formally established. It was only then officially recognized by Hanoi. At this time the Front re-leased its first program, the Ten Points, calling for gradual reunification with the north and a neutral foreign policy. The Front held its first formal Congress in 1962, at which leaders and a Four-Point program were announced.

"According to published accounts, the NLF congress not only grouped former Communist resistance members, but also other elements from the Vietnamese Democratic Party and the Radical Socialist Party, both of which, like all non-Communist Vietnamese political organizations, represented almost nothing."

"In the American official view, there can be no doubt but that the NLF is nothing but a suboffice of the Reuni-fication Commission operating under the Council of Min-isters of the Hanoi government. . . . But to many people, that can only be part of the story. There is, for example, the high-ranking spokesman of the Front who told *Le Monde's* Georges Chaffard that the NLF had got along without the North 'for a long time' and would 'prefer to settle our affairs among "southerners." ' " (Fall, "Viet-Cong—The Unseen Enemy in Viet-Nam," Raskin and Fall, *op. cit.*, pp. 258-260.)

"1. To cancel all unequal treaties signed with foreign countries by the U.S. henchmen which violate national sovereignty.

"2. To establish diplomatic relations with all countries irrespective of political regime, in accordance with the principles of peaceful co-existence as put forth at the Bandung Conference.

"3. To unite closely with the peace-loving and neutral countries. To expand friendly relations with Asian and African countries, first of all, with neighbouring Cambodia and Laos.

"4. To refrain from joining any bloc or military alliance or forming a military alliance with any country.

"5. To receive economic aid from any country ready to assist Vietnam without conditions attached." (Section VIII, The Ten-Point Program of the NLF, December 20, 1960, Kahin and Lewis, *op. cit.*, p. 394.)

". . . [A] broad National United Front directed against the U.S. and Diem and based on the worker-peasant alliance . . . must rally all the patriotic classes and sections of the people. . . ." ("Resolution of the Third National Congress of the Viet Nam Workers' Party on the tasks and line of the Party in the new stage," *Third National Congress of the Viet Nam Workers' Party: Documents, ibid.*, p. 116.)

"As citizens of the Democratic Republic of Viet Nam and natives of the South, we admit that, at the first reading, the program of the South Viet Nam Liberation National Front is not likely to get our full approval. The neutrality of the South means for Viet Nam a divergence of political character each side of the 17th parallel, while our country has always constituted a single entity." (Tran Van Giau and Le Van Chat, political leaders of North Vietnam, in *The South Vietnam Liberation National Front, ibid.*, p. 135.)

"The Liberation Front is Hanoi's creation; it is neither independent nor southern, and what it seeks is not liberation but subjugation of the South." (*Aggression from the North*, p. 20.)

1956-1963

Vietcong terrorism posed a serious threat to the government in Saigon, particularly from 1960 forward. (Vietcong derives from Viet-Nam Cong-San meaning simply Vietnamese Communist. NLF refers to the political organization itself.) The United States helped the Republic of Vietnam to implement a number of compensatory measures, among them the strategic hamlet program. The emphasis remained on aid rather than active U.S. commitment, although President Kennedy increased the strength of the American military advisory forces in Vietnam by a substantial number.

"We have been deeply disturbed by the assault on your country. Our indignation has mounted as the deliberate savagery of the Communist program of assassination, kidnapping, and wanton violence became clear." (President Kennedy to President Diem, *Department of State Bulletin,* January 1, 1962.)

"In the past 3 years . . . constructive achievements have been over-shadowed by the resumption of guerrilla warfare on a large scale. Once again, a large part of South Vietnam has become unsafe a short distance outside the cities. . . . In 1962, about 25,000 Vietnamese were killed in this conflict. The attacks of the Vietcong guerrillas averaged over 100 per week during the year and ranged in size from squad to battalion level." (Mansfield, *op. cit.,* p. 20.)

"By 1961 it was apparent that the prospects for a total collapse in South Vietnam had begun to come dangerously close. A joint reevaluation of the situation was undertaken in that year by the Vietnamese Government and the United States. . . . After special political, military, and economic missions had examined the situation, the United States enlarged its aid program—military and other—to the present annual level of more than $400 million. The United States also agreed to put about 10,000 men into South Vietnam in direct support of the Vietnamese armed forces in addition to the large military aid group which was already functioning in the country.

"The new U.S. support forces were designed to provide tactical advice on counterguerrilla operations and logistical and other specialized services—notably those of rapid mobility and communications. The forces were not intended for combat, but they have been in combat. More than 50 men have lost their lives—about half in battle—in Vietnam since the beginning of the program of intensified assistance." (*Ibid.*, p. 21.)

Year	United States	
	Killed	Wounded
1960...................		
1961...................	1	1
1962...................	31	74
1963...................	77	411
1964...................	146	1,038
1965...................	1,365	6,110
Total	1,620	7,634

(Defense Department casualty figures, *Congressional Record,* Senate, October 10, 1966.) [See page 201 for official figures as of July 1968.]

1963

Toward the end of the Kennedy administration, the President and his advisers expressed considerable optimism about progress in South Vietnam and the effectiveness of American aid. Notwithstanding,

the Diem regime was overthrown by a military coup on
November 1, 1963, and Diem himself was assassinated.

". . . [W]e are satisfied that we have a sound strategy;
progress is being made, and the Vietnamese have certainly demonstrated their capacity for sacrifice and their
determination to survive as a free people. As President
Kennedy said in his state of the Union message, 'The
spearpoint of aggression has been blunted in South Viet-
Nam.'" (Deputy Under Secretary U. Alexis Johnson,
Department of State Bulletin, September 2, 1963.)

"The numbers of incidents have been dropping rapidly
from last year. Such elements as sabotage, propaganda incidents, the larger sized attacks, those were dropping. Additional areas of the country were coming under Government control. The strategic-hamlet program had been
moving forward. I think it is still moving forward." (Secretary Rusk, *ibid.,* September 2, 1963.)

"This is the first time in Vietnamese history that ham-
let councils have been elected. It is also the first time in
Vietnamese history that the national Government has
been effectively 'plugged in' to hamlet-level society."
(Theodore J. C. Heavner, Deputy Director, Viet-Nam
Working Group, *ibid.,* September 9, 1963.)

". . . [W]e should experience elation as we pursue policies designed to exorcise . . . doubt in ways that lead
mankind not only to prevail but to prevail with the freedom of consent, the freedom of action, and the freedom
of mind that are the reasons why prevailing is worth the
battle." (Assistant Secretary for Public Affairs Robert J.
Manning, *ibid.,* September 23, 1963.)

"They [Secretary McNamara and General Taylor] reported that by the end of this year, the U.S. program for

training Vietnamese should have progressed to the point
where 1,000 U.S. military personnel assigned to South
Viet-Nam can be withdrawn." (White House statement
on Vietnam, *ibid.,* October 21, 1963.)

"It is with the Vietnamese peasant, of course, that the
'strategic hamlet' concept is primarily concerned. The
concept is based on the assumptions that the Vietcong are
sustained by the rural populace primarily out of fear, and
in part, because the peasants are not aware of the superior social, economic, and political advantages which are
offered by support of the Government. . . . *Assuming the
accuracy of the assumptions* successful military action
within the dimensions of the present effort is conceivable
within the foreseeable future." (Mansfield, *op. cit.,* p.
22.)

"Ngo Dinh Nhu [Diem's brother] made the strategic
hamlet program his personal project and published glow-
ing reports of spectacular success. . . . One might have
wondered whether Nhu was just the man to mobilize the
idealism of the villages; but Nolting and Harkins listened
uncritically to his reports and passed them back to Washington, where they were read with elation." (Arthur M.
Schlesinger, Jr. [Former Presidential Assistant], *A
Thousand Days.* Houghton Mifflin: 1965, p. 549.)

". . . Alexis Johnson, speaking for right-thinking
officials, cited the strategic hamlet program as 'the most
important reason for guarded optimism.' 'Perhaps the
most important result,' Johnson declared, 'is the intangible knitting together of Government and people.'
"Intangible the knitting together certainly was. Exactly
a month after this piece of official wisdom . . . Diem's
troops fired indiscriminately into [a] crowd, leaving a
moaning mass of dead and wounded." (*Ibid.,* p. 986.)

"In the final analysis, it is their war. They are the ones

to win it or lose it. We can help them, we can give them equipment, we can send our men out there as advisers, but they have to win it . . ." (President Kennedy, *Department of State Bulletin,* September 30, 1963.)

SUMMARY

> *During the ten years following the Geneva Conference, the Geneva Agreements were reduced to unenforceable scraps of paper; the SEATO pact gave South Vietnam a political identity; and the United States committed itself to building a strong state in the south. These developments were to provide the foundation for U.S. policy in the years to come.*

"Whether or not the initial decision was a mistake is now moot. The United States does have a commitment in South Vietnam. The flag is there. United States honor and prestige are there. And, most important of all, United States soldiers are there." (Senator Richard B. Russell, Chairman, Senate Armed Services Committee, *Congressional Record,* Senate, June 15, 1965.)

"Our men in Vietnam are there . . . to keep a promise that was made 12 years ago." (President Johnson, February 23, 1966, *Weekly Compilation of Presidential Documents,* February 28, 1966.)

". . . America keeps her word. We are steadfast in a policy which has been followed for 10 years in three administrations."

"In the case of Viet-Nam, our commitment today is just the same as the commitment made by President Eisenhower to President Diem in 1954—a commitment to help these people help themselves." (President Johnson, news conference, June 2, 1964, *Department of State Bulletin,* June 22, 1964.)

PART III: THE SIGNIFICANT YEAR, 1964

1964

> *Hope for a peaceful solution to the Vietnam conflict swelled briefly after Diem's death. Disaffection with the war and strong sentiment for a neutralist solution were expressed even in Saigon. Both Hanoi and the National Liberation Front broadcast appeals for negotiation.*

". . . [O]n many occasions anti-French demonstrations [in Saigon] were followed by counter-demonstrations favorable to neutralization without the police having received orders to intervene." (*Le Monde,* February 1, 1964.)

"[Plans to press for a negotiated settlement are] sabotaging us, killing us, drowning us in difficulties." (Premier Nguyen Ngoc Tho of South Vietnam, *The New York Times,* January 27, 1964.)

"The National Liberation Front of South Vietnam asserted that if the leaders of the South Vietnamese armed forces are concerned with the people's happiness and future, they must consider that internal conflicts can be settled by means of negotiations." (FBIS [CIA-sponsored Foreign Broadcast Information Service] *Daily Report,*

February 5, 1964, KKK2: Hanoi Radio Broadcast of January 28, 1964.)

". . . [T]he coup promoters are still able to change what one calls their fate, and they still have enough time to replan their future—a future which will be brilliant, which will have no more nightmares—if they draw from the scenes of the ruins in Saigon a useful lesson, if they know how to rely on the people's strength to resolutely separate themselves from the control of the U.S. imperialists. . . ." (*Ibid.*, November 13, 1963, KKK4: Appeal from the NLF to the Minh junta that had executed the coup against Diem.)

"The parties concerned in South Vietnam [should] negotiate with one another to reach a cease-fire and solve the important problems of the nation, to stabilize the basic internal and external policies, with a view to reaching free general elections to elect state organs and to form a national coalition government composed of representatives of all forces, parties, tendencies, and strata of the South Vietnamese people." (National Liberation Front statement, November 8, 1963, reported on Hanoi Radio, November 17, 1963, Kahin and Lewis, *op. cit.*, p. 401.)

1964

Internationally, France's President de Gaulle, Secretary General U Thant at the United Nations, the Soviet Government, and the Cambodian Chief of State, Prince Sihanouk, advanced plans for resolution of the conflict. These plans varied from proposals for direct negotiation among the protagonists, including the United States, to suggestions for reconvening the Geneva Conference.

". . . [I]t is clear that the existence of a Communist

state installed in Tonkin . . . and the shock caused in the South by the withdrawal of our administration and our forces, exposed the country to new perils. It was a question of discovering whether the country could find, in itself, a national cohesion and a solid government. It was then that the Americans arrived, bringing their aid, their policy, and their authority."

". . . [I]n North and South Viet-Nam, in Cambodia, and in Laos, no foreign power may any longer intervene in any way in the affairs of these unfortunate countries. A meeting of the same order and including, in principle, the same participants as the former Geneva Conference would certainly be qualified to make a decision and to organize a means for impartial control. That is what France is proposing to all the states concerned. . . ."

"No other road can be visualized which can lead to peace in Southeast Asia, provided that once the theoretical agreement is concluded, two practical conditions be realized. The first is that the powers which directly or indirectly bear a responsibility in what was or is the fate of Indochina . . . be effectively resolved to be involved there no longer. The second is that massive economic and technical aid be furnished to all of Indochina by the states which have the means for it, in order that development replace cruel division." (President Charles de Gaulle of France, news conference, July 23, 1964, Raskin and Fall, *op. cit.,* pp. 269-271.)

"In my view, there was a very good possibility in 1963 of arriving at a satisfactory political solution. In 1964 the situation deteriorated still further, and the prospects for a peaceful solution became more remote."

"I have been conducting private discussions on this question of Viet-Nam for a long time, as you all know. Of course, it will not be very helpful at this stage to reveal even some parts or some features of the negotiations. . . . I am sure the great American people, if only they

knew the true facts and the background to the developments in South Viet-Nam, will agree with me that further
bloodshed is unnecessary. . . . As you know, in times of
war and of hostilities the first casualty is truth."

"I have even presented concrete ideas and proposals."

"QUESTION: Have they been presented to the United
States among other interested parties?"

"THE SECRETARY-GENERAL: Yes." (Secretary-
General U Thant of the United Nations, "Press Conference on Southeast Asia and Related Matters," *ibid.,* pp.
263-267.)

"He wanted, personally and directly, as Adlai Stevenson the man, to help bring the world to safety. The Vietnam war deeply worried him."

"In the early autumn of 1964, [he said that] U Thant,
the UN Secretary-General, had privately obtained agreement from authorities in North Vietnam that they would
send an emissary to talk with an American emissary, in
Rangoon, Burma. Someone in Washington insisted that
this attempt be postponed until after the Presidential election. When the election was over, U Thant again pursued
the matter; Hanoi was still willing to send its man. But
Defense Secretary Robert McNamara, Adlai went on,
flatly opposed the attempt. He said the South Vietnamese
government would have to be informed and that this
would have a demoralizing effect on them; that government was shaky enough, as it was.

"Stevenson told me that U Thant was furious over this
failure of his patient efforts, but said nothing publicly."
(Eric Sevareid, "The Final Troubled Hours of Adlai Stevenson," *Look,* November 30, 1965.)

"It is true that last autumn Ambassador Stevenson was
informed by Secretary-General U Thant that he had been
informed indirectly that Hanoi would be willing to have a
contact with the United States and that the Secretary-

General had suggested Rangoon as a suitable site." (Secretary Rusk, news conference, November 26, 1965, *Department of State Bulletin,* December 13, 1965.)

" '[Neutralization] would have as its principal advantage the ending of the bloody war there. . . . Then if South Vietnam lives up to a statute of neutrality,' he said, 'Cambodia would agree to the creation of a confederation of associated states, on equal footing.' " (Prince Sihanouk of Cambodia, *The New York Times,* December 4, 1963.)

"The NLF is not opposed to the convening of an international conference in order to facilitate the search for a solution." (Nguyen Huu Tho, leader of the NLF, *Le Monde,* July 26, 1964.)

"The Soviet Government has once again underlined the need to call a new international conference on Laos. It suggested once before that such a conference be held in June 1964, in Geneva. Unfortunately this proposal did not get the support of the United States and certain other States."
"The Soviet Government . . . stresses that in conditions of crude and systematic undermining of the Geneva Agreement by certain States, the role of Co-Chairman loses all of its beneficial purpose and becomes fictitious." (*Documents Relating to British Involvement in the Indo-China Conflict, 1945-1965,* p. 239.)

1964

The United States, in line with its stated foreign policy, rejected all proposals for a neutralist settlement. Immediately after President Kennedy's assassination, President Johnson indicated that he still hoped to follow the schedule adopted under Kennedy that called for reduction of U.S. training forces by late 1965. However, early in 1964, the new administration an-

nounced that it would retain the major elements of both Eisenhower's and Kennedy's Southeast Asian policies— combating the spread of communism and implementing the growth of non-Communist regimes. And it added a third objective of its own, an aim much broader in its international implications: to demonstrate the ability of the free world to counter Communist wars of liberation.

"Neutralization of South Vietnam would only be another name for a Communist take-over." (President Johnson's New Year's message to General Duong Van Minh, *The New York Times,* January 1, 1964.)

"Under the shadow of Communist power, 'neutralization' would in reality be an interim device to permit Communist consolidation and eventual take-over." (Defense Secretary Robert McNamara, address before the James Forrestal Memorial Awards Dinner, National Security Industrial Association, Washington, D.C., March 26, 1964, *ibid.,* March 27, 1964.)

"We do not believe in conferences called to ratify terror, so our policy is unchanged." (President Johnson, news conference, *ibid.,* July 25, 1964.)

"The Republic of Vietnam categorically rejects the proposition directed toward the convening of a new Geneva conference, and is strongly resolved to pursue its struggle against the invaders, in spite of colonialist and communist maneuvers." (Response to French proposal and U Thant's proposal by the Saigon government, July 25, 1964, *Le Monde,* July 26, 1964.)

". . . President Johnson laid down a general policy line emphasizing the following:

"First, the central point of United States policy on South Vietnam remains: namely, to assist the new government there in winning the war against the Communist Vietcong insurgents. The adoption of all measures should be determined by their potential contribution to this overriding objective.

"Second, the White House statement of Oct. 2 on the withdrawal of American troops from South Vietnam remains in force. This statement, reflecting a decision of the National Security Council, said the program for training of Vietnamese troops should have progressed by the end of this year to the point 'where 1,000 United States military personnel' can be withdrawn.

"The United States now has 16,500 military men in South Vietnam.

"Third, all United States agencies represented in Vietnam are to assist the present Government in its tasks of consolidation and the development of public support for programs directed toward winning the war." (*The New York Times,* November 25, 1963.)

"The U.S. role in South Viet-Nam, then, is: *first,* to answer the call of the South Vietnamese, a member nation of our free-world family, to help them save their country for themselves; *second,* to help prevent the strategic danger which would exist if communism absorbed Southeast Asia's people and resources; and *third,* to prove in the Vietnamese test case that the free world can cope with Communist 'wars of liberation' as we have coped successfully with Communist aggression at other levels." (Secretary McNamara, speech on March 26, 1964, *ibid.,* March 27, 1964.)

1964

South Vietnamese political currents hampered achievement of these United States aims. Within a year and a half of Diem's fall, seven military dictatorships came to power in South Vietnam. The

United States lent the weight of its influence to maintain anti-neutralist regimes in power, at the same time urging more democratic procedures and greater rapport between government and people. Three political facts came to light during this period: first, no regime that the United States opposed could long survive in Saigon; second, those leaders promoted by the United States because of their anti-neutralist sentiments invariably lacked the support of large segments of the population; and third, even with strong United States backing, leaders who did not accommodate themselves to the demands of South Vietnam's powerful Buddhist groups soon fell from power. Strong popular opposition to the war continued to manifest itself, and the overt corruption of government officials contributed to political instability in Saigon.

"There is . . . a chance that political evolution within the country and developments upon the world scene could lead to some kind of a negotiated settlement based upon neutralization." (From a CIA study leaked to the newspapers, *The New York Times,* August 23, 1964.)

"The United States will continue to furnish you and your people with the fullest measure of support in this bitter fight. . . . We shall maintain in Vietnam American personnel and material as needed to assist you in achieving victory." (President Johnson's New Year's message to General Duong Van Minh, *ibid.,* January 2, 1964.)

"The army is determined to sweep out the Communist and Vietnamese traitors standing for neutralism." (Declaration by Major General Nguyen Khanh at the time of his military coup, *ibid.,* January 31, 1964.)

"The hand of Washington has again shifted the pawns on the South Vietnamese board." (*Izvestia,* January 30, 1964.)

"We have reaffirmed U.S. support for South Viet-Nam's government and pledged economic assistance and military training and logistical support for as long as it takes to bring the insurgency under control.

"We will support the government of South Viet-Nam in carrying out its Anti-Insurgency Plan. Under that plan, Prime Minister Khanh intends to implement a National Mobilization Program to mobilize all national resources in the struggle." (Secretary McNamara, speech on March 26, 1964, *The New York Times,* March 27, 1964.)

"Well, we're trying to get this area so that it can stand on its own feet without our help and with us on call, so that it isn't under the control of communism."

". . . [W]hen I arrived in Saigon . . . there was a great deal of police brutality and oppression and everything was pretty much at a standstill and I think if it had gone on much longer there was such a disintegration that I think you might have had a Communist takeover."

". . . [N]ow with General Khanh while there's lots, lots of problems, he's a very bright, able soldier. He's a broadminded soldier, he recognizes the importance of politics, he recognizes the importance of finance, economics, he studies, he works at these things; he's not a politician, he's not a financier, but he realizes this is important. He's in a great hurry." (Former Ambassador Henry Cabot Lodge, *ibid.,* June 30, 1964.)

"Every Prime Minister or even Minister said: 'I'm here for two months, so money, money, and if necessary I'll go abroad.' " (Premier Nguyen Cao Ky, describing the corruption of his predecessors, *ibid.,* December 3, 1966.)

"After the assassination of Ngo Dinh Diem, repeated coups had weakened the cohesiveness of the central authority and acted to stimulate public disaffection and indifference to the war." (Mansfield, *op. cit.*, p. 1.)

". . . [T]he war has consistently seen more civilians killed than Viet Cong. Between 1961 and 1964, even modest estimates of the casualties indicated that more than half a million . . . civilians had been killed. Under these circumstances, is it a matter for surprise that more and more Vietnamese are drawn to the ranks of the National Liberation Front?"

"We talked with some peasants . . . and when we had established confidence between ourselves I asked them the question: 'Whom would you follow: the government of South Vietnam or the National Liberation Front?'

"They replied: 'We do not follow either. We follow the one who can end the war and guarantee that we can live.' " (Thich Nhat Hanh, *Vietnam: Lotus in a Sea of Fire.* Hill and Wang: 1967, pp. 65-67.)

"Maj. General Khanh has accepted in general and in detail an immediate Buddhist formula for reforming his Government along new civilian lines." (*The New York Times,* September 13, 1964.)

"The nation was desperately weary of war, its people verging on such despair that they would soon accept anything to get it over with." (John Mecklin [American Public Affairs Officer in Saigon, 1962-1964], *Mission in Torment.* Doubleday: 1965, p. 290.)

1964

During 1964, the United States gradually shifted from limited to unlimited support for the Vietnam war. Within a month after Vice-President Johnson succeeded to the Presidency, there came the first indications of a change from the Kennedy policy. Little

*by little, both men and supplies to Vietnam were in-
creased. By January 1965, United States advisory personnel had been augmented by a large number of American
forces of all kinds and by some direct American air support. Although American troops at that time were not yet
engaged in field combat, helicopter companies supplied
tactical transportation to Vietnamese forces. Military control of South Vietnam by Saigon became increasingly dependent on the United States presence.*

"Secretary of Defense Robert S. McNamara gave
South Vietnam's leaders a pledge of support from President Johnson today. The United States will back the war
against Communist guerrillas as long as its help is needed
and wanted, the Vietnamese leaders were told."

". . . [T]he message did not specifically mention any
date for the withdrawal of American forces, but in effect
it eliminated the previously announced goal of withdrawing most of them by the end of 1965.

"Secretary McNamara also sought to allay Vietnamese
fears that the United States might permit proposals for
neutralizing Vietnam to become the subject of a possible
international conference on Cambodian neutrality." (*The
New York Times,* December 21, 1963.)

"[A] need has emerged in Vietnam. I now request that
the Congress provide $125 million in addition to the $3.4
million already proposed for foreign assistance. $70 mil-
lion is required for economic and $55 million for military
uses in Vietnam."

". . . [A]dditional equipment, ammunition, training
and supplies will be needed as the organization and functioning of the armed forces improves [in South
Vietnam]. Additional aircraft pilot training for the Vietnamese and airfield improvements are required. Increased
activity will require additional ammunition. Additional
support equipment is required for all forces."

"By our words and deeds in a decade of determined effort, we are pledged before all the world to stand with the free people of Vietnam. Sixteen thousand Americans are serving our country and the people of Vietnam. Daily they face danger in the cause of freedom. Duty requires, and the American people demand, that we give them the fullest measure of support." (President Johnson, message to Congress, May 18, 1964, *ibid.*, May 19, 1964.)

"Question: I take it from what you've said so far that you advocate the continuation of the present policies without either extending the war to North Vietnam or to Cambodia and without the commitment of U.S. tactical units within South Vietnam?

"Answer: Well, I haven't said that. No, I haven't said that."

". . . [W]e ought to step up the status of the, our military." (Former Ambassador Lodge, *ibid.*, June 30, 1964.)

". . . [T]he American force was still basically an advisory organization. Americans, in regular combat units, were not yet engaged on the ground." (Mansfield, *op. cit.*, p. 2.)

". . . [T]he large indigenous support that the Viet-Cong receives means that solutions must be as political and economic as military. Indeed, there can be no such thing as a purely 'military' solution to the war in South Viet-Nam."

"The road ahead in Viet-Nam is going to be long, difficult and frustrating. It will take work, courage, imagination and—perhaps more than anything else—patience to bear the burden of what President Kennedy called a 'long twilight struggle.' In Viet-Nam, it has not been finished in the first hundred days of President Johnson's Administration, and it may not be finished in the first 1,000 days. . . ." (Secretary McNamara, speech on March 26, 1964, *The New York Times,* March 27, 1964.)

"When the day comes that we can safely withdraw, we expect to leave an independent and stable South Viet-Nam, rich with resources and bright with prospects for contributing to the peace and prosperity of Southeast Asia and of the world." *(Ibid.)*

"Well, we're defoliating every day. We're doing a lot of defoliation. . . . It's a military measure. . . . You kill the bushes and the trees and it broadens it out and you can't be ambushed." (Former Ambassador Lodge, *ibid.,* June 30, 1964.)

". . . [C]rops may be grown only to be destroyed by one side or the other. . . . Planes of the United States and South Vietnamese air forces drop napalm bombs on these crops so that they may be burned rather than fall into the hands of the Viet Cong." (Thich Nhat Hanh, *op. cit.,* p. 75.)

1964

Concurrently, the successive Saigon governments entered a new military phase, stressing the need to carry the war into the north itself. To some extent, sabotage operations inside North Vietnam had been in effect since 1957, but not until 1964 did Saigon publicly urge extension of the war northward. The most publicized events reflecting this new strategy were a series of commando raids and bombing runs during July 1964 on North Vietnamese islands and fishing vessels in the Tonkin Gulf.

"South Vietnam's Premier led an orderly mass meeting in a central square in a shout of 'Bac Tien!' ('To the

North!') after a speech putting his Government on the side of those who see an expanded war as the only way to reduce Communist pressure on South Vietnam."

" 'We have often heard that the people have called for the war to be carried to the North.' "

" 'The Government cannot remain indifferent before the firm determination of all the people who are considering the push northward as an appropriate means to fulfill our national history.' " (*The New York Times,* July 20, 1964.)

"We are ready. We could go this afternoon. I cannot assure that all of North Vietnam would be destroyed, but Hanoi would certainly be destroyed." (Vice-Marshal Nguyen Cao Ky, Commander of the Air Force, *ibid.,* July 23, 1964.)

". . . General Taylor told General Khanh at a meeting that . . . an extension of the anti-Communist war would be contrary to the United States' policy.

"The Premier is reported to have replied that, regardless of American policy, an extension was now in fact South Vietnamese policy. This policy was proclaimed in a Government declaration Monday and in public speeches by Premier Khanh and other officials in the last few days."

". . . General Khanh assured General Taylor that there were no basic policy differences—only differences about timing and about what to announce publicly."

"The [South Vietnamese Defense Ministry] . . . did not deny Air Commodore Ky's acknowledgment that South Vietnamese 'combat teams' had been dropped inside North Vietnam on sabotage and intelligence missions in past years—and by implication recently." (Dispatch from Saigon, *ibid.,* July 24, 1964.)

"Yesterday the [North] Vietnamese protested what

they called an attack by United States and South Vietnamese warships on North Vietnamese islands last Thursday." (North Vietnamese protest to the International Control Commission, *ibid.*, August 3, 1964.)

1964

Immediately thereafter, the United States undertook retaliatory air action against North Vietnam in response to presumed Communist torpedo boat attacks on the destroyers Maddox *and* Turner Joy. *Congress gave immediate support to the President in this action. The Tonkin Gulf Resolution of August 7, 1964, passed unanimously in the House and with only two dissenting votes in the Senate, expressed strong Congressional approval of such retaliatory measures. This Resolution further authorized the President to take future military action as he saw fit to counteract attacks on United States forces and to assist SEATO members, including the protocol states, who requested aid for defense.*

"[The *Maddox*] was attacked approximately 2 days after this alleged South Vietnamese attack and at a time when she was well off the coast of North Viet-Nam, and the *Maddox* . . . had no connection whatever with whatever may have been going on in connection with these islands." (Assistant Secretary of State for Far Eastern Affairs William P. Bundy, *Department of State Bulletin,* September 7, 1964.)

"But this Gulf of Tonkin incident, if I may say so, was a very vague one. We were briefed on it, but we have no way of knowing, even to this day, what actually happened. I don't know whether we provoked that attack in connection with supervising or helping a raid by South Vietnamese or not. Our evidence was sketchy as to whether those PT boats, or some kind of boats, that were approaching were coming to investigate or whether they actually attacked. I have been *told* there was no physical damage. They weren't hit by anything. I heard one man say there was one bullet hole in one of those ships. One bullet hole!" (Senator J. William Fulbright, Chairman, Senate Foreign Relations Committee, "Why Our Foreign Policy Is Failing," *Look,* May 3, 1966.)

"High-ranking Defense officials . . . insist that on the basis of the evidence that there can be no question that the two destroyers came under torpedo attack on Aug. 4.

"In part, this conclusion rests on such circumstantial evidence as the sighting of a North Vietnamese torpedo boat by both radar and navy planes flying overhead."

"A Pentagon spokesman acknowledged that some of the sonar reports of incoming torpedoes undoubtedly were erroneous. But he contended that the sighting of the wake of one torpedo, which had already been spotted on sonar, provided direct and conclusive evidence that at least one torpedo had been fired." (*The New York Times,* December 22, 1967.)

"(a) Evaluation of info from various sources indicates DRV considers patrol directly involved with 34A ops [South Vietnamese attacks on North Vietnamese islands and installations in the Tonkin Gulf]. DRV considers U.S. ships present as enemies because of these ops and have already indicated their readiness to treat us in that category. (b) DRV very sensitive about Hon Me, believe this is PT operating base, and the cove there presently contains numerous patrol and PT craft which have been repositioned from northerly bases. (c) Defense against PT's very difficult when in close proximity to Hon Me in that they can hide behind it until the opportune moment and start their run leaving very little time for tracking and spotting and allowing no international water working space for aircraft. (d) Under these conditions 15 minutes reaction time for obtaining air cover is unaccceptable. Cover must be overhead and controlled by DD's at all times. (Cable from Commander Task Group 72.1, embarked in *Maddox,* fifteen hours before second Tonkin Gulf incident, August 4, 1964, U.S. Senate, *The Gulf of Tonkin, The 1964 Incidents,* 90th Congress, 2nd Session, Government Printing Office: 1968, p. 40.)

". . . '[T]he first boat to close the Maddox probably fired a torpedo at the Maddox which was heard but not seen. All subsequent torpedo reports are doubtful in that it is suspected that sonar man was hearing ship's own propeller beat.' " (Message from U.S.S. *Maddox,* 6 p.m., EDT, to commander in chief, Pacific fleet [received in Washington, D.C., at 10:59 p.m., approximately one hour before the beginning of air attacks on North Vietnam by U.S. planes], Los Angeles *Times,* February 23, 1968.)

"Review of action makes many recorded contacts and torpedoes fired appear doubtful. Freak weather effects and over-eager sonarman may have accounted for many reports. No actual visual sightings by *Maddox.* Suggest complete evaluation before any further action." (Message from Task Group Commander to CINCPAC Fleet immediately following the second Tonkin Gulf incident, August 4, 1964, U.S. Senate, *The Gulf of Tonkin, The 1964 Incidents,* p. 54.)

"The Security Council . . . [c]ondemns reprisals as incompatible with the purposes and principles of the United Nations. . . ." (U.N. Security Council Resolution, April 9, 1964, referring to complaint of the Yemen Arab Republic regarding British air attack on Yemeni territory.)

"That the Congress approves and supports the determination of the President, as Commander in Chief, to take all necessary measures to repel any armed attack against the forces of the United States and to prevent further aggression.

"SEC. 2. The United States regards as vital to its national interest and to world peace the maintenance of international peace and security in southeast Asia. . . . [T]he United States is, therefore, prepared, as the President determines, to take all necessary steps, including the use of armed force, to assist any member or protocol state of the Southeast Asia Collective Defense Treaty requesting assistance in defense of its freedom." (Joint Resolution, U.S. Congress ["Tonkin Gulf Resolution"], August 7, 1964, *Department of State Bulletin,* August 24, 1964.)

"Mr. FULBRIGHT: It was testified that they went in at least 11 miles in order to show that we do not recognize a 12-mile limit, which I believe North Viet-Nam has asserted.

"Mr. NELSON [Senator Gaylord Nelson of Wisconsin]: The patrolling was for the purpose of demonstrating to the North Vietnamese that we did not recognize a 12-mile limit?

"Mr. FULBRIGHT: . . . That was one reason given. . . .

"Mr. NELSON: . . . [I]t would be mighty risky, if Cuban PT boats were firing on Florida, for Russian armed ships or destroyers to be patrolling between us and Cuba, 11 miles out." (*Congressional Record,* Senate, August 6, 1964.)

"Mr. BREWSTER [Senator Daniel B. Brewster of Maryland]: . . . I would look with great dismay on a situation involving the landing of large land armies on the continent of Asia. So my question is whether there is anything in the resolution which would authorize or recommend or approve the landing of large American armies in Vietnam or in China.

"Mr. FULBRIGHT: There is nothing in the resolution, as I read it, that contemplates it. I agree with the Senator that that is the last thing we would want to do. However, the language of the resolution would not prevent it. It would authorize whatever the Commander in Chief feels is necessary. It does not restrain the Executive from doing it. . . . Speaking for my own committee, everyone I have heard has said that the last thing we want to do is to become involved in a land war in Asia. . . ." (*Ibid.*, Senate, August 5, 1964.)

1964

Because the United States would soon be preoccupied with the 1964 election campaign, the President had asked Congress for immediate action on the Tonkin Gulf Resolution to resolve the problem in advance. However, Vietnam policy did become a fundamental campaign issue, with the Republican candidate, Senator Barry Goldwater, advocating immediate offensive action by United States forces while President Johnson argued against enlarging the war. President Johnson won the election by an overwhelming margin.

"The supplies of the Communist invaders have got to be shut off.

"This means threatening or actually interdicting the supply routes from Red China, Laos, and Cambodia.

"It does not mean bombing Vietnamese, or even bombing Vietnamese cities.

"It could mean messing up some roads, hitting some depots, and stopping some shipping." ("Barry Goldwater, A Report in Depth," *Newsbook*. The National Observer: 1964, pp. 157-158.)

". . . '[T]en years ago we should have bombed North Vietnam, destroyed the only access they had to North Vietnam, with no risk to our lives' (the previous day he had mused aloud to the students how ten years ago we might have dropped a low-yield atom bomb on North Vietnam to defoliate the trees)." (Senator Goldwater quoted in Theodore H. White, *The Making of a President 1964*. Atheneum: 1965, p. 106.)

"Some of our people—Mr. Nixon, Mr. Rockefeller, Mr. Scranton, and Mr. Goldwater—have all, at some time or other, suggested the possible wisdom of going north in Viet-Nam. Well, now, before you start attacking someone and you launch a big offensive, you better give some consideration to how you are going to protect what you have." (President Johnson, speech in Manchester, New Hampshire, September 28, 1964, *The Public Papers of the President of the United States, Lyndon B. Johnson, 1963-1964,* Book II. Government Printing Office: 1965, p. 607.)

"I have had advice to load our planes with bombs and to drop them on certain areas that I think would enlarge the war and escalate the war, and result in our committing a good many American boys to fighting a war that I think ought to be fought by the boys of Asia to help protect their own land.

"And for that reason, I haven't chosen to enlarge the war." (President Johnson, speech in Stonewall, Texas, August 29, 1964, *ibid.,* p. 544).

"In order to make his opponent appear reckless and trigger happy, the President in several statements set limits to American participation in the Vietnamese conflict. . . . 'Perhaps,' Secretary Rusk was quoted in the New York *Times* as saying, 'the Communist world misunderstood our Presidential campaign.' Perhaps indeed, it did. But whose fault was that?" (Representative Goodell of New York, *Congressional Record,* House, August 25, 1965.)

". . . [W]e seek no wider war. . . . We have made it clear that we cannot exclude the possibility that wider action against the North might become necessary, and we have carefully studied what might be involved, and all the rest, but I think it is clear enough that anything in the nature of attacks on North Viet-Nam of a systematic character by the South Vietnamese or by ourselves would involve very grave issues and we would, therefore, prefer to pursue the policy we are now pursuing of maximum assistance in South Viet-Nam." (Assistant Secretary Bundy, *Department of State Bulletin,* September 7, 1964.)

"Expansion of the war outside South Viet-Nam, while not a course we want or seek, could be forced upon us by the increased external pressures of the Communists, including a rising scale of infiltration." (*Ibid.,* October 19, 1964.)

SUMMARY

Between the death of President Kennedy at the end of 1963 and the election of President Johnson a year later, various pressures worked in combination to change the character of the Vietnamese conflict. An augmented United States military presence sought to salvage the political failure of successive Saigon regimes and to hold the line against increasing NLF strength. Two developments during this short period forecast the course that the war would take in the immediate future. First, direct United States air attacks on North Vietnam indicated a shift of emphasis in American policy from supporting a democratic government in South Vietnam to defeating a hostile government in North Vietnam. Second, the Tonkin Gulf Resolution, although aimed at an immediate, specific threat, nonetheless gave the President wide dis-

cretionary powers for handling future general threats. Though the official American position remained that this was strictly a Vietnamese conflict, in practical terms the war was becoming more and more American, both in its direction and in its prosecution. Almost immediately after Johnson became President in his own right in January 1965, the practical results of these developments were to become apparent.

"We either have to get out or take some action to help the Vietnamese. They won't help themselves. We made a big mistake in going there, but I can't figure out any way to get out without scaring the rest of the world." (Senator Russell, *The New York Times,* November 27, 1964.

"It would be impossible for Max [General Taylor] to talk to these people [the press] without leaving the impression the situation is going to hell." (Secretary McNamara, *ibid.,* December 2, 1964.)

". . . [T]he survival of an independent government in South Viet-Nam is so important to the security of Southeast Asia and to the free world that I can conceive of no alternative other than to take all necessary measures within our capability to prevent a Communist victory." (Secretary McNamara, speech before the House Armed Services Committee, January 27, 1964, Raskin and Fall, *op. cit.,* p. 394.)

"We ought to carry on and never give up because we are frustrated and discouraged." (General Taylor, quoted in *Le Monde,* January 11, 1965.)

"The confidence of the peasants was inevitably shaken by the disruptions in leadership and the loss of physical security. Army and paramilitary desertion rates increased, and the morale of the hamlet militia . . . fell."

"Although we estimate that in South Viet-Nam's 14 million population, there are only 20 to 25 thousand 'hard core' Viet-Cong guerrillas, they have been able to recruit from among the South Vietnamese an irregular force of from 60 to 80 thousand. . . ." (Secretary Mc-Namara, speech March 26, 1964, *The New York Times*, March 27, 1964.)

"If you were to cut off all the help from North Vietnam the Vietcong north of Saigon would be very badly affected, because they depend on that line of supply to a considerable extent.

"The Vietcong south of Saigon could go on for a long, long time, because they can live off the country. It's one of the most fantastically rich food-growing areas I've ever seen in my life."

"There are such tremendous long coastlines and tremendous long frontiers—tremendously rough country. There isn't a superhighway that you can blow it up with bombs and stop the—and stop the supplies. . . ." (Former Ambassador Lodge, *ibid.*, June 30, 1964.)

". . . [I]t is clear to me that the time may come in our relations to Southeast Asia when we must declare our intention to attack the source of guerrilla aggression in North Vietnam and impose on the Hanoi government a price for participating in the current war which is commensurate with the damage being inflicted on its neighbors in the south." (General Taylor, quoted in a letter from President Johnson to Senator Henry M. Jackson, *ibid.*, March 3, 1967. Taylor's statement was written November 3, 1961.)

". . . [W]e must do the best we can with the forces we have deployed to Vietnam, keeping in mind the true meaning of strategy in global affairs. . . . On the other hand, tactical mistakes that are allowed to escalate at the

initiative of an enemy could be disastrously costly."
(Lt. Gen. James M. Gavin, "A Communication on Vietnam," *Harper's Magazine,* February, 1966.)

". . . Congress was asked to show its support for the
President in a crisis . . . without question or hesitation, it
did so. The Senate Foreign Relations and Armed Services
Committees endorsed the resolution [Tonkin Gulf
Resolution] after perfunctory hearings and with only one
dissenting vote on the morning of August 6."

"Since its adoption the Administration has converted
the Vietnamese conflict from a civil war in which some
American advisors were involved to a major international
war in which the principal fighting unit is an American
army of hundreds of thousands of men. Each time Senators have raised questions about successive escalations of
the war, we have the blank check of August 7, 1964,
waved in our faces as supposed evidence of the overwhelming support of the Congress for a policy in Southeast Asia which in fact has been radically changed since
the summer of 1964."

"Had we met our responsibility of careful examination
of a Presidential request, had the Senate Foreign Relations Committee held hearings on the resolution before
recommending its adoption, had the Senate debated the
resolution and considered its implications before giving its
overwhelming approval, and specifically had we investi-
gated carefully and thoroughly the alleged unprovoked
attacks on our ships, we might have put limits and qualifications on our endorsement of future uses of force in
Southeast Asia, if not in the resolution itself then in the
legislative history preceding its adoption. As it was, only
Senators Morse of Oregon and Gruening of Alaska opposed the resolution." (J. William Fulbright, *The Arrogance of Power.* Random House: 1966, pp. 50-51.)

". . . [I]t must be remembered that the resolution

was adopted during an election campaign in which the President was telling the American people that it would be a mistake for the United States to become involved in a major war in Asia while criticizing his opponent for proposing just that." (*Ibid.*, p. 52.)

". . . I feel that I was misled that this was an entirely unprovoked attack, that our ships were entirely on routine patrol. The fact stands from today that they were intelligence ships; that they were under instructions to agitate North Vietnam radar, that they were plying close to the shore within 4 miles of the islands under orders in the daytime, retiring at night; that they were covered with immediate air cover which, in itself—that they were covered with military aircraft which you said on television the other day which would be provocative off of North Korea. Why it would not be provocative off of North Vietnam I do not know.

". . . I think that from my tentative conclusion it is that the administration was hasty, acted precipitately, inadvisably, unwisely, out of proportion to the provocation in launching 64 bombing attacks on North Vietnam out of a confused, uncertain situation on a murky night, which one of the sailors described as one dark as the knob of hell; and, particularly, 5 hours after the task force commander had cabled that he doubted that there were any attacks, and recommended no further action be taken until it was thoroughly canvassed and reviewed." (Senator Albert Gore, U.S. Senate, *The Gulf of Tonkin, The 1964 Incidents*, p. 102.)

"We had contingent drafts [of the Tonkin Resolution] . . . for some time prior [to August 1964]."

"We had always anticipated . . . the possibility that things might take a more drastic turn at any time and that it would be wise to seek an affirmation of the desires of and intent of the Congress. But that is normal planning. I

am not sure that my drafts were even known to others."
(Assistant Secretary Bundy, *The New York Times,* December 22, 1967.)

". . . [I]nsofar as the use of our combat ground forces are concerned, that took place, of course, only in the spring of 1965.

"In the air, we had been participating more actively over two or three years." (General Taylor, U.S. Senate, *Supplemental Foreign Assistance Fiscal Year 1966 —Vietnam,* 89th Congress, 2nd Session, Government Printing Office: 1966, p. 450.)

"The American command emphasizes that U.S. forces in Vietnam are there to support the Vietnamese and their Armed Forces in the effort to resist aggression by infiltration from the north and terrorism and subversion from within. Vietnamese sovereignty and the paramount role of the Vietnamese are meticulously respected and the supporting nature of the U.S. role is stressed." (Mansfield, *op. cit.,* pp. 2-3.)

"The Vietnamese army is fed, clothed, and armed from the American budget; its guns, bullets, and planes all come from America. In Vietnam people refer to gasoline as being typical of the American control; the army would be powerless without the use of American gasoline. Without gasoline every army activity would be cut off. . . . Thus everyone knows that the Vietnam policy is made by Americans and that everything that Vietnam does, the United States is responsible for." (Thich Nhat Hanh, *op. cit.,* p. 63.)

PART IV: ESCALATION, 1965-1968

1965

*Since 1965, the Vietnamese conflict has stead-
ily escalated both in military practice and in
concept. The initial events that heralded an open-ended
policy of increasing American involvement took place
soon after the turn of the year in 1965. Within three
weeks of his inauguration, President Johnson ordered air
attacks on North Vietnam in retaliation for guerrilla raids
in South Vietnam. Twenty-three days later, the President
initiated the first non-retaliatory bombing raids on North
Vietnam. At approximately the same time the United
States employed planes against the Vietcong in the south.*

"Approximately 24 hours ago, at 2 a.m. Sunday morning, February 7, Saigon time, the Viet-Nam Communist
guerrillas carried out three attacks, one against installations in the Pleiku area, which is in the central part of
South Viet-Nam, a second at Tuy Hoa, with an airstrip
adjacent to it, an area near the coast, and a third against
Viet-Nam villages near Nha Trang."

". . . Immediately following, the United States representatives in Saigon met with representatives of the South
Vietnamese Government. They jointly agreed that joint
retaliatory action was required."

". . . [E]lements of the U.S. and South Vietnamese

Air Forces were directed to launch joint retaliatory attacks against barracks and staging areas in the southern portion of North Viet-Nam." (Secretary McNamara, *Department of State Bulletin,* February 22, 1965.)

"As in the case of the North Vietnamese attacks in the Gulf of Tonkin last August, the response is appropriate and fitting." (President Johnson, White House statement, February 7, 1965, *ibid.*)

"If we hadn't given an adequate response, we might have given the impression we might pull out." (Senate Minority Leader Everett Dirksen, *The New York Times,* February 9, 1965.)

". . . [W]ho gave the United States the right to retaliate against the actions of guerrillas in South Vietnam, the defeats that the occupationists and their henchmen are suffering there, by bombing the territory of a third country—the Democratic Republic of Vietnam? . . ."
". . . [T]he Soviet Union will be forced, together with its allies and friends, to take further measures to safeguard the security and strengthen the defense capability of the Democratic Republic of Vietnam." (Soviet Government statement, *ibid.,* February 9, 1965.)

"In point of fact, the United States has already embarked on the course of expanding the war beyond South Vietnam." (Peking statement, *ibid.,* February 9, 1965.)

". . . [E]arly in 1965, the President was advised that morale in South Vietnam could be revived only if we bombed military targets in North Vietnam. This would assure Saigon of our determination to stay the course, and perhaps, if we were lucky, would so weaken Hanoi's will to fight that we could avoid the unpleasant, looming need to send in large numbers of combat troops. Thus the most fateful decision of all was made. The war went North." (Richard N. Goodwin [former Assistant to the President], *Triumph or Tragedy: Reflections on Vietnam.* Random House: 1966, p. 31.)

"I do not know of any element in the Vietnamese situation which caused longer debate, longer discussions." (Maxwell D. Taylor, *Responsibility and Response.* Harper: 1967, pp. 25-26.)

"American commanders in Saigon were instructed to prepare for a continuing aerial offensive, but publicly and with announcements.

"Ambassador Maxwell D. Taylor argued for silence, but was overruled by the argument that clandestine raids would be politically unpopular in the United States." (Dispatch from Saigon, *The New York Times,* March 1, 1965.)

"The Administration described today's air strikes against North Vietnam as part of a 'continuing' effort to resist aggression and made no attempt, as in the past, to relate them to particular provocations." (*Ibid.,* March 3, 1965.)

"The Governments of the Republic of Vietnam and of the United States wish to avoid widening the conflict, but they are compelled to make clear to Hanoi that North Vietnam will be held fully accountable for continuing aggression against South Vietnam." (Statement by the Government of South Vietnam and the American Mission, *ibid.,* March 3, 1965.)

"The United States Embassy disclosed today that American jet aircraft were sent on air strikes against the Vietcong in South Vietnam during the last week."
" 'Such action was carried out because of the concen-

tration of Vietcong in this area as a result of increased infiltration of men and equipment in recent months.

" 'This is consistent with the Congressional resolution approving and supporting the determination of the President as Commander in Chief to prevent any further aggression and is in accordance with the Government's stated policy of continuous action that is appropriate, fitting and measured.' " (*Ibid.*, February 25, 1965.)

1965

Simultaneously, the administration issued a comprehensive reevaluation of the character of the conflict, defining it as a war of foreign aggression and rejecting the concept that it was, or had been, a civil war.

"Not too many years ago Viet-Nam was a peaceful, if troubled, land. In the North was an independent Communist government. In the South a people struggled to build a Nation with the friendly help of the United States.

"There were some in South Viet-Nam who wished to force Communist rule on their own people. But their progress was slight. Their hope of success was dim. Then, little more than 6 years ago, North Viet-Nam decided on conquest. And from that day to this, soldiers and supplies have moved from North to South in a swelling stream that swallowed the remnants of revolution in aggression." (President Johnson, State of the Union Message, January 12, 1966, *Weekly Compilation of Presidential Documents,* January 17, 1966.)

"The basic pattern of Viet Cong (Vietnamese Communist) activity is not new, of course. It operated, with minor variations, in China, and Mao Tse-tung's theories on the conduct of guerrilla warfare are known to every Viet Cong agent and cadre. Most of the same methods were used in Malaya, in Greece, in the Philippines, in

Cuba, and in Laos." (*A Threat to the Peace: North Viet-Nam's Effort to Conquer South Viet-Nam.* Department of State Publication No. 7308, 1961, p. 1.)

"Viet-Nam is *not* another Greece, where indigenous guerrilla forces used friendly neighboring territory as a sanctuary.

"Viet-Nam is *not* another Malaya, where Communist guerrillas were, for the most part, physically distinguishable from the peaceful majority they sought to control.

"Viet-Nam is *not* another Philippines, where Communist guerrillas were physically separated from the source of their moral and physical support." (*Aggression From the North* [1965], p. 1.)

"I continue to hear and see nonsense about the nature of the struggle there. . . . There is no evidence that the Viet Cong has any significant popular following in South Viet-Nam." (Secretary Rusk, *Department of State Bulletin,* May 10, 1965.)

"Guerrilla warfare requires a highly committed but covert civilian support which cannot be obtained at gun point."

"Politically and militarily, revolutionary guerrillas are, by and large, a self-sustaining group who can go on fighting indefinitely even if infiltration from across the border stops. . . . [T]he assumption that a guerrilla outfit, like a conventional army, can be controlled and commanded by a foreign or externally based government, ignores the organizational, psychological, and political facts of revolutionary warfare. The distrust of the 'home-based' guerrillas, even for their own government in exile, cannot be overstated. The resourceful and tough 'interior' leaders and cadres who face the enemy daily . . . are not easily controlled from abroad and make suspicious, exacting, and hard-to-please allies."

"In Vietnam, the signs are clear. The South Vietnamese regime has no legitimacy, and no government backed by a Western power can hope for popular support in a country where the Communists have capitalized on the nationalist appeal of restoring independence and unity, and where the pro-Western leaders have been Bao Dai, Diem, and the musical-chair generals."

". . . [A]rmies trained for conventional combat follow a vicious logic of escalation, which derives from acute frustration over an elusive war that puts in question not only their effectiveness but the very validity of their training and organization. . . . Hence the compulsion to believe that behind the popular behavior lies the terror of an army trained, equipped, and directed by a foreign power. . . ." (Eqbal Ahmad, "Revolutionary Warfare," Gettleman, *op. cit.,* pp. 357-361.)

"For if the Vietnam war were merely what the Communists say it is, an indigenous rebellion, then the United States has no business taking sides in the conflict and helping one side to defeat the other by force of arms." (Address by George W. Ball, January 30, 1966, *Congressional Record,* Senate, January 31, 1966.)

"There is no evidence of any action by North Viet-Nam which could be regarded as an armed attack upon the South prior to 1958, after Ho Chi Minh had engaged in four years of fruitless effort to carry out the resolutions of the Geneva Conference. In these circumstances Ho Chi Minh's action in support of the Viet-Cong did not constitute aggression or armed attack in international relations but civil strife within the domestic jurisdiction of Viet-Nam, similar to the action of the North against the South in the American Civil War. . . . [T]he United States response by bombings in North Viet-Nam, . . . violated international law. . . ." (Quincy Wright, "Legal Aspects of the Viet-Nam Situation," *The American Journal of International Law,* October, 1966.)

1965

Two months later, the President identified China as the real enemy behind the North Vietnamese aggression.

"Over this war—all Asia—is another reality: the deepening shadow of Communist China. The rulers in Hanoi are urged on by Peiping. . . . It is a nation which is helping the forces of violence in almost every continent. The contest in Viet-Nam is part of a wider pattern of aggressive purposes." (President Johnson, speech on April 7, 1965, *Department of State Bulletin*, April 26, 1965.)

1965

Hanoi's response to American and South Vietnamese escalation was initially conditioned by renewed international attempts to stimulate negotiations. As they had in 1964, Secretary General U Thant, Pope Paul, France, and the Soviet Union proposed separate plans for bringing the conflict to the negotiating table. North Vietnam signified its interest in these proposals, but the United States and South Vietnam did not. Significantly, the People's Republic of China declared that the "only way out" would be the immediate and complete withdrawal of American troops. Relations between the Soviet Union and China had seriously deteriorated by that time, and China's more extreme demands attested to a widening Sino-Soviet split.

". . . I do feel very strongly that means must be found, and found urgently, within or outside the United Nations, of shifting the quest for a solution away from the field of battle to the conference table.

"In this connection I believe that arrangements could

be devised under which a dialogue could take place between the principal parties with a view, among others, to
preparing the ground for wider and more formal discussions." (Secretary-General U Thant, *The New York
Times,* February 13, 1965.)

"I strongly hope that there will be a prompt follow-up
on the stated willingness of the parties directly involved to
enter into discussions and that no effort will be spared to
get discussions started with a minimum of delay. . . .
The world, which is gravely threatened by this conflict, is
certainly due this much." (Secretary-General U Thant,
UN Monthly Chronicle, May, 1965.)

"We have undertaken to approach, or to have approached, in a confidential manner, representative personalities of various governments to ask them with
insistence to contribute to an honorable and peaceful
solution to various international difficulties that cannot
but be gravely worrisome. . . ." (Pope Paul VI, *The New
York Times,* February 21, 1965.)

"We think that the negotiations should be engaged as
soon as possible.
"A long time, in our opinion, has already been lost,
and the more we wait the more, of course, the situation
deteriorates, and the more it is difficult to arrive at a satisfactory settlement." (Foreign Minister of France Maurice Couve de Murville, *ibid.,* February 22, 1965.)

"General de Gaulle proposed a meeting of the major
powers, including China, on the future of the United Nations on February 4. Six days later the French Cabinet
renewed its appeal for a meeting of the Geneva conference as a forum for a negotiated settlement of the war in
South Vietnam."
"North Vietnam recently urged France to intensify her

efforts for a negotiated settlement of the war in South
Vietnam, a reliable French source said today."

"Diplomatic sources have reported Foreign Minister
Maurice Couve de Murville as having said, as early as
last December, that President Ho Chi Minh had told
France that he wanted to discuss the basis for an accom-
modation with the United States. . . ." (*Ibid.,* February
23, 1965.)

"The friends of peace ask for a strict application of the
Geneva accords in order to prevent an escalation of the
conflict to all of Southeast Asia and to find at a conference table the measures permitting a solution of the Indo-
chinese problems. . . ." (Soviet Premier Kosygin, *Le
Monde,* March 3, 1965.)

"The Communist Government of North Vietnam has
notified the Secretary General, U Thant, that it is recep-
tive to his suggestion for informal negotiations on the
Vietnam situation." (*The New York Times,* February 26,
1965.)

"There is indeed an honorable way out for the United
States. . . . [I]mmediately stop its armed intervention,
and aggression in Vietnam, and immediately withdraw all
its armed forces from South Vietnam in accordance with
the 1954 Geneva Agreements. This is the only way for
the United States to save its face, and there is no other
way out." (Chinese Government statement, March 4,
1965, FBIS *Daily Report,* March 5, 1965, BBB5.)

"The Government [of South Vietnam] . . . said it
would reject 'any international solution which has not received the agreement of the Government and the people
of Vietnam.'

" 'The question of negotiation is entirely an internal
Vietnamese problem and one the South Vietnamese Gov-

ernment has never tackled.'" (Premier Quat of South Vietnam, *The New York Times,* March 2, 1965.)

"There are no authorized negotiations under way with Mr. Thant or any other government. . . .

"I am not going into any diplomatic chitchat that may be going forth, or way-out feelers, . . . But authorized or meaningful negotiations—no." (White House Press Secretary George E. Reedy, *ibid.,* February 25, 1965.)

"Political channels have been and are open, and a considerable number of governments are actively interested in keeping them open to explore the possibilities of a peaceful solution. But a negotiation aimed at the acceptance or the confirmation of aggression is not possible." (Secretary Rusk, February 25, 1965, *Department of State Bulletin,* March 15, 1965.)

". . . [W]hen we began the bombings there was no talk of negotiations." (President Johnson, *ibid.,* May 24, 1965.)

1965

Meanwhile, the United States intensified its military efforts. It began systematic heavy bombing in South Vietnam and adopted a schedule of continuous air raids on North Vietnam. Beginning with the assignment of small units of Marines for security purposes, the U.S. troop commitment climbed in 1965 from 23,000 to 170,000.

"At the request of the Government of Viet-Nam, U.S. Air Force F-100 and B-57 aircraft from Bien Hoa and Da Nang participated in a combined airstrike west of An Khe in Binh Dinh Province on the afternoon of February 24. This strike was launched in order to assist in an attack against large Viet Cong forces in the mountain pass between An Khe and Pleiku and to assist in the extrication of an isolated unit under heavy attack.

"U.S. jet aircraft have participated in similar combined operations on a number of occasions during the past week. Use of American aircraft stationed in Viet-Nam to reinforce the capability of the Vietnamese Air Force is in keeping with the announced U.S. policy of providing maximum assistance to the Government of South Viet-Nam in its effort to repel the Communist aggression directed and supported by the Hanoi regime." (Statement by American Embassy, Saigon, February 24, 1965, *Department of State Bulletin,* March 15, 1965.)

"More than 70 United States Air Force planes unleashed the greatest incendiary attack of the war on a Vietcong concentration 25 miles northwest of Saigon." (*The New York Times,* April 1, 1965.)

"United States and South Vietnamese fighter-bombers, in the largest air strike of the war, dropped 1,000 tons of bombs today on what was described as a major stronghold of the Vietcong.

"In a dawn-to-dusk raid, 230 aircraft saturated a heavily wooded area in Tayninh Province. . . ." (*Ibid.,* April 16, 1965.)

"The United States attack on North Vietnam today was another attempt to increase the pressure by which Washington hopes to force Hanoi to end its support of the Communist insurgency in South Vietnam."

"Thus far, officials reiterated, there has been no such sign, but the indications were that Washington would now give North Vietnam a few days' respite for further diplomatic activity." (*Ibid.,* March 16, 1965.)

"Apparently indicating that the strategy of bombing

targets in North Vietnam to force it to cease supporting the Vietcong would be maintained, the President said, 'We will try to take such measures as are appropriate and fitting, and measures that are calculated to deter the aggressor.' " (*Ibid., April 2, 1965.*)

"Early in 1965 we knew that the enemy hoped to deliver the *coup de grâce* by launching a major summer offensive to cut the Republic of Vietnam in two with a drive across the central highlands to the sea. I had to make a decision, and did. I chose a rapid build-up of combat forces, in the full knowledge that we should not have a very fully developed logistic base to support those forces." ("General Westmoreland Reports on Vietnam War," *U.S. News & World Report,* November 28, 1966.)

"*Mr. Niven:* Mr. Secretary, will the 3,500 U.S. Marines who are going into South Viet-Nam merely defend U.S. installations, or will they also be available for combat duty?

"*Secretary Rusk:* The purpose of those Marines is to provide local close-in security for the Marines who are already at Da Nang with the Hawk missiles and other American personnel there in connection with aircraft. It is not their mission to engage in the pacification operations. . . ."

"*Mr. Niven:* . . . Do you exclude the possibility of their getting into action against the Viet Cong?

"*Secretary Rusk:* Oh, I think there is no doubt . . . that if they are shot at, they will shoot back. But their mission is the security of the Da Nang Air Base." (*Department of State Bulletin,* March 29, 1965.)

"Well, as a matter of fact, the South Vietnamese themselves have felt that ground combat personnel is not what is needed. They have very substantial armed forces that are fighting with effectiveness and with gallantry. . . .

[T]he South Vietnamese Government has not asked for international ground forces to support their effort in South Viet-Nam." (Secretary Rusk, *ibid.*)

"Well, the South Korean personnel that are going into South Viet-Nam are not going there for combat purposes. They will be primarily engaged, I understand, on engineering tasks here and there." (Secretary Rusk, *ibid.*, March 15, 1965.)

"Senator GORE: . . . Will you tell us what aid other countries are providing in Vietnam, if any?
"Mr. BELL [David E. Bell, former Administrator, AID]: Yes, sir. Fortunately we are not doing all the fighting. . . . There is a Korean division which is fighting there. . . ." (U.S. Senate, *Supplemental Foreign Assistance Fiscal Year 1966—Vietnam,* p. 122.)

"By December 1965 . . . there were approximately 170,000 U.S. troops in South Vietnam. Additionally, there were about 21,000 soldiers and marines from the Republic of Korea. . . ."
"In the month of November 1965, alone, 469 Americans were killed in action, a figure representing about 35 percent of all Americans killed in action in the war until that date. In addition, 1,470 Americans were listed as wounded and 33 as missing." (Mansfield, *op. cit.,* pp. 2, 4.)

" . . . [F]urther increases in forces, military personnel, production and construction will be required if we are to deploy additional forces to Southeast Asia and provide for combat consumption while, at the same time, maintaining our capabilities to deal with crises elsewhere in the world." (Secretary McNamara, August 4, 1965, in *Why Vietnam.* Government Printing Office: 1965, p. 23.)

1965

In the middle of March, seventeen non-aligned nations, gathered in Belgrade under the guidance of Presidents Tito of Yugoslavia and Ben Bella of Algeria, issued a plea to all parties for immediate negotiations. The United States, while it hailed the motives of the signatories, replied that North Vietnam must first cease its "aggression" against South Vietnam before negotiations could begin. Both Hanoi and the National Liberation Front, under the pressure of increased bombing, categorically rejected the plea and enunciated, instead, the Chinese position. Moscow supported the positions of Hanoi and the Front, speaking in much harsher terms than previously.

"[W]e are firmly convinced that, irrespective of possible differences in appraising various elements in the existing situation in Vietnam, the only way leading to the termination of the conflict consists in seeking a peaceful solution through negotiations. We therefore make an urgent appeal to the parties concerned to start such negotiations, as soon as possible, without posing any preconditions. . . ." (Seventeen-Nation Appeal, March 15, 1965, *Department of State Bulletin,* April 26, 1965.)

"[I]n a letter . . . to President Tito of Yugoslavia . . . Mr. Johnson said negotiations could take place only if 'Hanoi shows itself willing to leave its neighbors alone.' " (*The New York Times,* March 14, 1965.)

"The signatory nations point out that they are 'deeply concerned' at the aggravation of the situation in Vietnam. And so are we. We should end the war by ensuring the independence of South Vietnam.

"The basic cause of the conflict in Vietnam is the at-

tack by North Vietnam on the independent nation of
South Vietnam. The object of that attack is total conquest."

"Peace in Southeast Asia demands an independent
South Vietnam—securely guaranteed and able to shape
its own relationships to all others—free from outside interference—tied to no alliance—a military base for no
other country.

"These are the essentials of a final settlement.

"We will never be second in the search for such a
peaceful settlement in Vietnam."

"We have stated this position over and over again, to
friend and foe alike. And we remain ready—with this
purpose—for unconditional discussions.

"We believe that peace can be achieved in Southeast
Asia the moment that aggression from North Vietnam is
eliminated." (Acting Secretary George W. Ball, reply to
the seventeen non-aligned nations, *Department of State
Bulletin,* April 26, 1965.)

"Tito has thus played the role of a stoolpigeon of the
United States in this peace fraud. . . . There can be no
question of negotiating with American imperialism at a
time when it openly declares and brazenly steps up the
war of aggression in South Vietnam and extends this war
to North Vietnam. . . ." (FBIS *Daily Report,* March
19, 1965, JJJ2; March 24, 1965, BBB9, JJJ11, Hanoi
reply to seventeen non-aligned nations.)

". . . All negotiations with the U.S. imperialists at this
moment are entirely useless if they still refuse to withdraw from South Vietnam all their troops and all kinds of
of war materials and means and those of their satellites. . . ." (Statement of the Central Committee,
National Liberation Front, March 22, 1965, Gettleman,
op. cit., p. 414.)

". . . [T]he United States Government [must] stop at once its aggressive acts against the DRV, withdraw all its troops and weapons from South Vietnam, and let the Vietnamese people decide their internal affairs by themselves." (Letter from Moscow for co-chairmen of the 1954 Geneva Conference, FBIS *Daily Report,* March 19, 1965, JJJ1.)

1965

> *During the remainder of the year, the international community made repeated appeals for a cessation of bombing and an end to hostilities.*

"QUESTION: Mr. Secretary, there have been reports that General de Gaulle is waiting for the right moment to try to personally negotiate an end to the Viet-Nam war. Would we welcome any such efforts by de Gaulle?

"ANSWER: . . . Neither we nor the other side has, so far as I know, nominated attorneys in this field. But, nevertheless, the fact that many governments are interested, that there are many contacts all over the world, is itself I think positive. . . . This is the way that other crises have been resolved. Thus far my own antennae have not picked up this key signal, but the antennae are very much alert." (Secretary Rusk's news conference, August 27, 1965, *Department of State Bulletin,* September 20, 1965.)

"If, then, a series of increasingly powerful retaliatory strikes against North Vietnam does not bring about this preliminary condition of cease-fire, surely serious consideration must be given to every other way in which the stalemate might be broken."

"There does appear to be at least a possibility that a pause in such air strikes against North Vietnam at the right time might provide the Hanoi authorities with an opportunity, if they wish to take it, to inject some flexibility into the policy without appearing to do so as the direct result of military pressure." (Canadian Prime Minister Lester B. Pearson, *The New York Times,* April 3, 1965.)

"Many Communist diplomats have expressed their belief that a pause in the American bombing would ultimately bring about negotiations. . . . Janos Peter [Hungarian Foreign Minister] said as much to Secretary of State Dean Rusk." (*Ibid.,* December 31, 1965.)

"Listen to the lucid words of the great departed John Kennedy, who proclaimed, four years ago: 'Mankind must put an end to war, or war will put an end to mankind.' "
"No more war, war never again! Peace, it is peace which must guide the destinies of peoples and of all mankind." (Pope Paul VI, address to the UN General Assembly, October 4, 1965, Los Angeles *Times,* October 5, 1965.)

"[The USSR] could not do much to arrange a settlement in Vietnam until the United States stopped bombing North Vietnamese targets." (USSR Ambassador Anatoliy F. Dobrynin, *ibid.,* March 27, 1965.)

"The Mission appointed by the Commonwealth Prime Minister's Meeting is to explore the circumstances in which a conference might be held to end the fighting in Viet-Nam."
"The Commonwealth as such is in no way committed to either side of the conflict in Viet-Nam and has formed no collective view except on the urgency of re-establishing conditions in which the people of Viet-Nam may be able to live in peace. Although within the Commonwealth

there is diversity of opinion on the Viet-Nam problem, there is complete unanimity as to the need to find a peaceful solution." *(Documents Relating to British Involvement in the Indo-China Conflict, 1945–1965*, pp. 261-262.)

1965

     North Vietnam alternated between more and less conciliatory stances, depending on the military circumstances. Each instance of American escalation stimulated a series of inflammatory declarations from Hanoi. These statements were often followed by more tempered, seemingly contradictory, avowals by North Vietnam of its willingness to negotiate, once the United States agreed to the minimum condition—ceasing its air attacks. At such times, Hanoi distinguished between the military *conditions necessary for a cease-fire and the* political *conditions essential to a long-term solution.*

"The President acknowledged that in the last five weeks there had been a change in American tactics and in some instances in strategy. He was referring to strikes by American planes against Communist targets in North and South Vietnam—steps intended to drive home to North Vietnam the demand that Hanoi halt support of the Vietcong." (*The New York Times,* March 14, 1965.)

"[We] demand that the U.S. Government respect and correctly implement the 1954 Geneva Agreements on Vietnam, put an immediate end to its war acts against the DRV, withdraw from South Vietnam all arms, military personnel and troops of the United States and its satellites, and let the South Vietnamese people settle by themselves their own affairs." (Letter from North Vietnam to members of the 1954 Geneva Conference, FBIS *Daily Report,* March 24, 1965, JJJ1).

"What then holds up a peace conference of interested parties, and the ending of slaughter in Vietnam? North Vietnamese insistence on withdrawal of American forces from South Vietnam as a pre-condition of their participation in a Conference? No. Mr. Pham Van Dong was emphatic that this was *not* a pre-condition; it was, he said, a subject to be discussed and arranged at the Conference itself. The only pre-condition is a cease-fire; the Americans and the South Vietnamese Air Force must stop their attacks on North Vietnam." (Interview by William Warbey, Labour M.P., with Pham Van Dong, reported in letter to London *Times,* April 1, 1965.)

"We have no desire to rush political re-unification. We want the opening up of trade and communications between the North and South and the reunion of the divided families, but political re-unification will result from a slow process of rapprochement between our Government and the new democratic Government in Saigon. This is a matter we shall settle between ourselves, in our time, and without outside interference." [Pham Van Dong.]
"For a political solution, and to achieve true peace in South Vietnam, the U.S. imperialists must first of all agree to the withdrawal of their forces. Concerning the way of conducting this withdrawal, the imperialist side has many experiences: the French have withdrawn from Indo-China and Algeria, and the Americans have withdrawn from Laos and other areas in the world." [General Nguyen Van Vinh.]
"The Americans also want to know what they will obtain in return for this withdrawal. Certainly, they will get something. They will, in return, obtain peace, friendship, honor for the U.S.A., and benefit for the American people's interests and lives." [Pham Van Dong.] (Quotations from North Vietnamese leaders, John Gittings, "A

Basis for Negotiation Exists," *The Nation,* September 6, 1965.)

1965

Of the communications from North Vietnam and the National Liberation Front during 1965 the most important were: first, Hanoi's Four-Point Program, broadcast by Premier Pham Van Dong as a basis for settlement on April 8 and endorsed by the NLF in September; and second, a proposal contained in a letter to President Johnson sent through Ambassador Goldberg from the President of the UN General Assembly, Italian Foreign Minister Fanfani, on November 20.

Essentially, the Four Points called for, first, withdrawal of the United States from Vietnam; second, respect for the military provisions of the Geneva Agreements pending reunification of Vietnam; third, settlement of South Vietnam's internal affairs by the South Vietnamese, in accordance with the program of the National Liberation Front; and, fourth, the exclusion of foreign interference in the eventual reunification of the country.

The Fanfani overture interpreted these four points as meaning simply a return to the principles of the Geneva Agreements.

"1—Recognition of the basic national rights of the Vietnamese people—peace, independence, sovereignty, unity, and territorial integrity. . . . [T]he U.S. Government must withdraw from South Vietnam U.S. troops, military personnel, and weapons of all kinds, dismantle all U.S. military bases there, and cancel its military alliance with South Vietnam."

"2— . . . The two zones must refrain from entering into any military alliance with foreign countries and there must be no foreign military bases, troops, or military personnel in their respective territory.

"3—The internal affairs of South Vietnam must be settled by the South Vietnamese people themselves in accordance with the program of the NFLSV without any foreign interference.

"4—The peaceful reunification of Vietnam is to be settled by the Vietnamese people in both zones, without any foreign interference." (Hanoi's Four Points, Kahin and Lewis, *op. cit.*, pp. 432-433.)

"The Government of the DRV is of the view that the stand expounded here is the basis for the soundest political settlement of the Vietnam problem.

"If this basis is recognized, favorable conditions will be created for the peaceful settlement of the Vietnam problem, and it will be possible to consider the reconvening of an international conference along the pattern of the 1954 Geneva conference on Vietnam." (Concluding statement to the Four-Point proposal by Prime Minister Pham Van Dong, *ibid.*, p. 433.)

". . . [I]n Hanoi, Ho Chi Minh and the President of the Council [Pham] Van Dong, expressed to two persons (known to me) the strong desire to find a peaceful solution to the conflict in Vietnam and, in summary, stated —according to what they wrote me—that 'in order for the peace negotiations to come about, there will be necessary (a) a cease-fire (by air, by sea, by land) in the entire territory of Vietnam (North and South); the cessation, that is, of all belligerent operations (including therefore also the cessation of debarkation of further American troops); (b) a declaration according to which the Geneva agreements of 1954 will be taken as the basis for the negotiations—a declaration made up of the four points formulated by Hanoi, points that are in reality the explanation of the Geneva text and which therefore can be reduced to a single point: application, in other words, of the Geneva accords.'

" '. . . [T]he Government in Hanoi is prepared to initiate negotiations without first requiring actual withdrawal of the American troops.'

"To the same interlocutors Ho Chi Minh said: 'I am prepared to go anywhere; to meet anyone.' " (Letter from Italian Foreign Minister Fanfani to President Johnson, *The New York Times,* December 18, 1965.)

1965

> *The United States rejected the Four-Point proposal, taking strong exception only to point three. Both Washington and Saigon interpreted point three, embodying the NLF's call for a coalition government, as a demand for the overthrow of the existing South Vietnamese regime, and they were adamant in refusing to recognize the autonomy of the National Liberation Front.*
>
> *The United States failed to accept the Fanfani overture as a sincere approach to negotiations. Furthermore, in his reply to the Italian Foreign Minister, the US Secretary of State made no mention of the National Liberation Front and limited America's willingness to enter discussions to "negotiations with any government." The correspondence broke off abruptly when details of the Fanfani letter were made public.*
>
> *During the exchange of letters, the United States bombed a major North Vietnamese industrial target for the first time.*

"The United States alleges that the four-point stand of the DRV could be accepted with the exception of point three. This point says the affairs of South Vietnam will be solved by the South Vietnamese themselves according to the program of the NLFSV without foreign interference. Everybody knows that . . . this program is to unite the entire people. . . . This program fully conforms to the

1954 Geneva agreements on Vietnam. . . ." (Hanoi Radio Broadcast, Kahin and Lewis, *op. cit.,* p. 211.)

" . . . [A] broad national democratic coalition administration [must be] formed including representatives of all strata of people, nationalities, political parties, religious communities, and patriotic personalities. We must wrest back the people's economic, political, social and cultural interests, realize independence and democracy, improve the people's living conditions, carry out a policy of peace and neutrality and advance toward peaceful reunification of the Fatherland." (Point 1 of the program of the National Liberation Front, *ibid.,* p. 390).

"The first point of this program [the National Liberation Front program] discloses the full Communist intention. It calls for the overthrow of the South Vietnamese Government in Saigon and the establishment of a coalition government from which the Government in Saigon would be totally excluded.

". . . [T]he Hanoi regime is demanding the following preconditions to which the United States must agree before the Communists will even condescend to negotiate:

"First, that the South Vietnamese Government be overthrown;

"Second, that the Liberation Front, the creature and agent of Hanoi, be accepted as the sole bargaining representative for the South Vietnamese people;

"Third, that South Vietnam be put under the control of a coalition government formed by the Communists and from which the South Vietnamese Government would be excluded." (Secretary Rusk, commenting on Hanoi's Four Points, U.S Senate, *Supplemental Foreign Assistance Fiscal Year 1966—Vietnam,* p. 576.)

"The government of the Republic of Viet Nam has never, and at the present time, does not, recognize the so-called 'South Viet Nam Liberation Front' which is only an instrument created by the Communist North Vietnamese with a view to carrying out their criminal schemes and imperialist aims."

"It is a matter of course that negotiations proper can only take place when preconditions (the withdrawal of Communist troops and cadres) laid out by the Republic of Viet-Nam during eventual preliminary talks will have been accepted and carried out." (Communiqué of the Republic of Vietnam Government, Kahin and Lewis, *op. cit.*, pp. 430-431.)

"1. . . . [T]he United States is prepared to enter into discussions or negotiations with any government at any time without any preconditions whatsoever."

"2. . . . Hanoi would agree that negotiations might be undertaken on the basis of the Geneva agreements of 1954 without any qualifications or conditions. We for our part would be willing to engage in negotiations on this basis without any qualifications or conditions.

"3. The United States does not, however, agree with the contention that the 'four points' advanced by Hanoi constitute an authentic interpretation of the Geneva agreements of 1954. Elements in the four points, notably the political program of the so-called National Liberation Front, have no basis in the Geneva agreements. . . .

"4. . . . [I]f a reduction or cessation of hostilities were to be arranged prior to negotiations, it seems self-evident that it would have to be on an equitable and reciprocal basis. . . . The formulation proposed by Hanoi's leaders does not appear to meet this test, for example, in that it imposes no restraint on the continued infiltration of forces and equipment from North to South Vietnam.

"5. . . . However, the clarification of this point, though not without significance in the light of conflicting public statements by Hanoi on the subject, still leaves the questions discussed in 2 and 3 above.

"We are, thus, far from persuaded that statements by Ho Chi Minh and Pham Van Dong quoted by your Italian sources indicate a real willingness for unconditional negotiations. . . . [I]n light of any further soundings your sources may make with Hanoi, to discuss this matter further with you, I have asked Ambassador Goldberg, who bears this letter, to make himself available to you at any time for this purpose." (Secretary Rusk, reply to Foreign Minister Fanfani, December 4, 1965, *The New York Times,* December 18, 1965.)

"According to Mr. Weiss [Peter Weiss, New York lawyer who talked over the Fanfani overture with one of the Italian emissaries, Professor Giorgio La Pira, former Mayor of Florence, and relayed the information to Ambassador Goldberg], the memorandum given to Mr. Goldberg stated that, if the contents were published, it would lead to a repudiation by Hanoi." (*Ibid.,* December 19, 1965.)

"Asked why the Administration had acted so quickly in publicizing the exchange of messages, Mr. Goldberg said one reason was that 'there has been great concern as to whether we . . . really are pursuing what has been said is a path to peace . . . and the credibility of our Government has been assailed.'" (*Ibid.,* December 20, 1965.)

"Some United Nations delegates have blamed the intensified air offensive against North Vietnam for yesterday's denial by Hanoi of its purported peace approach. They said the strikes had been accelerated after the United States' letter to Mr. Fanfani was relayed to Hanoi." (*Ibid.,* December 20, 1965.)

"Mr. Goldberg was asked whether the United States thought the stepping up of the bombing in North Vietnam —specifically of Haiphong—would help convince Ho Chi Minh to negotiate.

"He replied that the bombing had 'no relationship' to any possible negotiations. He added that 'our bombing program is laid on weeks in advance, and we didn't step it up.' " (*Ibid.*, December 20, 1965.)

"It is known to everybody that each time the United States imperialists jabbered about 'peaceful negotiations,' they intensified and expanded the war in Vietnam." (Hanoi radio broadcast, *ibid.*, December 19, 1965.)

1965

> *The first significant American appeal during this period was delivered by President Johnson in a speech at Baltimore on April 7 in which he announced his unwillingness to withdraw but his readiness to enter unconditional discussions provided that an independent South Vietnam was securely guaranteed.*

"The central lesson of our time is that the appetite of aggression is never satisfied. To withdraw from one battlefield means only to prepare for the next. We must say in Southeast Asia—as we did in Europe—in the words of the Bible: 'Hitherto shalt thou come, but no further.' "

"Our objective is the independence of South Viet-Nam and its freedom from attack. . . . We will do everything necessary to reach that objective, and we will do only what is absolutely necessary."

"We will not be defeated.

"We will not grow tired.

"We will not withdraw, either openly or under the cloak of a meaningless agreement."

". . . And we remain ready . . . for unconditional discussions." (President Johnson, speech at Baltimore, Md., April 7, 1965, *Department of State Bulletin,* April 26, 1965.)

1965

This speech was followed in May by a six-day bombing pause ordered, according to a secret communication from Secretary Rusk to Hanoi, to see if it would stimulate reduction in Hanoi's military activities in the south. Although the United States made the official announcement, immediately after it resumed bombing, that there had been no reaction from North Vietnam to the secret letter and the bombing pause, subsequent revelations contradicted these official statements. Eight months later, Secretary Rusk reversed himself and declared that North Vietnam had sent a "harsh rejection" to United States peace moves.

". . . [T]he United States Government has taken account of repeated suggestions from various quarters, including public statements by Hanoi representatives, that there can be no progress toward peace while there are air attacks on North Vietnam."

"But my Government is very hopeful that . . . this first pause in air attacks may meet with a response which will permit further and more extended suspension of this form of military action in expectation of equal constructive actions by the other side in the future." (Secretary Rusk, secret letter to Hanoi, May 12, 1965, later broadcast by Hanoi radio, *The New York Times,* December 12, 1965.)

"[The Administration was] disappointed at the fact that there was no reaction. . . . We must assume that the other side was aware that the strikes had not been carried out for a number of days, and we have seen no reaction to that fact." (Robert J. McCloskey, Director, State Department Office of News, *ibid.,* May 19, 1965.)

"[Mai Van Bo, North Vietnamese diplomat in Paris] called particular attention to a phrase that indicated that if the four points were recognized as a basis, 'favorable conditions will be created for a peaceful settlement of the Vietnam problem.' He then said that if the four points, including withdrawal of American troops and self-determination for South Vietnam, were accepted in principle, the application of the principle might be delayed over a very long time." (Joseph Kraft, reporting on North Vietnamese response to the secret letter and May bombing pause, Washington *Post,* January 5, 1966.)

"A Hanoi representative in an uncommitted capital announced that Dong's four points were not 'prior conditions' but general principles which, if accepted, would make the search for a settlement possible. A few hours later, however [on May 18], the bombings were resumed before the White House had been advised of the North Vietnamese diplomat's gesture." (Jean Lacoutre, *Vietnam Between Two Truces.* Random House: 1966, pp. 282-283.)

"Although French specialists concur with the American contention that the North Vietnamese feelers of last May were no valid offer of negotiation, they regret the resumption of the bombing of North Vietnam so soon afterward." (*The New York Times,* November 19, 1965.)

"Mr. SPIVAK: Well, Mr. Secretary, can you tell us whether the report that the Washington *Post* published on Saturday that there had been a response from North Vietnam but that we considered the response negative but ambiguous?

"Secretary RUSK: No, no, I have not had—and I think

I would know about it if there were such a response—I have not seen a response direct or indirect to the United States by Hanoi in this situation." (NBC-TV's "Meet the Press," January 23, 1966.)

"In May, there was a cessation of bombing which ended after a harsh rejection by the other side of any serious move toward peace." (Secretary Rusk, *The New York Times,* January 22, 1966.)

". . . [T]he details of time and place about contacts with particular capitals [were] the only point that I know of in which we have not given all of the detailed facts to the general public. . . ." (Secretary Rusk, *ibid.,* February 1, 1966.)

"Senator GORE. . . . I was not too favorably impressed in the last few days with the statements by administration leaders, including yourself this morning, that during the bombing pause infiltration had continued from the North. Has it not continued also from the South, and did you expect——

"Secretary RUSK. Senator, there is a fundamental difference——

"Senator GORE (continuing). Did you honestly expect that because there was a cessation of bombing of North Vietnam that they would ipso facto stop all their military movements? The question I am trying to pose is: Is this a realistic approach or is this a propagandistic approach?

"Secretary RUSK. No, Senator, I think it would be a great mistake to put those two forces on the same footing, and not just on the basis that we are on our side.

"The North Vietnamese armed forces have no right whatever to move from North Vietnam into South Vietnam to seize South Vietnam. That is aggression." (U.S. Senate, *Supplemental Foreign Assistance Fiscal Year 1966 —Vietnam,* p. 16.)

1965

In July, the President reiterated his willingness to start unconditional discussions with any government.

"We are ready now, as we have always been, to move from the battlefield to the conference table. I have stated publicly many times, again and again, America's willingness to begin unconditional discussions with any government at any place at any time. Fifteen efforts have been made to start these discussions with the help of 40 nations throughout the world, but there has been no answer."

"We are ready to discuss their proposals and our proposals and any proposals of any government whose people may be affected, for we fear the meeting room no more than we fear the battlefield."

"But we insist and we will always insist that the people of South Viet-Nam shall have the right of choice, the right to shape their own destiny in free elections in the South or throughout all Viet-Nam under international supervision, and they shall not have any government imposed upon them by force and terror so long as we can prevent it." (President Johnson, news conference, July 28, 1965, *Weekly Compilation of Presidential Documents,* August 2, 1965.)

" 'South Vietnam will unquestionably be liberated,' Ho said, adding, 'Both zones . . . will achieve national unification step by step, without any kind of foreign interference.' " (*Pravda,* July 31, 1965.)

1965

Several fixed patterns of action and response emerged in 1965. On the part of the United

States, "peace offensives" or attempts to bring about negotiations were, in each instance, accompanied or followed by an enlargement of the American troop commitment in South Vietnam and by an escalation of bombing. This American action pattern emerged clearly in April, at the time of the President's Baltimore speech, and was repeated in May, July, and December. In addition, the United States always stipulated that it would negotiate only with other governments, agreeing merely to have NLF views "reflected" and thus eliminating the National Liberation Front, which was not a formal government, as an equal partner to discussions. Also, the United States was consistent in requiring that North Vietnam cease aggression in South Vietnam as a prior condition for negotiation.

". . . [N]o nation need ever fear that we desire their land, or to impose our will, or to dictate their institutions. . . . But we dream of an end to war. And we will try to make it so. . . . The guns and the bombs, the rockets and the warships, are all symbols of human failure. . . . [T]hey are witnesses to human folly." (President Johnson, speech at Baltimore, April 7, 1965, *Department of State Bulletin,* April 26, 1965.)

"In February, we flew 160 strike sorties against military targets in North Vietnam. In April, we flew over 1,500 strike sorties against such targets.

"Prior to mid-February we flew no strike sorties inside South Vietnam. In March and April we flew more than 3,200 sorties against military targets in hostile areas inside the country." (President Johnson, message to Congress, May 4, 1965, *The New York Times,* May 5, 1965.)

"The highest authority in this Government has asked me to inform Hanoi that there will be no air attacks on North Vietnam for a period beginning at noon, Washington time, Wednesday the 12th of May, and running into next week." (Secretary Rusk, secret letter to Hanoi, May 12, 1965, *ibid.,* December 12, 1965.)

"I ask the Congress to appropriate at the earliest possible moment an additional $700 million to meet mounting military requirements in Vietnam." (President Johnson, message to Congress, May 4, 1965, *ibid.,* May 5, 1965.)

". . . If the United Nations and its officials or any of its 114 members can by deed or word, private initiative or public action, bring us nearer an honorable peace, then they will have the support and the gratitude of the United States of America." (President Johnson, news conference, July 28, 1965, *Weekly Compilation of Presidential Documents,* August 2, 1965.)

"I have today ordered to Viet-Nam the Air Mobile Division and certain other forces which will raise our fighting strength from 75,000 to 125,000 men almost immediately. Additional forces will be needed later, and they will be sent as requested." (*Ibid.*)

"QUESTION: Mr. Secretary, the Pope's Christmas message warned that perhaps the world was on the wrong path again and urged all nations 'to modify the direction of your steps, stop, think.' What's your reaction to that, sir?

"ANSWER: Well, I think that those words of His Holiness must be taken with the utmost seriousness by everyone concerned because the world is in a turbulent and indeed a very dangerous situation. . . . Our objective there [in Vietnam] *is* peace." (Secretary Rusk, interview for Canadian Broadcasting Corporation, December 23, 1965, *Department of State Bulletin,* January 17, 1966.)

"United States jet fighter-bombers destroyed a large power plant today 14 miles from Haiphong, North Vietnam's chief port, in the first American air strike against a

North Vietnamese target of major industrial importance."
(*The New York Times,* December 16, 1965.)

"Now the President in July has indicated that if Hanoi
is interested in peace there should be no insuperable
problem in having the views of the so-called Liberation
Front reflected. But that does not mean that they are the
representatives of the South Vietnamese people. . . ."
(Secretary Rusk, news conference, *ibid.,* January 22,
1966.)

"Even if the preconditions set by the Republic of Viet
Nam are fulfilled, the government of the Republic of Viet
Nam can only negotiate with recognized representatives
of the opponent." (Saigon Government statement, April
11, 1965, Kahin and Lewis, *op. cit.,* pp. 430-431.)

"Senator AIKEN. . . . [A]ccording to the Department of Defense we have killed 112,000 Vietcong. The
year-end strength of the Vietcong was 225,000 excluding
the North Vietnamese troops. . . . If you subtract from
that the total of 63,300 infiltrators from the North, that
still leaves 273,000 Vietcong recruited and trained in the
south, according to the Department of Defense statements.

"Does this indicate that there are civil war aspects to
this struggle, and that the appeal of the Vietcong to his
fellow countrymen in South Vietnam is quite strong?

"Secretary RUSK. There are elements of civil war in
this situation, but the heart of the problem of peace is the
external aggression." (U.S. Senate, *Supplemental Foreign
Assistance Fiscal Year 1966—Vietnam,* pp. 593-594.)

"Now, there wouldn't be a single American combat
soldier in South Vietnam had Hanoi not launched this
aggression against South Vietnam." (Secretary Rusk, in
ibid., p. 592.)

1965

*For its part, North Vietnam reacted to each
escalatory move by increasing its rate of infiltration into the South and by stiffening its minimum conditions for negotiation. Its many proposals for settlement
during 1965, no matter how divergent in other respects,
retained one central point: the NLF must be recognized
as the real representative of South Vietnam at the negotiating table. Later, other inflexible preconditions were
added—the unconditional, though not necessarily permanent, cessation of bombing and an end to all other acts of
war against North Vietnam.*

"An improvement in the morale and performance of
the South Vietnamese Government and its troops has
been the chief discernible result of the last month's air
strikes against North Vietnam, a senior American military
spokesman said today."

"There is no evidence that infiltration from the North
has declined recently." (*The New York Times,* April 7,
1965.)

"The clandestine infiltration of personnel and matériel
from North Viet-Nam into South Viet-Nam continues to
play a vital role in providing the Communist Viet Cong
with the leadership, with the technical competence, with
the weapons, and with the ammunition which they need
to carry on their insurgency directed against the established Government in South Viet-Nam.

"Recent evidence both from captured prisoners and
from captured documents has increased our estimates of
the number of infiltrators to a total of 39,000. Reports to
date confirm the infiltration of between 5,000 and 8,000
men in 1964 alone.

"In view of the normal timelag between the actual active infiltration and our confirmation of it, I think it is probable that we are in excess of 10,000 men infiltrated from the North into the South during the past year." (Secretary McNamara, news conference, April 26, 1965, *Department of State Bulletin,* May 17, 1965.)

"The bombing has failed to live up to its advanced billing in several respects.

"First, thousands upon thousands of tons of bombs have not blasted the North Vietnamese government out of its militant stance and toward the peace conference table.

"Second, it has not reduced the infiltration of troops from North to South Vietnam—by the Pentagon's own admission.

"Last February [1966], Rep. ROBERT L. F. SIKES (D. Fla.) asked McNamara during Senate Defense Appropriations Subcommittee hearings: 'What do our forces propose to do to seal off the Ho Chi Minh trail?' . . . 'Our bombing campaign against the North,' McNamara responded, 'has that as one of its primary objectives.'

"When this exchange took place, the Defense Department estimated that the infiltration rate was 4,500 troops a month. The department estimates that right now the infiltration rate is 5,000 a month. So by the Pentagon's own statistics, the bombing failed in this respect."

"This raises the question of why continue to bomb in the North at all. McNamara has said there are three basic objectives of the bombing: (1) raise the morale of the South Vietnamese; (2) reduce the flow of infiltration or increase its cost; (3) push North Vietnam's leaders toward the conference table.

"At most, only the first and half of the second of these objectives have been achieved. The Air Force line is that the infiltration of supplies has been greatly reduced." (Washington *Post* staff writer George C. Wilson, quoted in the *Congressional Record,* Senate, October 10, 1966.)

"Total Vietcong strength, apparently, is steadily increasing despite the serious casualties which these forces have suffered during the past few months." (Mansfield, *op. cit.*, p. 3.)

". . . I look upon this [strategic bombing] as one of the great illusions of all time, that through air power you can really win this way. I think the results of the strategic bombing survey will show that as our bombing [in World War II] was increased German production went up until we overran facilities. I don't think you can hold them by bombing . . . nor really win by bombing." (Lt.-Gen. Gavin, U.S. Senate, *Supplemental Foreign Assistance Fiscal Year 1966—Vietnam,* p. 244).

"Mr. MINSHALL [Representative William E. Minshall of Ohio]. You . . . said something about the North Vietnamese applying full power. What did you mean by that?

"How many more troops do you think they can send down there?

"Secretary McNAMARA. I do not believe we can predict accurately what their capabilities are for reinforcing the forces in South Vietnam under our air attacks. I believe that by recruitment in the South and infiltration from the North they probably can increase their forces roughly 50 percent above the levels of the end of last year. . . ."

"Mr. MINSHALL. Do you think that the number of troops we presently have in South Vietnam, and our present military commitment, will enable us to cope with a full power, all out North Vietnamese war effort?

"Secretary McNAMARA. Well, I think that if the North Vietnamese expand their forces by infiltration and by recruitment in the South to a level some 50 percent greater than their level at the end of last year, we would have to add to the strength we now have in South Vietnam." (Secretary McNamara, February 16, 1966, U.S. House of Representatives, *Department of Defense Appropriations for 1967,* Part I, 89th Congress, 2nd Session. Government Printing Office: 1966, pp. 274, 276.)

"If the United States really wants peace it must recognize the NLFSV as the sole genuine representative of the people of South Vietnam and engage in negotiations with it." (President Ho Chi Minh, letter to Communist leaders, Kahin and Lewis, *op. cit.,* p. 439.)

"If the U.S. Government truly wants to talk, it must . . . first of all stop unconditionally the bombing and all other acts of war. . . ." (Nguyen Duy Trinh, North Vietnamese Foreign Minister, *The New York Times,* January 3, 1968.)

1966

The patterns established in 1965 prevailed throughout 1966. Early in the year the United States launched a major peace offensive by releasing its Fourteen Points as a basis for settlement; at the same time it increased its troop commitment. The Fourteen Points were announced and publicized in the context of a short Christmas cease-fire, a longer New Year cease-fire, and a 37-day bombing pause.

Although the Fourteen Points closely approached North Vietnam's Four Points in many respects, President Ho Chi Minh rejected them on the grounds that the National Liberation Front was still denied full and distinct status as a combatant. Since 1960, when Hanoi formally recognized the National Liberation Front, the relationship between the Democratic Republic of Vietnam and the Front had been that of allies with separate political organizations and divergent foreign policies. Ho Chi Minh at all times insisted that the United States, contrary to its practice of re-

ferring to the Front as an appendage of Hanoi, recognize the Front's separate status as the real representative of the majority of South Vietnamese. He also questioned the sincerity of the Fourteen-Point offer in view of the American military build-up during the bombing pause.

Although President Johnson publicly noted some lull in the fighting during the bombing pause, air attacks were resumed on the last day of January and were continued throughout the year.

"The following statements are on the public record about elements which the United States believes can go into peace in Southeast Asia:

"1. The Geneva Agreements of 1954 and 1962 are an adequate basis for peace in Southeast Asia;

"2. We would welcome a conference on Southeast Asia or on any part thereof;

"3. We would welcome 'negotiations without preconditions' as the 17 nations put it;

"4. We would welcome unconditional discussions as President Johnson put it;

"5. A cessation of hostilities could be the first order of business at a conference or could be the subject of preliminary discussions;

"6. Hanoi's four points could be discussed along with other points which others might wish to propose;

"7. We want no U.S. bases in Southeast Asia;

"8. We do not desire to retain U.S. troops in South Viet-Nam after peace is assured;

"9. We support free elections in South Viet-Nam to give the South Vietnamese a government of their own choice;

"10. The question of reunification of Viet-Nam should be determined by the Vietnamese through their own free decision;

"11. The countries of Southeast Asia can be nonaligned or neutral if that be their option;

"12.   We would much prefer to use our resources for economic reconstruction of Southeast Asia than in War. If there is peace, North Viet-Nam could participate in a regional effort to which we would be prepared to contribute at least one billion dollars;

"13.   The President has said, 'The Viet Cong would not have difficulty being represented and having their views represented if for a moment Hanoi decided she wanted to cease aggression. I don't think that would be an insurmountable problem.'

"14.   We have said publicly and privately that we could stop the bombing of North Viet-Nam as a step toward peace although there has not been the slightest hint or suggestion from the other side as to what they would do if the bombing stopped." (Washington's Fourteen Points, January 7, 1966, *Department of State Bulletin,* February 14, 1966.)

"A United States spokesman announced today that there were about 197,000 American servicemen in South Vietnam."

"The spokesman said the figure represented an increase of 6,000 men in the last 10 days. . . . (*The New York Times,* January 29, 1966.)

"The recommendations in this budget will require $121.9 billion in new obligational authority for fiscal year 1967 in the administrative budget. The special costs of Vietnam represent $9.1 billion of this amount."

"In 1967, total obligational availability of $25.7 billion is estimated for these forces. . . . Both the Army and the Marine Corps will organize additional helicopter units. . . . The flexibility and mobility of Navy general purpose forces will be further enhanced in 1967. . . . Our superiority in tactical air forces will be maintained." (President Johnson's budget message, *ibid.,* January 25, 1966.)

"At the very moment when the U.S. Government puts forward the so-called new peace efforts, it is frantically

increasing the U.S. strength in South Vietnam. It is stepping up the terrorist raids, resorting to the scorched earth
policy, burning all, destroying all, killing all, using napalm bombs, poison gases, and toxic chemicals to burn
down villages and massacre the civilian population in vast
areas of South Vietnam." (President Ho Chi Minh, letter
to Communist leaders, Kahin and Lewis, *op. cit.,* p. 440.)

". . . [T]he NLFSV is fighting to achieve independence, democracy, peace, and neutrality in South Vietnam
and to advance toward the peaceful reunification of the
fatherland. If the United States really respects the right to
self-determination of the people of South Vietnam, it cannot but approve this correct program of the National
Front for Liberation. (President Ho Chi Minh, *The New
York Times,* January 29, 1966.)

"If the Vietcong come to the conference table as full
partners, they will be in a sense have been victorious in
the very aims that South Vietnam and the United States
are pledged to prevent." (Secretary Rusk, *ibid.,* January
29, 1966.)

"The number of incidents have dropped off some. I
don't say there is any connection with that and our peace
moves, but that is a fact." (President Johnson, *ibid.,* January 14, 1966.)

"Throughout these 37 days, even at moments of truce,
there has been continued violence against the people of
South Viet-Nam, against their Government, against their
soldiers, and against our own American forces."

"So on this Monday morning in Viet-Nam, at my direction, after complete and thorough consultation and
agreement with the Government of South Viet-Nam,
United States aircraft have resumed action in North
Viet-Nam.

"They struck the lines of supply which support the
continuing movement of men and arms against the people

and the Government of South Viet-Nam." (President Johnson, January 31, 1966, *Weekly Compilation of Presidential Documents,* February 7, 1966.)

1966

Unrest and demonstrations continued to disrupt the political scene in Saigon during this period. Outward signs to the contrary, the government remained military and undemocratic despite American efforts to liberalize it. In June, 1965, Air Vice Marshal Nguyen Cao Ky was installed as Premier. The Ky regime failed to enact significant reforms. A display of American-Vietnamese solidarity in Honolulu in May, 1966, was followed by unprecedented rioting and complaint in South Vietnam. As a result, elections were promised for the fall and took place on September 11, 1966. The electoral laws governing eligibility for nomination assured the return of the military to power.

"Well, we have been very deeply concerned, as you know, for some time about the question of the essential unity and solidarity of the Government in Saigon. . . . And undoubtedly disunity and confusion in Saigon increases the expectation of the other side that, if they persist, they have a chance of success.

"So we attach the highest possible priority to unity and solidarity among the South Vietnamese leaders and its Government." (Secretary Rusk, *Department of State Bulletin,* March 15, 1965.)

"As long as the Saigon government remains in the hands of the military junta, which at best represents only the interests of senior officers who fought with the French colonial forces during the 1945-1954 war of independence, the Viet Cong's claim sounds valid to many Vietnamese."

"A relatively competent, honest, respected and stable leadership and a relatively coherent and efficient administrative structure in South Vietnam is . . . [a] necessary condition. These are clearly missing today, and extensive bombings in the South, the use of defoliants and chemicals, and growing direct participation in the war by American troops will not help create that structure." (Tran Van Dinh [Chargé d'Affaires and Acting Ambassador of the Republic of Vietnam to the United States in 1963], "Elections in Vietnam," *The New Republic,* July 2, 1966.)

"If, in response to revolutionary activity, a government can only promise its people ten years of napalm or heavy artillery, there will not be government for long." (Senator Robert F. Kennedy, *Le Monde,* July 12, 1965.)

"To the increasing resentment of the Southerners, all the key posts in the government of South Vietnam are now held by men from North Vietnam. General Nguyen Cao Ky, the prime minister, is a Northerner; so are the secretary general of the National Leadership Committee which advises Ky; the minister for National Reconstruction (in charge of pacification); the director general of police and of military security; the ministers for information and for state security; the chief of staff; and the commander of the troops that surround Saigon and protect Ky against a *coup d'état.* Northerners control the Army, the police, the pacification, the propaganda, have all the money, all the power, and thus control 14 million South Vietnamese." (Tran Van Dinh, "The Ky Question," *The New Republic,* January 21, 1967.)

"People ask me who my hero is; I have only one—Hitler." (Premier Nguyen Cao Ky, quoted by Senator Claiborne Pell, *Congressional Record,* Senate, May 23, 1967.)

"The Republic of Vietnam and the United States of America jointly declare:

"their determination in defense against aggression,

"their dedication to the hopes of all the people of South Vietnam,

"and their commitment to the search for just and stable peace.

"In pursuit of these objectives the leaders of their governments have agreed upon this declaration, which sets forth:

"the purposes of the Government of Vietnam,

"the purposes of the Government of the United States,

"and the common commitment of both Governments." (Part I, Declaration of Honolulu, February 8, 1966, *Department of State Bulletin,* February 28, 1966.)

"A . . . statement by Ky on May 8 to the effect that he intended to remain in power set off more demonstrations; this time the Buddhists demanded Thieu's and Ky's resignations. Ky sent loyal marines to occupy Danang and Hue." (Tran Van Dinh, "Elections in Vietnam," *The New Republic,* July 2, 1966.)

"The resistance movement of the dissident army units of Da Nang and Hue in May, 1966, could not continue because of a lack of gasoline, and without American gasoline the troops of General Ky could not have suppressed it." (Thich Nhat Hanh, *op. cit.,* p. 63.)

"Article 10 of the electoral law excluded as possible candidates: 'Civil servants, servicemen, government personnel of all levels who are dismissed or discharged for disciplinary reasons' and those 'who work directly *or indirectly* for Communism or neutralism.'" (Kahin and Lewis, *op. cit.,* p. 259.)

1966

As prosecution of the war relied more and more heavily on American troops and their modern military hardware, North Vietnam reciprocated by utilizing advanced weapons supplied by the Soviet Union. This trend was apparent in 1965, and by 1966 the USSR, rather than China, was indisputably supplying the bulk of material aid to North Vietnam. Chinese aid was limited mainly to food supplies and engineering troops.

"From the mass of contradictory evidence it would be hazardous to guess the relative contributions of China, the U.S.S.R. and Eastern Europe, but such a guess, based on the relative participation of the Soviet Union in North Vietnam's foreign trade, would estimate that the Soviet Union contributed about half of the total amount of aid, and Eastern Europe roughly one-quarter, probably less. The Chinese contribution, mostly labour and experts, is probably exaggerated by enthusiasts of the Chinese model, especially regarding the repair of border-zone bridges, railroads and footpaths, an activity important in the 1955-60 period and again since 1965.

"The amount of aid in both periods looks quite modest in dollar terms: $380 million in grants (including the questionable $5 million Soviet anti-malaria 'grant') and $452 million in credits, a total of $832 million for the entire decade, compared with about $2 billion in United States support of the South Vietnamese economy from 1955-62. In 1963 alone, U.S. economic aid to South Vietnam amounted to over $200 million. One must consider also that Chinese aid pledges are notoriously overextended." (Jan S. Prybyla, "Soviet and Chinese Economic Aid to North Vietnam," *The China Quarterly,* July-September, 1966.)

"Tonnage from Red China may run higher, but the dollar-per-ton value and the strategic value of Russian aid is much greater." ("Russia: The Enemy in Vietnam?" *U.S. News & World Report,* January 30, 1967.)

"There's no question that the Soviet Union is the primary supplier of war goods to North Vietnam, even though rival China loudly disputes that fact. U.S. intelligence experts estimate that the Russians have supplied North Vietnam with more than $600 million in military aid, including $500 million in arms alone, since 1953; of that total, 85% has been sent since August 1964, when North Vietnamese ships attacked U.S. destroyers in the Gulf of Tonkin and the Vietnam war began heating up rapidly. Since 1953 the Chinese have given Hanoi only $150 million in military aid, 65% of that since August 1964.

"The Soviet arms aid, according to U.S estimates, has flowed like this: Before 1964, $50 million; in 1964, $25 million; in 1965, $200 million to $225 million; in 1966, about $200 million. Analysts figure Chinese military aid in 1965 was about $35 million and rose to $50 million or $60 million last year, most of it in small arms such as rifles and mortars that play a major role in the war in the south." (Frederick Taylor, *The Wall Street Journal,* February 14, 1967.)

"Senator CARLSON. Is it your thought that, despite the logistics problems the Red Chinese have, they are helping or not helping the North Vietnamese, the Vietcong, in this war?

"General GRIFFITH. Definitely, yes, sir; they are helping them, I should think, with advisers, technicians. They may be manning the antiaircraft guns around Haiphong and Hanoi. They probably sent doctors, medicines, they send everything from greaseguns to automatic rifles, ammunition grenades, explosives, I am sure they are doing all this. . . . [T]he Chinese are very happy to see us mired down in southeast Asia.

"If I were Mao Tse-tung I would just be up there drinking tea and smoking cigarettes and feeling quite content with the situation. It is not costing them anything." (Testimony of Brig. Gen. Samuel B. Griffith, USMC [Ret.], U.S. Senate, *U.S. Policy With Respect to Mainland China,* 89th Congress, 2nd Session, Government Printing Office: 1966, pp. 305-306. [General Griffith received his doctorate in Chinese military history from Oxford in 1960.]

"The Vietnam War is sometimes spoken of as if it were an example of Chinese military aggression, but, at the time of this writing, China had sent only some 40,000 noncombatant engineers into North Vietnam, which is less than a tenth as many men as the fighting forces we have sent halfway around the world to South Vietnam.

"Without doubt the Chinese Communists, and also probably the Soviets, have done what they could to promote Communist movements and stir up strife in all parts of Asia. But, except in Korea, their means have not been by the sort of open aggression against which military defense lines can be erected. Communist movements in Asia, whether or not they have been aided and abetted by China or the Soviet Union, have thrived primarily on local discontent." (Edwin O. Reischauer, *Beyond Vietnam.* Random House: 1967, p. 82.)

"Outside aid has compensated, on occasion more than compensated, for bombing losses. . . . Soviet aid has risen dramatically since 1964. According to estimates of civilian officials, it increased from $300-million in 1965 to $520-million in 1966 and an estimated level of $720-million this year. The military aid figures were $210-

million in 1965, $385-million in 1966 and about $520-million this year."

"By contrast, China's . . . military aid portion was about $50-million in both 1965 and 1966, rising to about $85-million this year." (Hedrick Smith, special report, *The New York Times,* November 5, 1967.

1966

Toward the end of the year, renewed hope arose that a settlement might be in sight. Although the October Manila Conference publicly announced that henceforth South Vietnamese troops would concentrate on clear-and-hold actions, thus reversing the previous roles of American and Vietnamese units, assurances at the same time that the United States intended no permanent Southeast Asian bases gave credence to rumors of pending negotiations. Polish attempts at mediation followed by a bombing pause in February 1967 reinforced these hopes. The Polish attempts failed, however.

"The Vietnamese leaders stated their intent to train and assign a substantial share of the armed forces to clear-and-hold actions in order to provide a shield behind which a new society can be built." (Paragraph 11, Manila Conference Documents, *Department of State Bulletin,* November 14, 1966.)

". . . [T]he entire Vietnamese Army will switch to a pacification role in 1967 and leave major fighting to American troops." (Statement by South Vietnamese Foreign Minister, Los Angeles *Times,* November 18, 1966.)

"They [allied troops] shall be withdrawn, after close consultation, as the other side withdraws its forces to the North, ceases infiltration, and the level of violence thus subsides. Those forces will be withdrawn as soon as possible and not later than six months after the above conditions have been fulfilled." (Paragraph 29, Manila Conference Documents.)

"Janusz Lewandowski, a Polish diplomat in the International Control Commission for Vietnam . . . told Mr. Lodge he believed North Vietnam was prepared to open secret exploratory discussions with the United States. . . . The Polish diplomat gave Ambassador Lodge a 10-point statement of topics and principles for the proposed talks."

"One of the 10 points provided that the United States would not insist that North Vietnam acknowledge publicly the presence of its forces in South Vietnam. The Johnson Administration decided this should be clarified to require that if the troop issue was to be covered up for face-saving purposes, then the North Vietnamese forces should be withdrawn from the South."

"Before any North Vietnamese representative showed up for the Warsaw meeting, United States planes carried out the Dec. 13-14 raids on the outskirts of Hanoi." (AP Dispatch, John M. Hightower, *The New York Times,* May 9, 1967.)

"Nothing has yet happened that would justify us as saying we have a serious offer to negotiate." (Special Presidential Assistant Walt W. Rostow, quoted by Hedrick Smith, *ibid.,* February 5, 1967.)

"Prime Minister Wilson said today that he thought 'a very considerable two-way misunderstanding' broke up efforts in December to arrange talks between the United States and North Vietnam.

"He spoke of 'the Polish discussions.' This gave substance to recent reports of a move by Henry Cabot Lodge, the United States Ambassador in Vietnam, to arrange contacts with Hanoi through a Polish diplomat."

(Prime Minister Harold Wilson of Great Britain, *ibid.*, February 8, 1967.)

1967

> *In February, during the bombing pause, President Johnson sent a secret communication to President Ho Chi Minh through Moscow, restating American terms for negotiation. At approximately the same time, senior State Department officials were sending a somewhat more conciliatory secret message to Ho Chi Minh through private channels. The resumption of American bombing before North Vietnam replied to either message ended the exchange, but there was later controversy over U.S. willingness to undertake negotiations.*

"QUESTION: Sir, we have said in the past that we would be willing to suspend the bombing of North Vietnam in exchange for some suitable step by the other side. Are you prepared at all to tell us what kind of other steps the other side should take for this suspension of bombing?

"ANSWER: Just almost any step." (President Johnson, news conference, *The New York Times,* February 3, 1967.)

"The Department decided that, while the direct channel in Moscow [used by President Johnson] was crucial and must at all costs be preserved, it would be useful to send a more general message through Messrs. Baggs and Ashmore, which would be consistent with the important messages being exchanged in Moscow. . . . Accordingly, the letter . . . was worked out with the representatives of the Department, and authorized to be sent on February 5. We were subsequently informed by Mr. Ashmore that this letter reached Phnom Penh on February 15."

"There was no change of basic position whatever be-

tween February 5 and February 8 [the respective transmittal dates of the two letters], but President Johnson's
letter did include a specific action proposal that speaks
for itself, as does the tone of his communication."

"I see no inconsistency between the two." (Assistant
Secretary William P. Bundy, official statement and text of
press conference, U.S. Department of State, September
18, 1967.)

"In our several discussions with senior officials of the
State Department . . . they emphasized that the U.S. remains prepared for secret discussions at any time, without
conditions, and that such discussions might cover the
whole range of topics relevant to a peaceful settlement.
They reiterated that the Geneva Accords might be the
framework for a peaceful solution.

"They expressed particular interest in your suggestion
to us that private talks could begin provided the U.S.
stopped bombing your country, and ceased introducing
additional U.S. troops into Vietnam. They expressed the
opinion that some reciprocal restraint to indicate that neither side intended to use the occasion of the talks for military advantage would provide tangible evidence of the
good faith of all parties in the prospects for a negotiated
settlement. . . ." (Harry S. Ashmore, "The Public Relations
of Peace," *The Center Magazine,* October-November,
1967. [Letter from Ashmore to President Ho Chi Minh,
February 4, 1967.])

"I am prepared to order a cessation of bombing against
your country and the stopping of further augmentation of
United States forces in South Vietnam as soon as I am
assured that infiltration into South Vietnam by land and
by sea has stopped." (Secret letter from President Johnson to President Ho Chi Minh, February 2, 1967, made
public, *The New York Times,* March 21, 1967.)

"They have three times rejected a bombing pause as a

means to open the way to ending the war and go together to the negotiating table." (President Johnson, speech to the Tennessee State Legislature, March 15, 1967, *Department of State Bulletin,* April 3, 1967.)

"In the past two weeks, I have noted public statements by representatives of your Government suggesting that you would be prepared to enter into direct bilateral talks with representatives of the United States Government provided that we ceased 'unconditionally' and permanently our bombing operations against your country and all military action against it. . . ."

"I see two great difficulties with this proposal. . . . [S]uch action on our part would inevitably produce worldwide speculation that discussions were under way and . . . there would inevitably be grave concern on our part whether your Government would make use of such action to improve its military position." (President Johnson, secret letter to President Ho Chi Minh, February 2, 1967, *The New York Times,* March 21, 1967.)

". . . [I]f the bombings cease completely, good and favorable conditions will be created for the talks. . . ." (North Vietnamese Foreign Minister Nguyen Duy Trinh, through Australian journalist Wilfred G. Burchett, *ibid.,* February 8, 1967.)

"Hanoi has just simply refused to consider coming to a peace table." (President Johnson, speech to Tennessee State Legislature, March 15, 1967, *Department of State Bulletin,* April 3, 1967.)

"In your message, you apparently deplore the sufferings and destructions in Vietnam. May I ask you: Who has perpetrated these monstrous crimes? It is the United States and satellite troops." (President Ho Chi Minh, February 15, 1967, reply to President Johnson's letter, *The New York Times,* March 21, 1967.)

"The United States resumed the bombing of North Vietnam today after a pause of nearly six days.

". . . President Johnson said the United States had 'no alternative but to resume full-scale hostilities' in view of the use of the truce by the North Vietnamese for 'major resupply efforts of their troops in South Vietnam'. . . ." *(Ibid.,* February 14, 1967.)

"When Hanoi made this correspondence public the State Department was moved to disclaim the virtually unanimous press interpretation that the President's blunt demand for advance evidence of a halt to infiltration actually constituted a new condition for negotiations, and that the letter was, as *The New York Times* described it, 'designed to convey a hardening of the U.S. position.' " (Ashmore, *op. cit.*)

1967

The events of 1967 accentuated and deepened the action and response patterns set in 1965. The United States expanded its aerial attacks on North Vietnam both in volume and in frequency, at the same time adding to its list of permissible targets. In South Vietnam similar escalation took place. North Vietnam gave increasingly strong indications that unconditional cessation of the bombing was in itself the key to talks, while the United States insisted on reciprocity for this action. Since North Vietnam was bombing neither South Vietnam nor the United States, the only reciprocity possible was for Hanoi to end its support of troops in the south. To North Vietnam, therefore, the demand for reciprocity meant a demand for surrender.

"United States warplanes flew through heavy antiaircraft fire and MIG interceptors yesterday to attack the

Hanoi area. One of the targets was a previously untouched military barracks south of the North Vietnamese
capital."

"Other targets included a strategic highway and rail
bridge running north of Hanoi toward the Chinese border."

"For the last four days, Hanoi has experienced an almost uninterrupted series of alerts, bomb explosions, antiaircraft barrages, falling planes and missile bursts."
(*The New York Times,* October 28, 1967.)

". . . [I]t has been General Westmoreland's strategy
over the past several months to attack the base areas,
particularly those in the II and III Corps, using B-52
strikes in some cases but in particular using a coordinated
ground and air attack against these base areas to destroy
the facilities, the stocks—the recuperation areas that the
Viet Cong and the North Vietnamese had used."

"There have been some very significant changes in
technology. I don't want to go into the details of them
other than to say they have greatly increased the capability of our forces to carry on all-weather attacks on the
lines of communication, both in South Viet-Nam and in
North Viet-Nam."

". . . I think some more U.S. military personnel will be
required. I am not sure how many."

"We have about 480,000 U.S. military personnel authorized for assignment to Viet-Nam at the present time,
and we have a strength of something in the order of
450,000 or 460,000 men there now. So there are an additional 20,000 or 30,000 men to be added under the
present program before any new program might take
effect." (Secretary McNamara, *Department of State
Bulletin,* August 7, 1967.)

"I do not think it [the bombing] has in any significant
way affected their war-making capability. . . . The North

Vietnamese still retain the capability to support activities in South Vietnam and Laos at present or increased combat levels and force structure."

"All of the evidence is so far that we have not been able to destroy a sufficient quantity [of war matériel in North Vietnam] to limit the activity in the South below the present level, and I do not know that we can in the future." (Secretary McNamara, *The New York Times,* October 11, 1967.)

"[Cessation of bombing] generally would be a disaster for the United States, in my opinion . . . a great boost for the morale of the North Vietnamese. . . ." (Admiral U. S. Grant Sharp, Commander, Naval Forces Pacific, *ibid.,* September 21, 1967.)

" 'If the American side really desires conversations, it should first cease unconditionally the bombings and every other act of war against the Democratic Republic of Vietnam.' "

"What the North Vietnamese Government asks the United States Government to do, according to the [Hanoi] source, is stop the bombing without imposing conditions: in other words, without specifying a length of time and without proclaiming that during the pause it will send observation planes into the air over North Vietnam." (Prime Minister Pham Van Dong, quoted by North Vietnamese source, *ibid.,* September 15, 1967.)

"In a very real sense, the objective of our air campaign is to change the will of the enemy leadership." (General Taylor, U.S. Senate, *Supplemental Foreign Assistance Fiscal Year 1966—Vietnam,* p. 437.)

". . . —[J]ust almost any reciprocal action on their part. We have said that we would be glad to stop our invasion of North Vietnam if they would stop their invasion of South Vietnam.

"We would be glad to halt our bombing if they would halt their aggression and their infiltration." (President Johnson, March 9, 1967, *Weekly Compilation of Presidential Documents,* March 13, 1967.)

"We are prepared to withdraw and categorically we intend to withdraw as and when the North Vietnamese get out." (Assistant Secretary Bundy, *The New York Times,* September 5, 1967.)

". . . [W]e shall continue to seek negotiations—confident that reason will at last prevail; that Hanoi will realize that it cannot win. . . ."

"Let the world know that the keepers of peace will endure through every trial—that with the full backing of their countrymen, they will prevail." (President Johnson, speech at San Antonio, Texas, September 29, 1967, *ibid.,* September 30, 1967.)

"We must convince Hanoi that its cause is hopeless. Only then will Hanoi be ready to negotiate.

"Then, when we do negotiate, we must, Mr. President, work for an honorable peace." (Premier Nguyen Cao Ky, Guam Conference, March 20-21, 1967, *ibid.,* March 21, 1967.)

"A peace that the weaker party is forced to accept is a surrender." (President Nguyen Van Thieu's inauguration address, *ibid.,* November 1, 1967.)

"If you stop bombing Hanoi, we will stop bombing Washington."

"Johnson and Rusk keep saying that they'll increase the pressure until they force us to the peace table. Well, you can note this. . . . We will not make peace under the heel of the aggressor."

". . . [W]e will not sell our fundamental right to independence for peace." (North Vietnamese Prime Minister Pham Van Dong, quoted in David Schoenbrun, *Vietnam: How We Got In; How To Get Out.* Atheneum: 1968, pp. 79, 202-203.)

"The Vietnamese people will never submit to force, they will never accept talks under the threat of bombs." (President Ho Chi Minh, letter to President Johnson, February 15, 1967, *The New York Times,* March 21, 1967.)

1967

In South Vietnam, military domination of the political atmosphere continued as in the past. The September elections, meticulously supervised on the spot, returned the military to power once more; as in the 1965 elections, the electoral laws and pre-election practices precluded any other result. Continued devastation of the countryside, with the accompanying dislocation of the rural population, negated many advances under the pacification program.

". . . [One] candidate, Au Truong Thanh, was barred because his advocacy of peace was considered to be evidence of Communist sympathies; he had served as the Government's Finance Minister until 1966. . . ."

"No candidate representing the views and interests of the militant Buddhists was allowed. No run-off between the two leading candidates—in the event no candidate won a majority—was permitted, since this would certainly have resulted in a civilian victory. . . . The military ticket used the full resources of the government to promote its own cause. Any voters inclined to doubt their power were reminded of it on the eve of the election, when two Saigon newspapers were closed down and a former National Police Chief who supported another candidate was arrested. It was in these and many similar ways, and not in the crude stuffing of ballot boxes, that the election . . . was such a disappointment." (Robert F. Kennedy, *To Seek a Newer World*. Doubleday: 1967, pp. 190-191.)

". . . [T]he Constituent Assembly was composed of members none of whom were permitted to advocate peace or neutrality and who were elected by a constituency from which potential voters with similar ideas were excluded."

"The American observers reported to the President that the elections had been 'reasonably fair.' They pointed to the fact that 83% of the registered voters had actually voted, as compared with 63% in the last Presidential election. . . ."

"The 83% who reportedly voted were 83% of the *registered* voters, not of the population. . . . By the American government's own figures (W. P. Bundy, *New York Times*, 9/8/67) 70% of South Vietnam's potential electorate were registered, so that approximately 56% voted. . . . Thus, even if the balloting itself was strictly honest, Generals Thieu and Ky were elected by the votes of 34% of 56% of the electorate, or a total of 19% of South Vietnam's citizens of voting age." (Senator Ernest Gruening, *Congressional Record*, Senate, September 26, 1967.)

"We destroyed about 59,000 acres in 1965-66 alone. The operation has been stepped up. It has been estimated that the total crops destroyed to date is in excess of 220,000 acres . . . [and] destruction of about 340,000 acres of non-crop land, which would be about 1,000 square miles, or an area equal to about the size of Rhode

Island." (Senator Vance Hartke, *ibid.*, February 6, 1967.)

"In the final analysis it appears that a ratio of two civilians [casualties] to one Vietcong is likely." (Representative Clement J. Zablocki, "Report on Vietnam," U.S. Senate, *U.S. Policy With Respect to Mainland China,* p. 349.)

" 'We just want to be free from the terror and weapons of soldiers. . . . We want our children to read, we don't want them to be sick all their lives, and we want to grow our own food on our own land.' " [Village chief, quoted by Senator Edward Kennedy.]

"By now, there are approximately 1 million . . . refugees in South Vietnam, or 6 percent of its population. It is as if the population of the six New England States were homeless in America." (Senator Edward Kennedy, U.S. Senate, *Supplemental Foreign Assistance Fiscal Year 1966 —Vietnam,* pp. 109–110.)

"[The peasants] see the war profiteers becoming rich in Saigon from foreign aid. They see that the profiteers have something to fight for. But what does the peasant have to fight for? . . . Everyone in Vietnam is a Communist under the criterion the police use. Using the police way, every Vietnamese would have to be killed and our villages repopulated with Americans if the war was to be won.

"I think we should give the hamlet, the community, the rights of law."

"It is ironic that in North Vietnam our bombers are driving all the educated elite from the cities into the safety of the countryside. In South Vietnam, the reverse is the case. . . . [T]here will [soon] be islands of Americans, Australians, Koreans, and Thais, all hostile and suspicious toward Vietnamese, because they'll believe every Vietnamese is a Communist.

"If we can't close the huge gap, then only the Communists can benefit, because the people will have no one else to turn to." (Major Nguyen Be, Commander, Revolutionary Development Cadre Training School, Vung Tau, South Vietnam, quoted by correspondent Peter Arnett, Santa Barbara *News-Press,* November 23, 1967.)

1967

> *The global implications of the Vietnamese conflict became increasingly clear during 1967. International proposals for settlement gave way to appeals for cessation of hostilities, particularly for an end to the bombing; the United States found itself separated from all but its closest allies. The deepening involvement of the Soviet Union on one side of the conflict and the United States on the other hand repercussions well beyond the area of hostilities. The tensions of Vietnam strained to the breaking point the détente with the USSR that had been the accomplishment of the earlier policy of Communist containment as practiced in Europe. As China developed preliminary nuclear capacities, the presence of large contingents of American troops on her borders presaged serious future complications. And, as 1967 drew to a close, the conflict threatened to engulf the other Southeast Asian nations.*

"If Vietnam is independent and militarily nonaligned, as I have been advocating, preferably with the guarantee of the big powers, including the United States, then I do not see how this could pose a threat to international peace or security or how Vietnam could be strategically vital to the interests and security of the West." (Secretary-General U Thant, statement, January 10, 1967, *The New York Times,* January 11, 1967.)

"Abdulrahim Abby Farah (Somalia), said the United States had an international and moral obligation to initiate negotiations under the Geneva Accords. . . ." (United Nations Press Services, AM Summary, Twenty-second General Assembly, Press Release, 27 September 1967.)

"On Viet-Nam, Mr. Miki [Japan] urged a cease-fire and talks on the basis of the 1954 Geneva Agreements, as well as international guarantees for the co-existence of the North and South, with an eventual withdrawal of foreign troops." (*Ibid.,* 22 September 1967.)

"The Foreign Minister of Sweden appealed to the United States to take [the] first step towards negotiations on Viet-Nam and stop the bombing of North Viet-Nam." (*Ibid.*)

"Mr. Gromyko said the Viet-Nam war was the most large scale since 1945 and the danger was that 'at any moment the fighting can overrun new areas and draw new States into its orbit.' " (*Ibid.*)

"Nicanor Costa Mendez, Foreign Minister of Argentina, said the United Nations should take up the problem of Viet-Nam. His delegation supported all efforts to establish peace in the region on solid political bases which would allow the people of south-east Asia to live in safety from all threats." (*Ibid.,* 27 September 1967.)

"Doudou Thiam, Foreign Minister of Senegal . . . urged a cessation of the bombing and a negotiated settlement." (*Ibid.*)

"Paul Martin, Secretary of State for External Affairs of Canada, said that the cessation of bombing of North

Viet-Nam was a matter of first priority to get negotiations started, but that reciprocal concessions were needed to end the war." (*Ibid.*)

"The first essential step . . . is the unconditional ending of the bombing of North Vietnam, and we are confident that if this is done it will lead to cessation of all hostile activities throughout Vietnam and a Geneva-type meeting. . . ." (Indian Defense Minister Swaran Singh in the UN General Assembly, *The New York Times,* October 7, 1967.)

"We hear about reciprocity for the stopping of the bombing, but what kind of reciprocity? . . . [T]he Americans started the bombing, and they must stop it. That is all there is to it." (Marian Dobrosielski, adviser to the Foreign Minister of Poland, statement at *Pacem in Terris* Convocation, Geneva, Switzerland, May 29, 1967.)

". . . [T]he Indonesian Government is still firmly of the opinion that it supports the struggle of the Vietnamese people against U.S. military intervention. . . . Indonesia maintains her demand that the U.S. withdraw its military forces from Vietnam, and leave the settlement of the Vietnamese problem to the Vietnamese people themselves." (Foreign Minister Adam Malik, address to Indonesian Parliament, May 5, 1966, Kahin and Lewis, *op. cit.,* pp. 309-310.)

"In this war the two most interested parties are primarily from Vietnam itself. Would it not be desirable, therefore, to have direct contacts between these leaders? This would place them beyond the reach of all outside interference, of all intermediaries, so that they might discover the basis on which a possible dialogue could begin." (Princess Moune Souvanna Phouma of Laos, statement at *Pacem in Terris* Convocation, May 29, 1967.)

"The era of the *concert Européen* is dead and gone as far as Asia is concerned. The West can no longer claim the right or the authority to shape the destiny of Asia." (Foreign Minister Thanat Khoman of Thailand, statement at *Pacem in Terris* Convocation, May 29, 1967.)

". . . [A] minority benefits from the American occupation, while the rest of the population, directly and indirectly victims of the war, wishes with all its heart for the end of the conflict." (Statement of the General Confederation of Free Associations of Vietnam [neutralist], Paris, 1967.)

"Regardless of the ideological motives that may have been put forth by one side to justify the military intervention, in the eyes of the Vietnamese people, from North to South, all who fight do so only to defend—in their name and with their support—the national soil which is attacked and occupied by foreign troops." (Tran Van Huu, Prime Minister in the Bao Dai Government, Nguyen Manh Ha, former minister, and Nghiem Van Tri, former minister, statement at *Pacem in Terris* Convocation, June, 1967.)

"We have declared many times that if the United States wants to develop mutually beneficial relations with the Soviet Union—in principle, we also would like this— it is necessary to clear major obstacles from the path. The piratical bombing attacks against a socialist country, the Democratic Republic of Vietnam, must be halted and the aggression against the Vietnam people stopped." (First Secretary Leonid Brezhnev, USSR, *The New York Times,* October 16, 1966.)

"I would have to say that the Soviet position, with respect to bilateral relations and the general situation, is a difficult one under the circumstances of the Vietnam situation. We regret that. We would like to find ways to improve our bilateral relations with the Soviet Union, but we cannot do so by giving away South Vietnam." (Secretary Rusk, *ibid.*, August 6, 1966.)

"I think that we have more important problems than Vietnam to thrash out eventually with the Soviet Union, problems of disarmament, and problems of the halting of the proliferation of nuclear weaponry, and the still great and vital problem of Germany, which is, to my mind, the most important specific political geographic problem in the world.

"All of this, as I see it, is in suspense while this Vietnam conflict proceeds, and the effect of the Vietnam conflict on the Soviet Union has been, I fear, to make it more difficult for us to discuss these things in a useful way with the Soviet leaders." (Former Ambassador George F. Kennan, U.S. Senate, *Supplemental Foreign Assistance Fiscal Year 1966—Vietnam,* p. 346.)

"Within the next decade or two, there will be a billion Chinese on the mainland, armed with nuclear weapons, with no certainty about what their attitude toward the rest of Asia will be." (Secretary Rusk, news conference, *The New York Times,* October 13, 1967.)

"[T]he threat to world peace is militant, aggressive Asian Communism, with its headquarters in Peking, China." (Vice-President Hubert H. Humphrey, *ibid.,* October 16, 1967.)

"If U.S. imperialism should impose a war upon us . . . millions of people and millions of militia will shoot from all directions, lay mines, blockade the enemy, cut off the enemy's rear, and drown the enemy in the ocean of a people's war." (Jen-min Jih-pao [*People's Daily*], Peking, September 21, 1965, Kahin and Lewis, *op. cit.,* pp. 295-296.)

". . . [N]o man in his right mind would advocate sending our ground forces into continental China. . . ." (Douglas MacArthur, *Reminiscences.* McGraw-Hill: 1964, p. 403. [Speech to Congress, 1951.].)

". . . [B]ehold, new, terrible obstacles arise to complicate, with new problems and new threats, this intricate question, increasing dangers, rancors, ruins, tears and victims.

"We would wish to ward off the tremendous disaster of a spreading war, an needless war." (Pope Paul VI, *The New York Times,* January 2, 1968.)

"The State Department expressed concern today that Communist forces were seeking to increase military pressures in Laos, Cambodia and Thailand, but it discounted speculation that the United States was attempting to lay the basis for an expansion of the war in Vietnam." (*Ibid.,* December 28, 1967.)

". . . [T]here was widespread speculation that the Johnson Administration was proposing to counter the enemy's use of Cambodian territory by giving American military commanders authority for 'hot pursuit' from Vietnam."

"The State Department spokesman, Robert J. McCloskey, . . . said the United States had stated that 'it continues to respect the neutrality, sovereignty and territorial integrity of Cambodia. . . .' " (*Ibid.,* December 27, 1967.)

"EISENHOWER: . . . [I]f you're chasing some people and they just step over into Cambodia or Laos, I wouldn't—it wouldn't bother me. I'd go at 'em as long as they'd come in there in the first place. . . . I'd go in wherever his base was. As far as I'm concerned.

"Q.—Including China?

"EISENHOWER: Yes, wherever his base comes." (Former President Eisenhower, TV interview on CBS, *ibid.,* November 30, 1967.)

1967-1968

As the struggle entered 1968, the dominant issues remained unchanged, and the inflexible positions of the adversaries still did not admit of compromise. North Vietnam insisted as before on unconditional cessation of the bombing as a preliminary to discussions, indicating this to be the single condition; the United States continued to demand reciprocity for this gesture until late in January when it modified its stand.

"Now, if they are talking about our stopping our half of the war while they continue their half of the war unabated, then this is not on. . . ." (Secretary Rusk, news conference, *The New York Times,* September 9, 1967.)

"Our quiet support for Asian regional initiatives and our economic-assistance programs are essential underpinnings for progress in Southeast Asia."

"But—to repeat once more the crucial point—all this hinges on the maintenance of confidence. And that confidence in turn depends on the collective determination of South Vietnam and its allies to see the conflict through to an honorable settlement that will insure the right of the South Vietnamese people to determine their own future without external interference.

"These are the stakes the Administration sees in Vietnam. They are very grave indeed, but also very hopeful. And behind these stakes lies . . . the calculation of our own national interest, and a belief that that national interest is at one with the desires and hopes of the peoples of the area themselves." (Assistant Secretary William P. Bundy, "Why U.S. Is in Vietnam—An Official Explanation," *U.S. News & World Report,* December 18, 1967.)

"Your servicemen in Vietnam . . . are determined to provide the shield of security behind which the Republic of Vietnam can develop and prosper for its own sake and for the future and freedom of all Southeast Asia." (General William C. Westmoreland, "Vietnam, The Situation Today," *Vital Speeches of the Day,* May 15, 1967.)

"The Government of the Democratic Republic of Vietnam . . . demands that the United States stop unconditionally and definitively its bombing and all other acts of war against the Democratic Republic of Vietnam . . . let the south Vietnamese people decide themselves their own internal affairs, and strictly respect the independence, sovereignty, unity and territorial integrity of Vietnam as stipulated in the Geneva agreements of 1954." ("DRV Government Statement," *Peking Review,* November 10, 1967.)

"After the United States has ended unconditionally the bombing and all other acts of war, [North Vietnam] will hold talks with the United States on questions concerned." (Nguyen Duy Trinh, North Vietnamese Foreign Minister, statement, *The New York Times,* January 3, 1968.)

"The United States has directly informed North Vietnam that it would be willing to stop bombing North Vietnamese territory and talk peace if Hanoi did not take advantage of this move to raise infiltration of men and supplies to South Vietnam beyond 'normal' levels. . . ."

"But they emphasized that Washington would tolerate neither an intensified resupply effort from North to South Vietnam nor halt the bombing in the face of a major build-up of North Vietnamese forces in the South. . . ."

"[T]he State Department, through its spokesman, asserted that the terms recently proposed to Hanoi were consistent with Mr. Johnson's position as voiced at San Antonio. In what has become known as the San Antonio formula, he offered to halt air and naval bombardment of North Vietnam 'when this will lead promptly to productive discussion' and on the assumption that Hanoi would 'not take advantage' of the bombing suspension." (*Ibid.*, January 30, 1968.)

1967-1968

Politically, the divergent aims of the combatants promised little hope for settlement. Hanoi still showed no disposition to depart from its demand for genuine NLF representation in the political affairs of the South. The Front itself promulgated its program with increased vigor, while Saigon's attitude remained unyielding in spite of increasing pressure for compromise from within South Vietnam. For its part, the U.S. administration stood firm in its insistence on an independent South Vietnam, securely guaranteed, accepting the National Liberation Front not as a full-fledged combatant, but only as an expedient creation of the North.

"The Saigon puppet administration has sold out South Vietnam to the U.S. imperialists. . . . The cruel U.S. aggressors are trampling upon our homeland. We, people of South Vietnam, must stand up to make revolution and wage a people's war with a view to annihilating them, driving them out of our borders, and wresting back national independence and sovereignty."

"To achieve these objectives, the South Vietnam National Front for Liberation lays down the following concrete policies: . . . To abolish the disguised colonial regime established by the U.S. imperialists in South Vietnam. . . . To hold free general elections, to elect the National Assembly in a really democratic way in accordance with the principle of universal, equal, direct suffrage and secret ballot. . . . To proclaim and enforce broad democratic freedoms: freedom of speech, freedom of the press and publication, freedom of assembly, trade-union freedom, freedom of association, freedom to form political parties, freedom of creed, freedom of demonstration." (Excerpts from *Political Programme of the South Vietnam National Front for Liberation,* published by the Permanent Representation of the South Vietnam National Front for Liberation in Czechoslovakia, 1967.)

"We would accept any representative of the front who came back to us as a returnee. We will never recognize the front as a government or even as a legitimate political party." (President Nguyen Van Thieu of South Vietnam, *The New York Times,* December 21, 1967.)

"AMBASSADOR BUNKER: I don't think that the Vietnamese government will accept them as a political entity. I think they have made that quite clear.

"MR. NOYES: Will they accept them at a conference?

"AMBASSADOR BUNKER: They will do as we have said, that their position can be represented at a conference. It will be no problem having their views presented at a conference." (Interview by Crosby Noyes of the Washington *Star* with U.S. Ambassador to South Vietnam Ellsworth Bunker, NBC-TV's "Meet the Press," November 19, 1967.)

"In the name of God, we cry, stop! The North and South Vietnamese Governments must meet together, begin serious negotiations."

"How can there be peace when those in responsible places mask their false promises behind rhetoric? How can there be peace if laziness, hypocrisy and corruption prevail everywhere in society?"

"It is necessary that the bombing of the North cease and that at the same time infiltration of arms and war materials in the South cease. It is now that the conflict must be settled." (Vietnamese Council of Bishops [Roman Catholic], meeting in Saigon, *The New York Times,* January 9, 1968.)

"President Thieu has said that the South Vietnamese Government is not prepared to recognize the N.L.F. as a government, and it knows well that N.L.F.'s control is by Hanoi. And so do we.

"But he also has said that he is prepared for informal talks with members of the N.L.F. and these could bring good results.

"I think that is a statesmanlike position and I hope the other side will respond." (President Johnson, *ibid.,* December 21, 1967.)

1968

Even as the United States was offering a more conciliatory interpretation of reciprocity, the National Liberation Front launched widespread, coordinated attacks on major urban areas throughout South Vietnam. This unexpected Lunar New Year (Tet) offensive changed the United States assessment of the military picture and cast further doubt on the possibility of a clear-cut military victory for either side.

"More than 5,000 United States marines have been concentrated at Khesanh amid indications that one of the major battles of the Vietnam war may be in the offing.

"The marines were rushed in because of an increasingly obvious concentration of North Vietnamese troops in the area." (*The New York Times,* January 24, 1968.)

"Vietcong commando units wearing South Vietnamese Army uniforms smashed into the grounds of the Presidential Palace and the United States Embassy here today behind a barrage of mortar fire and rockets."

"At the same time the United States mission reported that assaults had been made on the Bienhoa air base and the headquarters of the American II Field Force at Longbinh, north of the city.

"Danang, the second-largest city in South Vietnam, came under heavy attack, a day after it was rocked by rocket and mortar barrages.

"The whereabouts of President Thieu and Vice President Ky could not be immediately determined."

"Ground attacks, following mortar and rocket barrages had struck eight major cities—Danang, Nhatrang, Quinhon, Kontum, Hoian, Pleiku, Banmethout and Tuyhoa—between midnight and 4 A.M."

"The attack was said to have begun at about 2 A.M.; it was led by the 401st Vietcong battalion, supported by two companies of demolition men who had apparently infiltrated the city the previous day."

"American forces at Khesanh and elsewhere along the demilitarized zone . . . had gone on full alert as soon as word of the attacks in the rear areas was received. But there was no attempt by the North Vietnamese units opposing them to stage coordinated assaults." (*Ibid.,* January 31, 1968.)

"*Mr. Frankel* [Max Frankel of *The New York*

Times]: . . . [T]hese attacks were not organized by the North Vietnamese, were they?

"*Secretary Rusk:* Of course they were. There were North Vietnamese regiments involved in these attacks. . . ." (NBC-TV's "Meet the Press" interview, February 4, 1968, *Department of State Bulletin,* February 26, 1968.)

"General William C. Westmoreland, the United States commander, said at a news conference in Saigon yesterday that the Vietcong could continue their nationwide offensive against cities and towns for several more days but that there was some evidence that it was 'about to run out of steam.'" (*The New York Times,* February 2, 1968.)

"An enemy force of more than 300 today seized a village within easy mortar range of Tansonnhut Airport and Gen. William C. Westmoreland's quarters."

"The attack came as the Hanoi radio asserted that offensives against South Vietnamese centers had diverted allied attention from the rural areas and given Vietcong and North Vietnamese forces 'mastery over extremely large areas of the countryside.'" (*Ibid.,* February 21, 1968.)

"We have known for several months now that the Communists planned a massive winter-spring offensive. We have detailed information on Ho Chi Minh's order governing that offensive. Part of it is called a 'general uprising.'" (President Johnson, news conference, February 2, 1968, *Department of State Bulletin,* February 19, 1968.)

"In a year-end report submitted 29 days before the Communist offensive against South Vietnam's cities and major towns, Gen. William C. Westmoreland predicted that the allied war gains of last year would be increased many-fold in 1968.

". . . Excerpts from the classified document . . . make clear that not only was the offensive unexpected but that also United States military planning did not envision the possibility of a setback on the scale of that inflicted by the enemy attacks at Tet, the Lunar New Year holiday.

"General Westmoreland also said that as a result of allied military action and the pacification effort, the destruction of the political and administrative structure of the Vietcong guerrillas in South Vietnam 'is expected to gain considerable headway during the next six months.

" 'Impact on the enemy should be increased casualties, desertions, sickness and lowered morale. . . . His incountry recruiting potential will be reduced by acceleration of our military offensive and pacification efforts.' "

"Intelligence analysts have now tentatively concluded, however, that Vietcong recruiting began to rise substantially in the latter half of 1967 back toward the former level." (*The New York Times,* March 21, 1968.)

"A former official on Gen. William C. Westmoreland's staff who has worked for the United States mission for more than a year is leaving South Vietnam to protest 'failures' of the American effort here.

"The official, Sidney J. Roche, issued a report to the mission saying that United States programs were being frustrated by massive corruption, an 'ineffectual' South Vietnamese Army, badly managed aid policies and 'unsound' American military efforts. . . ."

" 'I had hoped that the Tet offensive would produce some changes in policies. . . . However, it appears that we are going to follow the same old road and pursue the same old policies.' " (*Ibid.,* March 26, 1968.)

1967-1968

And, throughout the country, powerful voices, including those of a number of retired military men, were raised, questioning the wisdom of our Asian policy.

"This is a terribly costly war—in lives and money and in a sense that can't be measured in money.

"This cost can be justified if the war is about the United States and not just Vietnam."

"From a strategic standpoint, if the Communists won we would have the world cut in half.

"It's not worth killing American boys to have Vietnam have free elections." (Former Vice-President Richard M. Nixon, Los Angeles *Times,* December 31, 1967.)

"The Senate approved today a resolution calling upon President Johnson to seek United Nations help in ending the war in Vietnam.

"By an 82-to-0 vote, the Senate urged the President to 'consider taking the appropriate initiative' in bringing the Vietnam issue before the Security Council." (*Ibid.,* December 1, 1967.)

"I believe that if we had gone in 1965 and really pounded them when they didn't have any defenses, that we would have been better off today." (General John P. Mc-Connell, Chief of Staff, USAF, *ibid.,* October 5, 1967.)

"[We must] destroy the ability of the North Vietnamese to wage war and then, if necessary, their entire productive capacity." (General Curtis LeMay, USAF [Ret.], speech to the Channel City Club, Santa Barbara *News-Press,* March 27, 1967.)

". . . General Lauris Norstad, retired Supreme Allied Commander in Europe . . . disclosed that last March he tried, through an intermediary, to sell President Johnson on a highly unorthodox peace plan. It called for the U.S. to announce an unconditional bombing pause. After that, the President himself would fly to Geneva and hole up in a hotel room to await representatives from the other side

—presumably including agents from Red China and the Viet Cong.

". . . 'If I were President, I would get down on my knees three times a day and pray' for somebody to appear. But if nothing happened after a week, he added, 'the President would have to stand up and say, "This is not leading anywhere and I'm going back to Washington to get on with the business of running my country." ' Having proved his good faith, said Norstad, the President would then be able to increase the pressure on Hanoi without qualms." ("The War," *Time,* September 29, 1967.)

"[W]e are prosecuting an immoral war in support of a government that is a dictatorship by design."

"It represents nothing but a ruling clique and is composed of morally corrupt leaders who adhere to a warlord philosophy."

"This is one hell of a war to be fighting. We must disengage from this tragic war. It is the only one in which we have committed troops without first being aggressed against."

"We cannot afford a major confrontation with the people of Asia if we want to dedicate this country to our sons and future generations." (Brig. Gen. Robert L. Hughes, USAR, Memorial Day Speech, Madison, Wisconsin, *Capital Times,* May 30, 1967.)

"They don't look at time the way we do. So there's no substitute for negotiations, but if we are really sincere, it will have to be done through secret, private contacts. When we put on one of our big public peace offensives, Peking considers this a snowstorm." (Brig. Gen. Samuel B. Griffith, USMC [Ret.].)

"It is an immoral business, and we shouldn't be in it. We are crucifying our souls. We are pursuing a war that has no moral or political justification." (Brig. Gen. William Wallace Ford, USA [Ret.].)

"Johnson is on a collision course. The Chinese will not stand by and watch North Vietnam destroyed. . . . We are in the wrong in Vietnam, morally and from a military standpoint. It is against the national interests of the United States." (Brig. Gen. Hugh B. Hester, USA [Ret.].)

"Our anti-Communist adventures bring us no return, while social programs suffer at home and twenty million of our citizens are in such despair that there is rioting in the streets. . . . [T]he only way to settle it is for the Vietnamese to negotiate. We can't make peace with Hanoi from Washington." (Admiral Arnold True, USN [Ret.].) (*Congressional Record,* Senate, November 15, 1967.)

"In Vietnam we have lost sight of our national objectives and let what started as a limited war expand in time, cost and effort. We have ended up killing more people and fighting far longer than we had planned, and the added death and destruction so transform the fabric of Vietnamese society that they make impossible the attainment of the objectives for which we entered the war. At the same time this excess of violence poisons our domestic life." (James M. Gavin, *Crisis Now,* p. 174.)

"You read, you're televised to, you're radioed to, you're preached to, that it is necessary that we have our armed forces fight, get killed and maimed, and kill and maim other human beings including women and children because now is the time we must stop some kind of unwanted ideology from creeping up on this nation. The place we chose to do this is 8000 miles away with water in between. I believe there's record of but two men walking on water and one of them failed."

"I want to tell you, I don't think the whole of South

East Asia, as related to the present and future safety and freedom of the people of this country, is worth the life or limb of a single American."

"I believe that if we had and would keep our dirty, bloody, dollar-crooked fingers out of the business of these nations so full of depressed, exploited people, they will arrive at a solution of their own. That they design and want. That they fight and work for . . . and not the American style, which they don't want and above all don't want crammed down their throats by Americans." (Gen. David M. Shoup, USMC [Ret.], [former Commandant of the Marine Corps], *Congressional Record,* Senate, February 20, 1967.)

"We live in a world very unlike the one we were raised in. We have a potential for wholesale destruction so indescribably vast that many words, including 'victory,' lose their meaning."

"With no clear-cut limit upon our immediate military objective, we commit ourselves to an upward-spiraling course that may approach annihilation." (Gen. Matthew B. Ridgway, "Pull-out, All-out, or Stand Fast in Vietnam?" *Look,* April 5, 1966.)

1968

The first promise of a break in the military-political impasse came in a speech to the nation by President Johnson on March 31. The President announced, first, that he had ordered American bombing of North Vietnam limited to the area immediately north of the demilitarized zone; second, he called upon Hanoi to respond to this unilateral initiative by agreeing to immediate, substantive peace talks; and third, he made known his decision to step down and to refuse the nomination for another term in the White House.

"Tonight I have ordered our aircraft and our naval vessels to make no attacks on North Viet-Nam, except in the area north of the demilitarized zone where the continuing enemy buildup directly threatens Allied forward positions and where the movements of their troops and supplies are clearly related to that threat." (President Johnson, address to the nation on March 31, 1968, *Department of State Bulletin,* April 15, 1968.)

"I call upon President Ho Chi Minh to respond positively and favorably to this new step toward peace." (*Ibid.*)

". . . I shall not seek, and I will not accept, the nomination of my party for another term as your President." (*Ibid.*)

1968

This peace offer, in the established pattern, was accompanied by plans for a further U.S. military buildup and was followed by an intensified ground campaign with an increase in the volume, if not the scope, of the bombing. However, the Democratic Republic of Vietnam accepted the President's suggestion for immediate preliminary negotiations. After six weeks of wrangling over the site while the fighting continued unabated, talks opened in Paris on May 10, 1968.

". . . [T]he Joint Chiefs of Staff have recommended to me that we should prepare to send during the next 5 months support troops totaling approximately 13,500 men."

"The tentative estimate of those additional expenditures is $2.5 billion in this fiscal year and $2.6 billion in the next fiscal year." (President Johnson, address to the

nation on March 31, 1968, *Department of State Bulletin,*
April 15, 1968.)

"The largest allied offensive of the war in Vietnam, involving the use of more than 100,000 troops to clear
enemy forces out of 11 provinces, was announced yesterday by the military command.

"The operation, code-named Complete Victory, is directed against enemy units in the III Corps area, which
surrounds Saigon." (*The New York Times,* April 11,
1968.)

"United States pilots have mounted their second heaviest attack of the year on North Vietnam. The pilots flew
143 missions, one fewer than the record number on Jan.
6, an American military spokesman said." (*Ibid.,* April
16, 1968.)

"The restriction of the bombing . . . has not done us
much damage. We are concentrating our forces on a
much smaller area. . . ."

"We are increasing the number of missions over that
area very substantially." (Secretary of Defense Clark
Clifford, testimony on May 28, 1968, U.S. House, *1969
Second Supplemental Appropriation Hearings,* 90th
Congress, 2nd Session. Government Printing Office:
1968, p. 727.)

"It is obvious that the U.S. Government has not seriously and fully met the legitimate demands of the Government of the Democratic Republic of Vietnam, of
progressive American opinion and of world opinion.

"However, for its part, the Government of the Democratic Republic of Vietnam declares its readiness to appoint its representative with a view to determining with
the American side the unconditional cessation of the U.S.
bombing raids and all other acts of war against the Dem-

ocratic Republic of Vietnam so that talks may start."
(Statement by Democratic Republic of Vietnam in re-
sponse to President Johnson's address, *The New York
Times,* April 4, 1968.)

"American and North Vietnamese delegates met in
formal conference today, after years of fencing and unofficial contacts, in what could be the start of negotiations
toward peace in Vietnam." (Dispatch from Paris, May
10, 1968, *ibid.,* May 11, 1968.)

1968

*As yet ostensibly unproductive, these talks
nevertheless mark the first mutual attempt by
Americans and North Vietnamese to move their conflict
from the battlefield to the conference table, an effort never
before realized during the eighteen years since the United
States entered the Southeast Asian arena.*

"The path toward restoration of the 1954 accords is
clear. It is to abandon the resort to force, to reestablish
the demilitarized zone and systematically to withdraw all
forces other than those of South Vietnam from its territory, and for the issue of reunification to be settled peace-
fully by the people in North Vietnam and the people in
[the] South."

"From the end of the Geneva conference until today,
three American Presidents have repeatedly made clear that
we would have to take action in support of the people of
the South if North Vietnam violated the accords. . . .
Accordingly, we have responded to the request of the
Government of the Republic of Vietnam for assistance as
North Vietnam increased its aggression."

"Let us now look to the future and seek a basis for
peace. I am struck by some similarities in our respective
positions. . . . First, we both speak of an independent,

democratic, peaceful and prosperous South Vietnam. . . . Second, we both speak of peace on the basis of respect of the Geneva accords of 1954—to which we add the 1962 agreements on Laos. Third, we both speak of letting the internal affairs of South Vietnam be settled by the South Vietnamese themselves—which we would clarify by adding, 'without outside interference or coercion.' Fourth, we both speak of the reunification of Vietnam by peaceful means. . . . Fifth, we both speak of the need for strict respect of the military provisions of the 1954 Geneva accords."

". . . [L]et me emphasize that the people of South Vietnam must be free from coercion. Nowhere is this more important than in Saigon, where vicious attacks are being directed against a civilian population. The continuation of such attacks on civilians in Saigon and elsewhere does not contribute to the atmosphere for successful talks." (Ambassador W. Averell Harriman, U.S. envoy to Paris talks, *The New York Times,* May 16, 1968.)

"Allow me to recall that the U.S. Government, which unleashed the aggression, has to stop it. The U.S. Government has no right to demand any price from the Vietnamese people for the cessation of its aggression against the Democratic Republic of Vietnam."

"The stand of independence and peace of the Vietnamese people, still is the four points of the Democratic Republic of Vietnam Government and the political program of the South Vietnam National Front for Liberation. To reach a peaceful settlement of the Vietnam problem, the U.S. Government must first of all stop definitively and unconditionally the bombing raids and all other acts of war on the whole territory of the Democratic Republic of Vietnam."

"On its part, the Government of the Democratic Republic of Vietnam has shown its goodwill before the whole world by having appointed its representative to come here for official conversations with the representatives of the Government of the U.S.A. and we are ready to have serious conversations.

"But, so long as the U.S. continues its aggression and continues to infringe upon the sovereignty and territory of the Democratic Republic of Vietnam, the Vietnamese people have to resolutely resist." (North Vietnamese Chief Delegate Xuan Thuy, *ibid.*, May 16, 1968.)

This is the story of the American involvement in Vietnam, from simple economic aid to French forces in 1950 to the massive military operation taking place in 1968. The aims of American policy emerge clearly from the record, as do the methods the administration has felt were best to implement these aims.

The record also shows how deep are the concern and the dissent among the nation's leaders and its lawmakers, how seriously they question the direction of our policy. More than in 1964, the Vietnam issue dominates the political atmosphere of this election year, emphasizing by contrast the depth of our neglect of the nation's domestic problems, long sidetracked by the overriding demands of an escalating war.

Within both major political parties, the Vietnam issue has caused deep ideological rifts. Democratic Senators Eugene McCarthy of Minnesota and the late Robert Kennedy of New York emerged in the party primaries as symbols of the rising popular discontent. Both drew countrywide support for their advocacy of an immediate cessation of bombing, a coalition government in South Vietnam, and a negotiated settlement. With the withdrawal of President Johnson, Vice-President Humphrey was left, with organized party support, to face rank-and-file dissat-

isfaction, reflected in the primary returns from New Hampshire to California.

Similar, though less insistent, dissident sentiment on the Vietnam war has accentuated the prior cleavage between liberal and conservative elements in the Republican Party. First Governor George Romney of Michigan and later Governor Nelson Rockefeller of New York championed the position of Republican moderates; their proposals for solution, though somewhat cautious regarding the political future of South Vietnam, have represented nevertheless a sharp challenge to the position of the leading contender, former Vice-President Richard Nixon, who has favored continued military pressure, particularly by sea and by air, and declared that he would "rule out any kind of settlement which would be interpreted as an American defeat or a victory for the Communists."

As the election nears, the issue of Vietnam brings into question wider foreign policy considerations, questions concerning America's future role in Asia and her relationship to emerging nationalism throughout the world. A new national concern bridges party lines and binds Americans of all persuasions—to avoid another Vietnam at another time, in another place.

BIBLIOGRAPHY

Books

Chaffard, Georges, *Indochine: dix ans d'indépendance*. Calmann-Lévy: 1964.
> A first-hand account of developments from 1954 to 1964 by a well-known French journalist.

Devillers, Philippe, *Histoire du Vietnam de 1940 à 1952*. Editions du Seuil: 1952.
> A comprehensive and scholarly study by a recognized authority on French Indochina.

Documents Relating to British Involvement in the Indo-China Conflict, 1945–1965, Cmd. 2834, Miscellaneous No. 25. Her Majesty's Stationery Office: 1965.

Draper, Theodore, *Abuse of Power*. Viking: 1967.
> A thorough analysis of the political considerations that have influenced American policy in Southeast Asia, with emphasis on the misuse of Executive power, by a well-known author-journalist and expert on world communism. Full documentation, at times inaccurately quoted.

Eckstein, Alexander, *Communist China's Economic Growth and Foreign Trade: Implications for U.S. Policy*. Mc-Graw-Hill: 1966.
> One of a series of publications on the United States and China in World Affairs published for the Council on Foreign Relations. Dr. Eckstein, a professor of economics at the University of Michigan, is well-known in the field of China's economic development.

Eden, Sir Anthony, *Full Circle: The Memoirs of Anthony Eden*. Houghton Mifflin: 1960.

Particularly valuable for the diplomatic context of the Geneva Conference of 1954.

Eisenhower, Dwight D., *Mandate for Change: The White House Years, 1953–1956*. Doubleday: 1963.

Eisenhower, Dwight D., *Waging Peace: The White House Years, 1956–1961*. Doubleday: 1965.

Illuminating accounts of the factors influencing foreign policy decisions during the Republican period of our involvement in Vietnam.

Fall, Bernard B., *The Two Viet-Nams: A Political and Military Analysis*. Praeger: 1964.

A thorough study of the nationalistic currents and political developments in all of Vietnam from 1945 to 1964. Fall, now dead, is recognized as the foremost authority on indigenous political movements in Vietnam, particularly the Vietcong.

Foreign Relations of the United States, Diplomatic Papers, The Conference of Berlin (The Potsdam Conference). Two Vols. Government Printing Office: 1960.

Fulbright, J. William, *The Arrogance of Power*. Random House: 1966.

A critical analysis of the weaknesses and dangers in our foreign policy by the Chairman of the Senate Foreign Relations Committee. Contains his proposal for peace in Vietnam.

Further Documents Relating to the Discussion of Indo-China at the Geneva Conference, June 16–July 21, 1954. Miscellaneous No. 20 (1954), Command Paper 9239. Her Majesty's Stationery Office: 1954.

For text of the Geneva Agreements.

Gavin, James M., *Crisis Now*. Random House: 1968.

A critical assessment of the major issues, foreign and domestic, facing the American people by a well-known former soldier-diplomat who has long been concerned with United States policy in Asia. General Gavin sees a direct relationship between United States policies abroad and its difficulties at home and recommends a massive, coordinated effort to set American affairs in order.

Gettleman, Marvin E., ed., *Viet Nam: History, Documents, and Opinions on a Major World Crisis.* Fawcett: 1965.
 Used chiefly for its documentary reprints.

Goodwin, Richard N., *Triumph or Tragedy: Reflections on Vietnam.* Random House: 1966.
 An appraisal of American involvement in Vietnam by a former Presidential assistant.

Gruening, Ernest, and Beaser, Herbert W., *Vietnam Folly.* National Press: 1968.
 A study of events and tactics leading to present American large-scale involvement in Vietnam by one of the earliest Senate critics of the war and his top legislative aide. Includes a plan for resolving the dilemma.

Halberstam, David, *The Making of a Quagmire.* Random House: 1965.
 A Pulitzer Prize-winning, first-hand account of events in South Vietnam from 1961 to 1964 by a *New York Times* correspondent.

Hammer, Ellen J., *The Struggle for Indochina.* Stanford University Press: 1954.
 An English language counterpart of Devillers' work, particularly comprehensive in its treatment of the Vietnamese struggle for independence through 1953.

Isaacs, Harold R., *New Cycle in Asia, Selected Documents in the Far East, 1943–1947.* American Institute for Pacific Affairs: 1947.

Kahin, George McT., and Lewis, John W., *The United States in Vietnam.* Dell: 1967.
 A comprehensive, thoroughly documented history of American involvement in Southeast Asia by two reputable Asian scholars. Contains reprints of Vietnamese documents and broadcasts not readily available elsewhere.

Kennedy, John F., *The Strategy of Peace.* Harper: 1960.
 A collection of major speeches by the late President, edited by Allan Nevins.

Kennedy, Robert F., *To Seek a Newer World.* Doubleday: 1967.
 An analysis of the human as well as the political factors involved in American foreign policy by an outspoken administration critic. Contains clearly articulated proposals for solutions to the conflict.

Lacoutre, Jean, *Vietnam Between Two Truces*. Random House: 1966.
    An analysis by one of the most reliable French correspondents, exceptionally familiar with Vietnam, both North and South.

Lancaster, Donald, *The Emancipation of French Indochina*. Oxford University Press: 1961.
    A political history by a former British legation official in Saigon. Particularly valuable for its treatment of the political maneuvering by the major powers at the time of the Geneva Conference.

MacArthur, Douglas, *Reminiscences*. McGraw-Hill: 1964.
    Valuable for its thorough exposition of the military dilemma in the nuclear age, as it was forcefully dramatized in the MacArthur-Truman controversy.

McCarthy, Mary, *Vietnam*. Harcourt, Brace & World: 1967.
    Lucid, critical account, from first-hand observation, of American policy and practices in South Vietnam. Frankly unsympathetic to American involvement in the area. Includes section called "Solutions," which is primarily a discussion of measures open to those who disapprove of present policy.

Mecklin, John, *Mission in Torment*. Doubleday: 1965.
    A critical account of the effects of United States involvement by a former U.S. Information Service Officer in Saigon.

Montgomery, John D., *The Politics of Foreign Aid*. Praeger: 1962.
    Used chiefly for its coverage of land problems and land reform in South Vietnam.

Morgenthau, Hans, *Vietnam and the United States*. Public Affairs Press: 1965.
    A collection of essays by an influential critic of American policy.

Murti, B. S. N., *Vietnam Divided*. Asia Publishing House: 1964.
    A comprehensive account of the difficulties encountered by the International Control Commission by one of its former members.

Raskin, Marcus G., and Fall, Bernard B., eds., *The Viet-Nam Reader*. Random House: 1965.

Valuable collection of articles and documents relating to American involvement in Vietnam.

Reischauer, Edwin O., *Beyond Vietnam*. Random House: 1967.

A study of Asian developments which places the Vietnam conflict in the context of movements taking place throughout the Far East, by a former Ambassador to Japan and lifelong student of Asian affairs. His suggestions for resolving the Vietnam war give consideration primarily to the productive future role of the United States in Asia.

Reischauer, Edwin O., *Wanted: An Asian Policy*. Knopf: 1955.

An earlier study of the misconceptions and miscalculations of American Asian policy that have resulted in the present dilemma.

Reston, James, *The Artillery of the Press*. Harper: 1967.

An analysis of the dilemma facing the press in reporting foreign and diplomatic affairs, with suggestions for more informative coverage of international affairs.

Ridgway, Matthew B., *Soldier: The Memoirs of Matthew B. Ridgway*. Harper: 1956.

The former Chairman of the Joint Chiefs of Staff discusses in detail his conception of the roles of the various military services in modern warfare and defends his objections to United States involvement in Indochina.

Schlesinger, Arthur M., Jr., *A Thousand Days*. Houghton Mifflin: 1965.

A biography of Kennedy as President, with insights into the reasons for his Vietnam decisions.

Schoenbrun, David, *Vietnam: How We Got In; How To Get Out*. Atheneum: 1968.

A detailed presentation of the case for American military disengagement and an immediate negotiated settlement of the war in Vietnam by a well-known American correspondent. David Schoenbrun covered the Vietnamese conflict from the French-Vietminh negotiations in 1946 through the Geneva Conferences of 1954 and 1962; his visit to Hanoi in 1967 places him among the limited number of American correspondents to have recent first-hand information on the Democratic Republic of Vietnam and the NLF.

Schurmann, Franz; Scott, Peter Dale; and Zelnik, Reginald, *The Politics of Escalation in Vietnam*. Fawcett: 1966.

Snow, Edgar, *The Other Side of the River: Red China Today*. Random House: 1961.
> The author, a lifelong student of Chinese affairs, is one of the few Americans still welcome in China today. One of his chief contributions is his insight into the thinking of the Chinese revolutionaries.

Taylor, Maxwell D., *Responsibility and Response*. Harper: 1967.
> A defense of American involvement by the general who was Ambassador to South Vietnam 1964–1965.

Thich Nhat Hanh, *Vietnam: Lotus in a Sea of Fire*. Hill and Wang: 1967.
> One of South Vietnam's foremost Buddhist scholars describes the impact of the war on his countrymen and offers his solution to the conflict.

Truman, Harry S., *Memoirs*. Doubleday: 1956. Vol. 2.
> Important for its summation of the legacy inherited by the Eisenhower administration.

U.S. House of Representatives, *Department of Defense Appropriations for 1967*, Part I, 89th Congress, 2nd Session. Government Printing Office: 1966.

U.S. Senate, *The Southeast Asia Collective Defense Treaty*, 83rd Congress, 2nd Session. Government Printing Office: 1954.

U.S. Senate, *Supplemental Foreign Assistance Fiscal 1966—Vietnam*, 89th Congress, 2nd Session. Government Printing Office: 1966.

U.S. Senate, *U.S. Policy With Respect to Mainland China*, 89th Congress, 2nd Session. Government Printing Office: 1966.

Vietnam Hearings, The. Random House: 1966.
> The major portions of the statements and testimony of Secretary Rusk, General Taylor, General Gavin, and George F. Kennan before the Senate Foreign Relations Committee in 1966, with an introduction by the Chairman, Senator J. William Fulbright.

White, Theodore H., *The Making of a President 1964*. Atheneum: 1965.
   Provides many insights into the 1964 election campaign.

Periodicals

Ahmad, Eqbal, "Revolutionary Warfare: How to Tell When the Rebels Have Won," *The Nation*, August 30, 1965.

Ashmore, Harry S., "The Public Relations of Peace," *The Center Magazine*, Fund for the Republic, October-November, 1967.

Baldwin, Hanson W.; Kahn, Herman; Kissinger, Henry; Morgenthau, Hans; and Schlesinger, Arthur, Jr., "Why Vietnam?" *Look*, August 9, 1966.

Bundy, McGeorge, "The End of Either/Or," *Foreign Affairs*, January, 1967.

Bundy, William P., "Bundy Comments on Galbraith's Plan," *The New York Times Magazine*, November 12, 1967.

Bundy, William P., "Why U.S. Is in Vietnam—An Official Explanation," *U.S. News & World Report*, December 18, 1967.

Carver, George A., "The Faceless Viet Cong," *Foreign Affairs*, April, 1966.
   A statement of the administration position that the Vietcong is an expedient of the North by a former CIA officer.

"DRV Government Statement," *Peking Review*, November 10, 1967.

"Escalation Means Getting Closer and Closer to the Grave," *Peking Review*, April 30, 1965.

Fall, Bernard B., "How the French Got Out of Vietnam," *The New York Times Magazine*, May 2, 1965.

Fulbright, J. William, "Why Our Foreign Policy Is Failing," *Look*, May 3, 1966.

Gavin, James M., "A Communication on Vietnam," *Harper's Magazine*, February, 1966.

"General Westmoreland Reports on Vietnam War," *U.S. News & World Report*, November 28, 1966.

Gittings, John, "A Basis for Negotiation Exists," *The Nation*, September 6, 1965.

Goldberg, Arthur J., "Vietnam Settlement: Relations With Red China," *Vital Speeches of the Day,* November 1, 1966.

"Go On Fighting in Vietnam?" (An interview with Henry Cabot Lodge), *U.S. News & World Report,* February 15, 1965.

McGovern, George, "Vietnam: A Proposal," *The New York Review,* July 7, 1966.

Osborne, John, "The Tough Miracle Man of Vietnam," *Life,* May 13, 1957.

"Peking Government Statement," *Peking Review,* November 10, 1967.

Pepper, William F., "The Following Acts . . . Are Crimes," *Columbia University Forum,* Fall, 1966.

Prybyla, Jan S., "Soviet and Chinese Economic Aid to North Vietnam," *The China Quarterly,* July-September, 1966.

Ridgway, Matthew B., "Pull-out, All-out, or Stand Fast in Vietnam?" *Look,* April 5, 1966.

Roberts, Chalmers M., "The Day We Didn't Go to War," *The Reporter,* September 14, 1954.

"Russia: The Enemy in Vietnam?" *U.S. News & World Report,* January 30, 1967.

Sevareid, Eric, "The Final Troubled Hours of Adlai Stevenson," *Look,* November 30, 1965.

Sorensen, Theodore C., "The War in Vietnam: How We Can End It," *Saturday Review,* October 21, 1967.

"The War," *Time,* September 29, 1967.

Tran Van Dinh, "Elections in Vietnam," *The New Republic,* July 2, 1966.

Tran Van Dinh, "The Ky Question," *The New Republic,* January 21, 1967.

UN Monthly Chronicle, May, 1965.

Westmoreland, William C., "Vietnam, The Situation Today," *Vital Speeches of the Day,* May 15, 1967.

Wheeler, Earle G., "The Challenge Came in Vietnam," *Vital Speeches of the Day,* December 15, 1966.

Wright, Quincy, "Legal Aspects of the Viet-Nam Situation," *The American Journal of International Law,* October, 1966.

Other

Aggression From the North: The Record of North Viet-Nam's Campaign to Conquer South Viet-Nam, Department of State Publication 7839. Government Printing Office: 1965.

A Threat to the Peace: North Viet-Nam's Effort to Conquer South Viet-Nam, Department of State Publication No. 7308. Government Printing Office: 1961.

Galbraith, J. K., *How to Get Out of Vietnam.* New American Library: 1967.

Great Britain, 5 Parliamentary Debates (Commons), Vol. 529.

Interim Reports of the International Commission for Supervision and Control in Vietnam, Great Britain Parliamentary Sessional Papers: 1954–1962, Vols. 19–39.

Komer, R. W., *The Other War in Vietnam—A Progress Report.* Agency for International Development, Washington, D.C.: 1966.

Mansfield, Mike, *The Vietnam Conflict: The Substance and the Shadow.* Government Printing Office: 1966.
> A first-hand comprehensive report on conditions in South Vietnam by Senators Mansfield, Muskie, Inouye, Aiken, Boggs to the Senate Committee on Foreign Relations.

Perry, James M., *Barry Goldwater: A New Look at a Presidential Candidate.* National Observer: 1964.

Political Programme of the South Vietnam National Front for Liberation. Published by the Permanent Representation of the South Vietnam National Front for Liberation in Czechoslovakia, 1967.

Public Papers of the President of the United States, The, Lyndon B. Johnson, 1963–1964, Book II. Government Printing Office: 1965.

Scheer, Robert, *How the United States Got Involved in Vietnam.* Fund for the Republic: 1965.

United States and Eastern Asia, The. Freedom House: December, 1967.

U.S. Senate, *Asia, the Pacific, and the United States,* 90th

Congress, 1st Session. Government Printing Office: 1967.

U.S. Senate, *Changing American Attitudes Toward Foreign Policy,* 90th Congress, 1st Session. Government Printing Office: 1967.

U.S. Senate, *Conflicts Between United States Capabilities and Foreign Commitments,* 90th Congress, 1st Session. Government Printing Office: 1967.

U.S. Senate, *The Communist World in 1967,* 90th Congress, 1st Session. Government Printing Office: 1967.

U.S. Senate, *The Gulf of Tonkin, The 1964 Incidents,* 90th Congress, 2nd Session. Government Printing Office: 1968.

Weekly Compilation of Presidential Documents. Government Printing Office: August 2, 1965, to date.

Whipple, Charles L., *The War in Vietnam.* Boston Globe: 1967.

A series of editorials appearing May 29 through June 3, 1967, in the *Boston Globe.*

Why Vietnam. Government Printing Office: 1965.

A collection of official statements justifying United States commitments in Vietnam.

Woito, Robert S., ed., *Vietnam Peace Proposals.* World Without War Council: 1967.

An exceptional collection of viable proposals for ending the war and solving the political problems of Vietnam.

Wormuth, Francis D., *The Vietnam War: The President versus the Constitution.* Fund for the Republic: 1968.